Pledge to Destiny

PLEDGE
TO
DESTINY

Charles de Gaulle
and the
Rise of the Free French

BY ROBERT SMITH THOMPSON

McGraw-Hill Book Company

New York   *St. Louis*   *San Francisco*

Düsseldorf   *London*   *Mexico*   *Sydney*   *Toronto*

*123456789*BPBP*7987654*

Library of Congress Cataloging in Publication Data

Thompson, Robert S.
    Pledge to destiny.

    Bibliography: p.
    1. France combattante.   2. Gaulle, Charles de,
Pres. France, 1890–1970. I. Title.
D761.9.F7T4   940.53'44'0924 [B]   73-19695
ISBN 0–07–064390–3

Acknowledgments

The author is grateful to the following for permission to quote passages from copyrighted material:

ATLANTIC MONTHLY COMPANY, for Arthur Mills Stratton, "Ambulance at Bir Hacheim," from *Atlantic*, Nov. 1942, Copyright © 1942, 1970, by the Atlantic Monthly Company, Boston, Mass.

MARY BORDEN, for excerpts from her book *Journey Down a Blind Alley.*

E. P. DUTTON, for material adapted from the book *Ten Thousand Eyes* by Richard Collier, Copyright © 1958 by Richard Collier.

EIRE AND SPOTTISWOODE, for Major General Sir Edward Spears, *Two Men Who Saved France.*

FARRAR, STRAUS AND GIROUX, for Robert Mengin, *No Laurels for de Gaulle*, Copyright © 1966 by Farrar, Straus and Giroux, Inc.

FOR

Judy and Polly

"Glory gives herself only to those who have always dreamed of her."
Charles de Gaulle

Contents

Foreword

THE GENERAL SPENT NOVEMBER 9, 1970, MUCH AS HE HAD SPENT EVERY OTHER DAY IN THE PRECEDING YEAR AND A HALF. AT NINE-THIRTY IN THE MORNING HE BEGAN WORK ON THE SECOND VOLUME OF HIS *Memoirs of Hope*, jotting down details from his prodigious memory. At noon he ate his usual robust lunch, topped off with a favorite cream pastry and a cup of extra-strong French coffee. That afternoon he took a stroll around his estate with his wife, Yvonne, then had a chat with a neighboring farmer, René Piot, about fencing a piece of land he had recently added to the grounds. Later, after returning to his two-story stone house, la Boisserie, he dictated from his notes to his secretary, staring while he spoke out the tall, narrow window at the thick trees and the meadows where once he had strolled hand in hand with his retarded daughter, Anne.

Early in the evening he checked over the typed manuscript, making corrections in his heavy, nearly illegible scrawl, and then he played a game of solitaire on the two-cushioned couch in the living room while he waited for the nighttime televised news. Shortly after seven o'clock he put down the cards and stood up to look for the television programming guide.

He had just started across the room when he clutched at his side and slumped back onto the couch. "Yvonne," he managed to whisper, "I hurt on my right side. Call a doctor."

Seventeen and a half hours later, after Yvonne had placed a call to her daughter Elizabeth in Paris, and had located her son, Philippe, a naval Captain, in Brest, her husband's former protégé spoke to the nation from a television studio in Paris.

"General de Gaulle is dead," Premier Pompidou said in a trembling voice, "France is a widow."

A crowd of several hundred veterans, wearing the moth-eaten red berets of the North African spahis and the faded blue caps of certain

French colonial regiments, marched that afternoon at the height of rush hour up the slope of the Champs-Elysées. Despite the many who still opposed him, a quarter of a million Parisians, soldiers and businessmen, housewives and clerks, students and matrons, followed them through the chill November rain and wind that rustled in the chestnut trees. The greats of the world—Indira Gandhi, Archbishop Makarios, Edward Heath, Anthony Eden, Harold Macmillan, Haile Selassie, Prince Rainier, the Shah of Iran, Prince Charles of England, and Richard Nixon from the United States—filed down the main aisle of Notre Dame Cathedral in Paris to hear the funeral mass. France mourned.

Some thirty years before, however, on August 2, 1940, a French military tribunal in Clermont-Ferrand, near Vichy, had heard charges against the obscure, self-exiled, and virtually friendless Brigadier General de Gaulle, found him *in absentia* guilty of insubordination and disobedience, and sentenced him to death by the guillotine. And for nearly two years thereafter he remained virtually unknown to the French public and a traitor in the eyes of the Vichy government of Marshal Pétain.

Yet by the end of those two years he had begun to emerge as a hero and the symbol of the Resistance in France, and from the summer of 1942 until the present day, the Gaullist movement has been the most potent single force in French politics. By mid-1942, of course, he was still an exile in London, and formidable obstacles still clogged his road up to power, but, nonetheless, he *had* launched his movement, his name *was* becoming revered in France, and his style of behavior, now crystallized and visible to all, was presaging bitter conflicts with allies in the postwar world.

How did he do it? How did he vault from obscurity to fame, imposing new political arrangements upon France and charting new directions in foreign policy? How did he so build his support that, upon his death, the greats of the world would fly to France and the people of Paris would march in the rain to the Arc de Triomphe? What combination of character, strategy, experience, circumstance, and luck enabled him to triumph over all the doubts and conflicts and drama that pressed in upon him?

Broader questions still lie behind these: How do leaders fashion new responses when old ideas have led to disaster? How do statesmen restructure the thinking of nations and turn countries in radically new directions? How do men and their movements create order out of chaos—and what are the costs of such creation?

Our story cannot answer these questions completely (although it is based upon an exhaustive study of the relevant documentation), since it focuses on a limited segment of General de Gaulle's career. But, as it begins to unfold with the German invasion of France on May 10, 1940, and rises to its climax on the desert of Libya where, in May and June of 1942, de Gaulle's men confronted the full might of Rommel's army, it does shine a light on the myterious workings of the charismatic movement that creates a new political order.

I should like not only to give thanks to the many in England, France and America who have helped me shape this book and to the Institute of International Studies of the University of South Carolina for its generous financial support, but also to single out four persons to whom I owe special gratitude: my parents, for their help of many kinds down through the years; the late Turner C. Cameron, Jr., of the United States Foreign Service, for having pointed me in sensible directions during this book's inception; and my wife, Judy, above all else, for having somehow put up with me during my three-year absence under the skin of another man.

September, 1973
Columbia, South Carolina

PART ONE
The Fall of France

Chapter 1

(1)

FROM A POINT IN THE MAGINOT LINE, JUST OUTSIDE STRASBOURG IN FRANCE, A PAIR OF YOUNG FRENCH SENTRIES HUNCHED THEIR HEADS DOWN TO GLANCE THROUGH THE SLOT IN THEIR CONCRETE PILLBOX. IT was shortly before dawn on May 10, 1940. The sun was about to peek over the hills of Germany to the east, and the bridge that led across the Rhine to the Nazi fortifications at Kehl was glittering with innumerable little lights. Soon the river would ripple and flash in the sunshine, the air would become dry and flawlessly clear and the sky would grow blue and cloudless and warm. One of the sentries leaned against the barrel of his 75-mm, thinking that soon he could be off duty far below, sleeping soundly between the sheets of his bunk in the Maginot Line. In the underground barracks deep beneath him, his comrades were already stretching and yawning as they climbed out of bed, waking to another day of ease and contentment and certain that all they would do that day would be to sit in their canteen, drink glasses of beer and wine, and wish they were listening to Maurice Chevalier singing his latest hit, *"Paris sera toujours Paris."* Like the sentries in the pillbox high above them, these men felt bored, restless—and safe.

This was the Phony War, the *Sitzkrieg, la drôle de guerre.* During the preceding eight months, the Nazi tanks had driven the government of Poland into exile, blitzed up through Denmark and along the fjords of Norway, and then turned to face the French across the guns of the Maginot Line. But the French soldiers at Strasbourg had grown complacent.

Under orders to hold their fire and so to avoid angering the Reich, they had become used to standing about with crossed arms and staring at the German munitions convoys that rumbled along the opposite bank. Only one piece of news had brightened their days at all throughout that long, black and dreary winter: the tale of the great Christmas-tree theft.

Although the bridge across the Rhine to Kehl had been only eight hundred feet long, the French machine gunners had been forbidden to shoot at the figures on the other side, and, in mockery, the Germans had sometimes taunted them in French through the speakers of a public address system. Then, on Christmas Eve, the Germans had gone further. They had placed a small Christmas tree, glowing with lights, atop their own pillbox beside the Kehl bridge. They had done it, of course, to make fun of the French.

By midnight the young sentry on duty on the French side had been unable to bear it any longer. He had pulled off his boots, crawled over his 75-mm, and, face down on his stomach, begun to slither across the bridge toward Kehl. A white frost had formed on the trestle bridge, making his handholds slippery, and a single mistake could have sent him hurtling onto the glistening ice below. But the sentry had kept on going. He had reached the German half of the bridge when another problem had come up: the moon had emerged from behind a cloud, silhouetting his body against the white on the bridge. But, again, he had kept on going. Minutes had gone by, and as he crept along the sentry had kept alert for sounds from the German pillbox ahead. Suddenly he had heard a rustling beneath his hands.

It had been a pile of newspapers in German, for he had reached the wall of the Nazi pillbox, and directly above him had glowed the lights on the branches of the Germans' Christmas tree.

In the morning, when the German sentries, hung over and groggy from their Christmas Eve carousing, had climbed again to their pillbox and had looked across the Rhine at the top of the Maginot Line, they had seen perched there, decorated with strips of the newspapers, their own little Christmas tree, safe now in the hands of the French.

So the first round of the Phony War had gone to France, and now that spring had come to the Maginot Line, the soldiers there had every reason to think that the next round, too, would belong to them. They had an alliance with England, they had an army of two million men, they had the biggest cannon in Europe, and, above all, they had the Maginot Line.

It was an impregnable wall. Named for André Maginot, a Minister of Defense in the 1920's, the plan for the line had been debated and studied in the Supreme War Council for nearly a decade. Paul Painlevé, a later

Defense Minister, had approved its final details, and by 1935 the Army's engineers had created the mightiest fortress in the long history of warfare.

The members of the High Command were proud of their Line—it had become a fixation with them. Its underground barracks and commissaries provided the soldiers with comfort, its bristling guns and turrets allowed them an unassailable safety and its location—it paralleled the border of Germany from Switzerland in the south to Belgium in the north —protected the northeastern corner of France, the corner that jutted straight into the heart of Germany. No known bomb could harm the Line, no known tank could cross it, and its only weakness, the fact that it stopped far short of the Belgian coast, seemed trivial because stationed above the Line and protecting it from the north were the mighty First and Seventh French Armies and the nine divisions of the British Expeditionary Force.

The Germans, moreover, had seemed to respect that strength: they had made no effort to cross the Line and their major maneuvers of the winter had been carried out far to the north and east, on the slopes of the Eifel Mountains.

And so, as the two bored sentries squinted past the lights that twinkled along the Kehl bridge and saw the first band of daylight above the hills to the east, there seemed every reason in the world for them to be relaxed, comfortable and assured of the good day's sleep, on that clear and lovely morning of May 10, 1940.

(2)

Before dawn on that same morning, the *Panzer* tanks of the 19th German Armored Corps under the command of General Heinz Guderian were rumbling along with their lights extinguished through the Eifel Mountains of Germany, just east of Luxembourg and just north of the top end of the Maginot Line. In the lead came the tanks, the armored cars and the reinforced motorcycles, next came the troop trucks, the heavy artillery and the supply echelons, and finally, stretching fifty miles to the rear, came the columns of the German athletes, the elite corps of the Nazi infantry, the blond supermen of the *Wehrmacht*.

It was pitch dark in the Eifel Mountains and the drivers had to exert the utmost powers of vision to avoid ending up in the roadside ditches. The noise of the motors was getting on everyone's nerves. More and more troops who had been quartered in the Eifel were getting under way; more and more armored vehicles were emerging from the approach roads to join the main columns of tanks. The men were uneasy and nervous: tempers were beginning to flare. At last the men understood why they had so often come to these mountain roads to carry out peacetime maneuvers.

Luftwaffe crews, too, were up and about that morning, tumbling from their bunks, taking no time to shave, scrambling into their flight jackets and racing to get to their briefing sessions on time. Even before sunrise, the *Stukas,* the *Junkers,* the *Heinkels,* and all other aircraft available to the Germans had climbed to the sky, most of them droning off toward Holland and Belgium, hoping to divert the attention of the French from where the main *Panzer* thrust was aimed.

The German code name for the operation was *Sichelschnitt*—the sweeping cut of a scythe. Its purpose was to trick the French.

When the Germans had invaded France in 1914, they had marched across the fields of Flanders, swinging their infantry down from northern Belgium so that, in theory at least, the last man on the right would brush the English Channel with his sleeve. And throughout the long years that followed their defeat in 1918, the German General Staff had continued, in secret, to develop contingency plans that foresaw their soldiers, once again, crossing the plains of northern Belgium. But early in 1940 the airplane of a German officer who was carrying a copy of one such plan had crash-landed behind the Maginot Line, and French military intelligence, the *Deuxième Bureau,* had captured and studied the revealing documents. So the Germans had dreamed up a new plan called OPERATION *Sichelschnitt.*

They had decided this time to feint toward the Channel, sending waves of planes to drop bombs over Rotterdam and directing a few *Panzer* columns toward the Albert Canal in Belgium, while sending most of their *Panzers* elsewhere: down from the Eifel Mountains, through the Duchy of Luxembourg, and across the Ardennes Forest in *southern* Belgium. The objective of these southern columns was the town of Sedan in the gap between the top end of the Maginot Line and the strong First and Seventh French Armies that, presumably, would be marching away into Belgium to meet the assault there.

The Germans had an excellent reason for trying to reach Sedan: once past it they would find little to stop them from conquering France. Above Sedan stood the Ninth French Army, below Sedan stood the Second French Army—the two least trained and mobilized in the French military system—and beyond Sedan stood nothing at all, nothing, that is, but rolling hills, the city of Paris and the shores of the English Channel. But first the Germans had to reach Sedan, and blocking their way was the Ardennes Forest.

Its trees were thick, its hills were steep, its valleys were narrow, and its twisting roads could hold a tank to a pace both slow and vulnerable to assault. A few anti-tank cannon hidden among the trees or a few airplanes swooping down through the valleys could destroy a division of *Panzers* within minutes. Marshal Philippe Pétain, a Commander-in-Chief of the French Army during the First World War, had called the Ardennes Forest "impenetrable."

The *Panzers* could penetrate the Ardennes Forest and reach Sedan, therefore, only if the French did not expect them, only if the strongest French Armies, the First and the Seventh, had snapped at the bait and marched up to Belgium.

So the Germans were gambling, and at four-thirty on the morning of May 10, 1940, as General Guderian drove the lead *Panzer* across a bridge into Luxembourg, he kept a nervous eye upon the brightening sky for any signs of approaching Allied aircraft.

He had his eye on something else, too: on his right was the Seventh *Panzer* Division under the command of a new Major General, Erwin Rommel, fresh, untried and inexperienced.

(3)

For two years the French High Command had been hearing the warnings.

In 1938 the French Army had conducted maneuvers that were identical to OPERATION *Sichelschnitt*. Four motorized divisions and two tank brigades, pretending to be German, had swept down the western slopes of the Ardennes Forest and had shattered the imaginary French defenses beyond hope of recovery. The implication has been clear: the French should have prepared for an assault at Sedan. But, lest the troops grow too worried, the general who had run the test had begged the High Command not to publicize the maneuver's results. The High Command had complied.

In the early spring of 1940, a few French officers had raised doubts again about the strength of the Sedan defenses. A Major Sarraz-Bournet had discovered that a series of new concrete bunkers lacked embrasures that faced the River Meuse and the Ardennes Forest. A Major Barlone had found an anti-tank ditch so poorly prepared that a quarter of an hour's bombardment could crumble the earth away and leave free passage for any German tank or motorcycle. A General Ruby had estimated that the Second Army, below the Sedan, had no more than 15 percent of the number of land mines it needed to slow a German attack. And a General Huntziger, in command of the Second Army, had begged Commander-in-Chief Maurice Gamelin to give him four reserve divisions with which he could begin the buildup at Sedan. Gamelin had refused the request.

On the morning of April 30, 1940, the French Military Attaché in Berne, Switzerland, had learned from a contact there that the German Army would launch an attack against France on May 8, 9, or 10, and that the "principal axis of the movement" would be Sedan. He had immediately flashed the warning to France and the *Deuxième Bureau* in turn had passed it along to Gamelin. But it had been one report among many: Gamelin had paid it little heed.

On May 9, 1940, the *Deuxième Bureau* had wired to Gamelin: "Be ready! Attack tomorrow at dawn!" The assault was to come through the Ardennes Forest. But once again, Gamelin, orthodox to the end, had ignored the message.

And, on the morning of May 10, 1940, upon learning that the war had begun, he ordered his armies to march up into Belgium.

(4)

As his *Panzer* crossed into Luxembourg, General Guderian peered out of his cockpit toward the end of the bridge below. He was, as always, expecting trouble.

No soldiers from Luxembourg had appeared that morning, but the Duchy had tried to slow the coming *Panzer* advance by erecting, parallel to the River Sauer, a series of high concrete walls reinforced with deeply imbedded iron poles. These could scarcely keep the invaders out—German engineers had come equipped with wooden ramps designed to fit over the walls and allow the tanks to climb up and over but they did force Guderian to stop his advance for more than half an hour. And every moment was precious.

Then, for a time, he relaxed. Through the slit in his turret he could see cows munching away in contentment and farmers trudging onto their fields with scarcely a glance at the oncoming columns of tanks. By ten o'clock in the morning Guderian had crossed the thirty-some miles of Luxembourg and had reached the Ardennes Forest in the southwest corner of Belgium. There he ran into trouble.

The Belgians had thrown trees and wooden barricades across the roads and had dynamited the bridges so skillfully that the Germans were having to rely entirely on their own pontoon systems to get across the rivers. And Guderian's engines were breaking down. Occasionally a tank would stall or run out of gas and would force the tanks in the column behind it to spend priceless minutes of their own pushing it into a ditch by the side of the road. Such slowdowns seemed increasingly frequent and Guderian found them nerve-wracking: the more slowly his columns progressed, the more inviting they became as targets for the planes of the French Air Force.

But to his great surprise none appeared—the only planes he saw that day bore the reassuring black crosses of the *Luftwaffe*—and by nightfall he was encamped on the wooded slopes of the Ardennes.

Guderian had still another surprise. Just a few miles up on his right and farther into the Forest, General Rommel's Seventh *Panzer* Division had penetrated closer toward France that day than any other unit in the German Army.

(5)

"Are they letting us walk into a trap?"

The Ministers seated at the ornate table in the Quai d'Orsay, in Paris, turned around in their chairs to look at the speaker, Paul Reynaud. He was wiry and dapper, and someone had said, referring both to his highly arched eyebrows and also to his bristling disposition, that he resembled a jockey, or, better yet, a gamecock. He had been a brilliant young lawyer in Paris and, in 1919, had entered politics by winning a seat in the Chamber of Deputies, representing the mountain folk of a district in the Basses-Alpes. After 1930 he had served seven times as Minister of Finance, Colonies or Justice, and now, in the spring of 1940, at the age of sixty-two, he had become the Premier of France. He was determined to stop the German advance.

Everyone in the room could sense his mood. He had always been bursting with energy, eager to seek solutions, restless to get things moving, determined to throw aside old ideas and start all over again. And now, in the face of the German invasion, Reynaud was convinced that they must reassess their tactics.

In his sharp and precise voice Reynaud explained the reasons for his fears.

Commander-in-Chief Gamelin, he said, was a fool. Like all the rest of the High Command, Gamelin had believed that the Germans would march down on foot across the plains of Belgium, as in 1914, and that the French could defend themselves with an equally large infantry and a long, continuous, fortified line of defense, again as in 1914. So Gamelin had ignored the warnings about the Ardennes Forest and the Sedan sector, and had confidently ordered the Allied troops to march ahead into Belgium. Gamelin was smart to do this, Reynaud admitted, if he was right in his assumption that the Germans were prepared to refight the First World War. But what, Reynaud demanded, if they were not?

Reynaud went on. The Allied advance into Belgium was starting well, yes, but what if that was just what the Germans had wanted? What if it was a trick? What if the German tanks and half-tracks did penetrate the Ardennes Forest, did break through at Sedan and did catch the ponderous Allied armies from the rear? Then what would happen? The answer, Renaud said, was obvious. The French and the British troops would be trapped in Belgium without hope of escape.

Now was the time to act, he continued. He had recently asked the Cabinet for support in firing Gamelin but the Commander-in-Chief had had friends among the Ministers—including the powerful former Premier Edouard Daladier—and Reynaud had let the matter ride. But this time, Reynaud said, the crisis had come: this time he was going to act on his own. The next time they heard from him, he assured his Ministers, he would have replaced Gamelin and ordered a retreat from Belgium.

But the news that spread that afternoon among the Ministries around the Seine and the Ile de la Cité was different. Reynaud had gone to his office, telephoned Daladier and, hearing the rasp of Daladier's voice, once again decided to stick with Gamelin. About the call for retreat the Ministers heard nothing at all.

(6)

General Guderian was still nervous. Although his tanks had encountered no hostile gunfire the next morning and although he himself had seen only a few enemy horsemen flitting among the trees, he had remained certain that trouble would come.

His engines were becoming overheated on the narrow, twisting roads of the Ardennes Forest and, while his military police tried frantically to unsnarl the enormous traffic jams that stretched across the woods, he kept a continuous watch on the dazzlingly clear sky above. Surely, he thought, the French must realize that now, with the Germans bogged down on these mountain roads, they had their great chance to destroy the most powerful divisions of the Third Reich and win the war with one quick strike from the air.

After he had stopped his tank that night in Neufchâteau, a village two-thirds of the way across the Ardennes Forest, he stayed awake until dawn listening to the French reconnaissance planes overhead and waiting for the bombs to fall.

To his great surprise, the Forest that night remained empty and silent: most of the Allied bombers had flown up to Belgium.

Something else, too, came as a shock. Miles ahead now of all its sister units, almost up to the border of France, stood the Seventh *Panzer* Division under the lead of General Rommel.

(7)

On the morning of May 11, the warnings began to reach the French High Command. Overnight air reconnaissance, reported General d'Astier de la Vigerie of the French Air Force, had revealed a heavy concentration of German "motorized elements" pushing through the Ardennes Forest.

General Gamelin saw no reason to worry. As his armies marched in the sunshine through towns in northeastern France, he had learned, they had seen French flags and tricolor garlands hanging from all the windows, and women with sweets in their aprons had come rushing toward them from the cottage doorways. In Belgium, too, the roads had been clear, and as they trooped in the direction of Holland, the French and British retaliatory forces had encountered no trace of opposition, either from the German infantry or from the *Panzer* columns or from the mighty Nazi air fleet. Things were going well, perhaps too well, and Kim Philby, a British journalist assigned to the march, who later would betray his country to the Soviets, asked a companion why the Germans might be holding back.

Someone else had seen the answer. After studying his late-morning, air-reconnaissance photographs, General d'Astier de la Vigerie sent off an urgent wire to Gamelin's headquarters in Paris. "The enemy appears to be preparing an energetic action," the message said, "in the general direction of Givet"—still in Belgium but just opposite the town of Sedan.

But the High Command was still looking toward the north. The French soldiers, said all the reports, were singing as they marched along the roads and the British Tommies were greeting passersby with their thumbs stuck up in the air, the new gesture that meant, "OK! Everything is jolly good!" "We shall have saved the Belgian Army," wrote the British General William Ironside that night. "On the whole the advantage is with us."

One Allied General, Alphonse Georges, the French second-in-command, did realize that something was wrong. He too had seen the intelligence reports from the Ardennes Forest and before retiring that night he issued Instruction No. 12 in which he foresaw the need to send seven fresh divisions "into the second position behind Sedan."

But the headquarters at the ancient Vincennes castle in Paris where Georges was stationed had no radio-communications center: his order did go out over the telephone, and it did reach the appropriate reserve camps, but it did not reach the divisional commanders there for another forty-eight hours.

(8)

"Keep going! Keep going! Don't stop!"

General Guderian was standing in the turret of his tank before dawn on May 12, as nervous as ever, shouting down to his men, waving them on with his Luger, and urging them to go faster and faster toward Sedan. But that morning, for the first time, he ran into real difficulty: the Belgian Air Force was starting to fight back.

He had just driven his tank over a bridge across the Semois, a river winding down the western side of the Ardennes Forest, and had started to push along the steep gorge toward Sedan when his problems began. Mines in the roadbed forced him to turn back to Bouillon, a Belgian town above the river, and there a Belgian air squadron came swooping down upon his position.

They managed only to set a house or two on fire and Guderian was soon able to drive along the Semois again to watch the Tenth *Panzer* Division ford the river. He returned to Bouillon within the hour and in an alcove of the Hôtel Panorama sat down with his staff to plan for the next stage of their attack. He was in his chair, however, for only a moment.

From the courtyard outside he heard a violent explosion and in the same instant a boar's head on the wall just behind his desk broke loose and missed him by less than a foot. Guderian sprawled flat on the floor. Other trophies along the walls came tumbling down and another set of explosions shattered the window that gave onto the Semois River. Splinters of glass shot across the room.

Guderian knew what had happened: the Belgian planes had found him again. Twice more that morning Guderian shifted his base; twice more that morning the Belgian bombers appeared overhead.

The Allied bombardment was growing heavy. French artillery along the Meuse, a few miles to the southwest, was lobbing shells at the German pontoon bridges over the Semois and British Royal Air Force fighters began running up and down the twisting Semois valley to finish off the marooned *Panzers.* Two times that morning a squadron of French-owned, American-made Curtiss fighter planes flew toward oncoming waves of *Stukas,* engaged them in dogfights, and, in spite of being grossly outnumbered, managed to shoot every one of them down.

But the *Stukas* kept coming, the *Panzers* kept moving, and by the end of the afternoon Guderian had stopped his tank on a hillside from which he could see the medieval spires of Sedan. His *Panzers* had just done the impossible: they had just penetrated the Forest that Marshal Pétain had called "impenetrable." With a yell and a wave Guderian led his tanks down the slopes and out across the valley of the Meuse toward Sedan.

Someone else had beaten him there. Erwin Rommel's Seventh *Panzer* Division had already reached the Meuse at Sedan and was starting its drive against the defenses of the Second French Army.

(9)

In 1914, the German juggernaut had crashed through Belgium, wheeled down from the Channel and marched on toward Paris, but the French had held at the Marne. In 1916, the Germans had thrown every man and gun they could spare at the French fortress at Verdun and launched against the positions there the heaviest bombardment of the war, but General Philippe Pétain, the hero of Verdun, had held and driven them back. In 1918, the Germans had launched an even greater assault: in late March they had pushed fourteen miles into French territory; in early April they had forced their way another ten miles toward Paris; in late May and early June, they had hurtled on to the Compiègne-Soissons railway, less than sixty miles from Paris; and in mid-July one German division had reached a road five miles beyond the Marne and less than forty miles from Paris. General Ludendorff, the German Commander-in-Chief, had drunk a toast to victory. Then, under the command of Marshal Ferdinand Foch, the French and the Americans had driven the enemy back. Four months later German emissaries had climbed aboard Foch's railway coach at Compiègne to sign the Armistice.

In 1940, Erwin Rommel accomplished in three days what the earlier generation of German Generals had failed to do in four years.

On May 13 he forded the Meuse, on May 14 he broke through at

Sedan, and on May 15 he set out again, leading the way for all other *Panzers* into France and closing the trap upon the Allied forces in Belgium.

In the rout that followed only one French unit took effective steps to save the troops in Belgium. That was the Fourth Armored Division, fancifully titled, hastily assembled, below strength and lacking in divisional training. Its commander was Colonel Charles de Gaulle.

Chapter 2

(1)

ONCE AGAIN A DE GAULLE WAS ABOUT TO DO BATTLE IN A LOSING CAUSE. THE FIRST KNOWN DE GAULLE (ACCORDING TO THE FAMILY'S GENE-ALOGY), A KNIGHT NAMED JEAN, HAD RIDDEN OUT OF THE MISTS OF Flanders to do battle against the English longbowmen on the fields at Agincourt. The family then sank from the ranks of nobility—a sixteenth-century de Gaulle was a miller in Burgundy—but surfaced again in Louis XIV's Paris as lawyers and clerks of the state. A portly, shrewd-eyed Jean-Baptiste-Philippe de Gaulle barely escaped the guillotine during the French Revolution and wound up Director of Promotions in the *Grande Armée* of Napoleon. But his son, Julien, was a monkish and threadbare scholar who wrote a history of Paris and compiled the de Gaulle genealogy. Julien's son, Henri, however, had always dreamed of being a soldier and, after graduating from the Ecole Polytechnique and becoming a Lieutenant in the artillery, he fought against the armies of Bismarck at Le Bourget, outside Paris. A Prussian bullet struck him in the kneecap. But it was his lack of independent wealth, necessary for an officer's expensive life, which forced him out of the service.

Henri de Gaulle never forgot that he had fallen in the service of France. Nor did he let others forget.

Year after year Henri appeared in the classrooms of the Parisian Catholic schools in which he taught, dressed in a black frock coast and sharply pressed striped trousers. Before lecturing he would peel off his butter-colored gloves and place his top hat on the desk before him. Henri wrote Greek elegies with bone-white fingers and once, when the Duc de Guise, the Pretender to the Throne, visited the College of the Immaculate Conception, Professor de Gaulle fainted dead away in front of his students.

But Henri had a gift as well: he knew how to make the past come alive. A generation of students attested to this. When you listened to Professor de Gaulle, the heroes of French history had real faces and real voices, and the bullets from their enemies' guns drew real blood. Henri's ability to mime brought his students and children alike to an understanding of, and a deep love for, the history of France—the bygone France of knights and cathedral builders and stained-glass kings.

His wife, Jeanne, had a different kind of effect upon their children: she taught them self-control. This tiny woman, *née* Jeanne Maillot, the daughter of a tobacco importer in Lille, was inwardly passionate, vibrant and warm, but she was also a perfectionist. She hated the careless and the slovenly, and she tried above all else to instill in her children the desire to serve others. As would her son, Charles, in maturity, she hid her feelings behind a mask of ice.

Jeanne and Henri de Gaulle reinforced each other's parental guidance. Over dinnertime plates of soup, on visits after school to the tomb of Napoleon, during carriage rides outside Paris to the farm where Henri had been wounded, whenever and wherever the family was together, they hammered and hammered upon a single theme: their children must devote their lives to the service of France.

Charles added his own dimension to this theme: a determination to live and act on a wider stage than that of his parents.

This breadth of spirit, perhaps, had come down from his grandmother, Josephine Maillot-Delannoy. Tall and gangling like her grandson, and a mid-nineteenth-century bluestocking, she had written novels, biographies (of Châteaubriand and Daniel O'Connell) and had edited a magazine in which she published essays by Proudhon, a French socialist thinker. Her grandson Charles would seem to have inherited both her literary bent and her independence of mind. After his birth on November 22, 1890, in his grandparents' home in Lille (he was the second of five children), the family moved back to Paris where he grew into a skinny, uncontrollable brat. "Lower your eyes," his teachers would tell him, for the boy had an insolent stare, and, along with his sisters and three brothers, he was a great practical joker. In spite of, or perhaps because of, his prodigious memory, his homework had bored him and, much to his grave father's consternation, instead of doing his lessons, at night he had often tussled with his brothers in the back bedrooms of the family's Paris apartment.

During the family holidays by the Dordogne, in the foothills east of Bordeaux, he had delighted in organizing imaginary wars in which boys from the neighboring villages had played the parts of foot soldiers and he, naturally, the role of commanding general.

With the onset of adolescence, he grew taller than his brothers, with no chin, a small pouting mouth, a long drooping nose, hooded eyes and a high receding forehead topped with flat black hair. And he began to act, his sister said, as if he had fallen into an icebox.

To an extent his environment had forced this upon him. His father was poorly paid—he could afford a summer cottage only by living on a fifth-floor flat (it was fashionable then to live on the first) in the Place de Président Mithouard in Paris—and such perpetual insolvency set young de Gaulle apart in school. But something else, too, was in his makeup.

The pieties he had heard from his father in praise of honor, the lessons he had learned from his teachers in praise of service, the themes from his many books in praise of devotion had taught him not only ideals but also the value of independence. No longer had he been content with membership in an old—and uncelebrated—family; no longer had he been happy with deferring to his teachers' judgments; no longer had he been able to accept the optimistic patriotism of his history books. He wanted to remake an imperfect world and to leave his mark upon it—but entirely in his own way.

Shy, awkward boys have often wished to reform their world and then, faced with the taunts of schoolmates more worldly than they and with the need of earning a living, have given way to the teasing and finished their adolescence as "grown-up" and "down-to-earth" as their friends. Not so with de Gaulle. In the three years before his career at Saint-Cyr, his longing to be himself and to leave his mark on affairs neither changed nor diminished. It hardened. Aware of his height (six feet, four inches) he began to stand as tall and erect as he could; sensing his strangeness he became even colder and more aloof than before. He became proud, indifferent, remote from others—and, thought many, in danger of losing touch with reality.

"My older brother, Xavier," de Gaulle himself once said, "was crazy. The others were normal. I was in between."

In 1910, he entered Saint-Cyr, the West Point of France. His family tradition, his father and his personality alike had suggested this step. In the Army, his stiffness and size would act to his benefit; in the Army, his shyness could hide in formality and rank; in the Army, his remoteness could help his command. But he seemed odd even to his Saint-Cyr classmates. He was a good student, and courteous, and he took part in several class plays, but something always seemed to keep him apart. There was a haughtiness about him, a disdain, a refusal to reveal his inner thoughts. Sometimes his fellow cadets call him "Cyrano," after the size of his nose, but more often simply the "Constable of France."

In 1912 came graduation and Second Lieutenant de Gaulle joined the 33rd Infantry Regiment at Arras under the command of Colonel Philippe Pétain.

Pétain had been born on April 24, 1856, into a peasant family, near Cauchy-à-la-Tour just south of Calais. He had studied hard and well in his youth and at Saint-Cyr he had compiled an excellent record. Upon graduation, he had had every reason to anticipate a brilliant career with the infantry, but Pétain had been difficult, both personally and intellect-ually. Toward his fellow officers, most of whom derived from the upper middle classes and who sneered at this tense and graceless peasant boy, he had shown little but contempt; toward the official Army doctrine at the time, the ideology of offensive war based upon swift cavalry charges and massive bayonet assults, he had revealed little but scorn. He had be-lieved, and had publicly stated his belief, in defensive war, in which the infantry would move slowly and always with the support of firepower from artillery and machine guns. Because Pétain had been bright, un-orthodox and outspoken, his rate of promotion had been uncommonly slow. When Lieutenant de Gaulle joined his regiment in 1912, Pétain was fifty-six, and still only a Colonel.

At Arras, de Gaulle continued the habits of earlier years: he pored over his histories of France (the trunk in his quarters was always crammed tight with books) and he resumed his custom of taking long walks by him-self through the fields and villages outside the base. He soon came to Pétain's attention.

One night the Colonel was lecturing the young officers of the Regi-ment on a siege of Arras in 1654, and had just described the tactics the rebel Condé had used to encircle the town, when de Gaulle leaped im-petuously to his feet and exclaimed: "But Turenne [Louis XIV's command-ing general] was there, and made his presence known by the sound of his cannon. Arras was saved." Pétain gave de Gaulle the job of teaching French history to the new recruits—a task that Charles relished—and in October, 1913, saw to it that he was promoted to First Lieutenant.

De Gaulle did not teach for long. On June 28, 1914, in a street of Sarajevo, in Bosnia, a member of the Serbian secret society called the Black Hand shot and killed Archduke Francis Ferdinand, heir to the throne of the Hapsburg Empire. Two months later, the men of de Gaulles's regi-ment, dressed in the infantry's traditional red trousers, blue great-coats and scarlet topped kepis, searched for the enemy in the neighborhood of Dinant, on the Meuse, engaged him, and then fell back into a long retreat.

Two years later de Gaulle fell wounded near Verdun and was captured by the Germans.

(2)

Three years later, in April, 1917, the new French Commander-in-Chief, Robert Nivelle, had gathered virtually the last scraps of equipment and manpower in France to launch a final offensive against the German lines. Nivelle knew that if he could not break the stalemate in the trenches, and break it soon, if he could not justify all the sacrifice, all the dying, through victory, his men would mutiny and the Germans would win. He decided, therefore, to risk an all-out attack near the village of Chemin-des-Dames. French intelligence had learned of the strengthened German defenses at Chemin-des-Dames: the clusters of mutually reinforcing machine-gun nests, the dugouts where troops could hide in safety until they were ready to counterattack, the divisions so beefed-up that they outnumbered all divisions Nivelle had collected. The odds were greatly against his succeeding, but Nivelle was determined, and the offensive began in a barrage of artillery fire on the morning of April 15.

It was sleeting and cold, the mud was deep, and the soldiers' feet were sore, but all that seemed perfectly normal. Movement along the roads toward the front lines was becoming slower and slower, but that too had happened before. Then the sleet turned to snow, and the French troops had their first premonition of disaster: they could hardly see through the storm.

The offensive collapsed. French guns fell too short or too long, much of the infantry stayed in the trenches, unable to move in the face of the withering machine-gun fire; those who left their positions got stuck in the barbed wire on the other side, presenting easy targets to the machine-gun nests; and some, advancing against all hope, looked ahead, and saw the line of their own exploding shells reappear from the German side and roll and right back over them. "It's all up," the troops said that night, "we can't do it, we never shall do it."

The next morning the Germans counterattacked and within days Nivelle had resigned. Two weeks later, on April 29, 1917, the men who Nivelle had thought would mutiny if he did not attack, mutinied precisely because he had. Fortunately the Army still had Pétain.

On April 29, 1917, the 2d Battalion of the 18th Infantry Regiment of the 1st Colonial Division got drunk on wine and refused to march. "Down with the war!" they shouted, and "Lets's go to Paris!" and "Kill all the officers!" The mutiny spread quickly; whole divisions laid down their arms.

> Camps were placarded with notices declaring the intention of the soldiers to refuse to go back again to the trenches. . . . A battalion ordered to the front dispersed in a wood. Soldiers coming home on leave sang the *Internationale* in the trains and demanded peace. Mutinies occurred in sixteen different Army Corps. . . . A number of young infantrymen marched through the streets of a French town, "baaing" like sheep to indicate they were being driven like lambs to the slaughter.

The mutinies became so extensive that, by the middle of June, 1917, the Army possessed a mere *two divisions* that it considered wholly and absolutely reliable. The High Command was desperate. Strikes were spreading through the munitions factories, the country was defenseless, and over the trenches there was an ominous silence that could mean only one thing: the Germans were preparing to attack.

The High Command, in its desperation, turned to the man it had despised the most before the war: Henri Philippe Pétain, once Colonel of the 33rd, then, in 1916, winner of the bloody battle at Verdun and now, Commander-in-Chief of France. Pétain worked fast; administration was his strength. To soothe the men he issued longer leaves and better food, to cool their tongues he cut off their wine, and to teach them a lesson he ordered fifty-five of the ringleaders shot before their eyes. Gradually, by the end of the summer, the men had returned to the front, and, at home, Premier Clemenceau had put an end to the strikes. But to quell rebellion was one thing; to stop the Germans was quite another.

The French felt frightened and defenseless: frightened, because German airplanes were strafing them at will and because in late July, for the first time, the enemy had used the blistering, choking chemical called "mustard gas" which, combined with the mud and the water, caused persistent casualties long after its release; defenseless, because civil war had broken out in Russia, France's former ally, causing Lenin to sign a treaty of peace with Germany, and because Lloyd George, the British Prime Minister, had decided to keep large numbers of his own troops safe on British soil. The French were scared, admitted their fear, and all they could do about it was to peer over their sandbags and wait for the dreaded attack. They knew the Germans would come, they knew when and approximately where; they did not know how long they themselves could hold on.

Erich Ludendorff, the German Commander-in-Chief, knew that in America, which had declared war on Germany, training camps had sprung out of the fields and forests, and factories were working three shifts a day; he also knew that soon a million Yanks would be boarding their ships for France and taking the troop trains to reinforce the front. He saw, therefore, that he had little time left. To his senior generals, he revealed his tactics: a series of sledgehammer blows, with short, intensive, artillery preparations, massive assaults and continued forward movement, designed to crash through the front, defeat the remaining British armies and force the surrender of France—all before the Yanks arrived. The bulk of the American army was due in July, 1918.

The Germans came for the first time on March 21, 1918. They launched their attack with gas and artillery fire, and then, under the cover of fog, they clawed over the barbed wire, raced through the machine-gun fire, jabbed their bayonets into the trenches below and, finally, pushed beyond toward the second lines of defense. In four days of fighting, the Germans had made their longest gain since 1914: they had advanced fourteen miles into French territory, threatening the vital rail junction at Amiens, and they had wheeled their new long-range gun close enough to Paris to lob shells onto its streets and rooftops. Then they paused to prepare for their second blow.

The Allies had to replace Pétain. "You are not fighting," the French General Foch had screamed at him after Pétain had proposed a retreat to Paris; "I would fight without stopping. I would fight before Amiens. I would fight at Amiens. I would fight behind Amiens. I would fight all the time." On April 13, the British and French governments asked Ferdinand Foch to be the new Commander-in-Chief and the first head of all the Allied armies. Foch had long lectured at the War College about the coming war and there he had coined his famous aphorisms:

> "The will to conquer is the first condition of victory" . . . and "A battle in which one will not confess oneself beaten". . . . But the idea
> that morale alone could conquer, Foch warned, was an "infantile
> notion". . . . From his flights of metaphysics he would descend at
> once to the earth of tactics, the placing of advance guards, the necessity of *sûreté*, or protection.

Now Foch had his chance to test his ideas. His job was to hold on, to slow the attack, to stop the retreat at any cost until the Americans arrived in July. He had three months to go.

---

*Foch later commented: "If the job requires that nothing be done, Pétain is your man."

The Germans came for the second time on April 9. They raced toward the important rail junction of Hazebrouck, near Ypres, pushing a British division out of their way and moving so fast that Haig, the top British General, felt compelled to issue his "backs-to-the-wall" command!

> There is no other course open to us but to fight it out. Every position must be held to the last man. . . . With our backs to the wall and believing in the justice of our cause each one must fight on to the end.

Foch rushed seven divisions into the attackers' path and his planes strafed and bombed the Germans, but the enemy kept on coming. On the front the Allied soldiers were being decimated; in the rear the reserves were gasping and gangrenous. Premier Georges Clemenceau, the "Old Tiger," shook his fist at the Chamber of Deputies and cried out that from then on the Germans would face "War—nothing but war!" France had two months to go.

The Germans came for the third time on May 27. Nineteen divisions made up the initial assault; twenty-three followed immediately. By the end of the first day they had crossed ten miles beyond the River Aisne; by June 2, they had reached Château-Thierry on the Marne, just fifty-six miles from Paris.

The Allied troops staggered. In some units as many as 40 percent of the men died. Even Foch saw little reason for hope—except for one encounter that most observers had overlooked. At 6:45 A.M., on May 28, after an hour of artillery preparation, the First American Division, already in France, had attacked the village of Cantigny, high on a hill above the Avre valley. The attack had been a complete success and Foch sent his congratulations to the First. He had one month to go.

The Germans came for the fourth time on June 9. Thirteen divisions poured over the lines, driving toward the Montdidier-Compiègne-Soissons railway, trying to link the salient at the Marne with the bulge at Amiens. They gained six miles this time, less than before, but enough to persuade General Ludendorff to drink his toast to victory.

Foch's help was on the way. American troop ships were anchored off Cherbourg and Le Havre and trains stood in lines beside the piers, ready to steam off toward the front. The Yanks were almost there.

The Germans came for the fifth, and final, time on July 15. One division reached a road five miles beyond the Marne, and everywhere the Germans hurtled across the Allied trenches at will—except where the Americans were stationed. There, they did not advance. The Germans paused to regroup; Foch and the Yanks hit back. The Second Battle of the

Marne had begun, but without American help the French would have lost it.

Four months later, in a clearing in the forest of Compiègne, German emissaries climbed aboard the railway coach of Marshal Foch to sign the Armistice. It was November 11, 1918. Foch rode to Paris that day: Cheering mobs recognized him, cheered him and pummeled him. The victor of the Marne waved back and shook their hands all along the route to the War Office. There, at the top of the stairs, he saw the Old Tiger, Premier Clemenceau, standing amidst a crowd of dignitaries, and the two men fell into each other's arms. That afternoon, at half past two, Clemenceau entered the Chamber of Deputies, his shoulders limp and his head bowed in exhaustion as he moved through the rows of Deputies. The applause grew to a frenzy. Clemenceau mounted the rostrum and painfully raised his hand for quiet.

He read out the terms of the Armistice, and when he had finished, he called for gratitude to Foch and the armies of France.

"Thanks to them," he cried, "France, yesterday the soldier of God, today the soldier of humanity, will be forever the soldier of the ideal."

The citizens streaming toward Paris that night could see, for the first time in four years, the glow of the city's lights against the darkening sky. In the streets outside the War Office, where Clemenceau had returned, the men and women of Paris milled by the thousands. "Clemenceau!" they chanted, "Cle-men-ceau! Cle-men-ceau!" The Old Tiger was silhouetted in the window. He threw it open and for a moment looked down upon his people in silence. Then he answered them: *"Vive la France!"* He went back into his room and sat down in his chair again, utterly worn out.

For he knew the price of survival had been too high. Artillery fire and German sabotage had gutted the homes of northern France and had made the fields unfit for crops. Four years of war had emptied the treasury and had left France with debts stacked so high that they were virtually beyond counting. In the horror of the trenches, 1,357,800 Frenchmen died, 4,266,000 were wounded and 537,000 were imprisoned or missing in action—a whole generation of young men maimed or destroyed. France would have lost without outside help, and without the spirit of Foch.

(3)

After becoming a prisoner in 1916—he had been wounded twice before—Charles de Gaulle had tried five times to escape but on each occasion his unusual height betrayed him. On his last attempt his stolen German uniform reached only to his elbows and knees and he landed in a German reprisal camp at Ingolstadt in Bavaria. "The toughest, most stubborn prisoner in the whole camp," a German guard said later, "was that mulehead de Gaulle."

There, embittered by isolation, de Gaulle had buried his nose in books and, when it was his turn to stretch his legs, usually strolled alone in the exercise yard. But, upon his release, he began to soften, to relax.

In 1919, after the Bolshevik Revolution and the outbreak of civil war in Russia, in which the Western Allies aided Lenin's enemies, the Soviets attacked Poland in the hope of linking forces with German Communists and so bringing a new wave of revolution to Europe. The conservative French government countered by appointing "advisers" to the Polish troops at the front. Captain de Gaulle volunteered for the job—and fell in love with Warsaw.

He often appeared at the home of the beautiful Countess Rose Tyszkiewicz, whose eighteenth-century mansion adjoined a park in the heart of Warsaw and whose furniture had come from the French Renaissance. De Gaulle sharpened his wit and found that, when he wished, he could both charm and amuse his Polish hosts. Even more often he strolled down Novy Swiat Street to the Blikie Café, where the fritters were famous and the pastries were gorgeous and the women were luscious. He became accustomed to spending a whole month's pay in a week, then taking all meals on the officer's mess on post, and finally, on the next payday, charging right back to the fleshpots for which Warsaw was renowned throughout Europe.

In 1921 de Gaulle was back in France, and Yvonne Vendroux, the daughter of a Calais biscuit maker, came into his life.

The year before, she had still been in Paris at a convent school where the girls wore sailor collars and wide Breton hats. She had already turned down a proposal from an officer because, as she told her friends, "When I start my family I want it to be in my own hometown. Traipsing from garrison to garrison is not the life for me." But a friend, a Mme. Denquin, who had known de Gaulle since childhood, had unexpectedly found him having lunch in her parent's home in Paris. "The *enfant terrible*," she said, "had grown up into a handsome young Captain. A curious thought came into my mind: Yvonne Vendroux doesn't want to marry an officer but I'll bet she would change her mind if she met Charles."

The couple was married on April 7, 1921, in the church of Notre-Dame in Calais.

For a time their life was quiet. They lived in a small pleasant flat on the Left Bank in Paris—de Gaulle began to teach history at Saint-Cyr—and soon Yvonne gave birth to their first child, Philippe; the boy's godfather was Marshal Philippe Pétain. The Marshal had had his eye on de Gaulle since before the First World War. He respected the younger officer's earnestness and ability, and during this period just after the war frequently invited Charles and Yvonne for Sunday dinners in his home in suburban Paris. Years later, after the two men had become enemies, Pétain would still remember de Gaulle as "one of the best." And, during the early 1920's, young de Gaulle felt it a privilege to have Pétain as his mentor. De Gaulle seemed happy in his work and contented in his home.

But, someone has said, before he wed Yvonne he had been married to France. Two years later an explosion occured.

In November, 1922, recognizing de Gaulle as a potential General, his superiors assigned him to a two-year course of study at the War College in Paris.

Another officer, André Lafargue, serving on the same assignment, has recalled his first memory of de Gaulle: "At the opening convocation, in the conference ampitheater, I saw a tall, very tall Captain in a blue uniform, coming down the steps to take his place in the seat below mine. He was very erect, stiff, grave, seeming overly dignified, as if he were taking the place of his own statue." Later Lafargue had become friends with de Gaulle, finding him friendly, polite and, at times, even witty.

But to his professors de Gaulle seemed unbearable. Their first critiques were gentle: "He should work out well," the first year's recommendation said, "if he just learns to listen more readily to the opinions of others. He should succeed in any branch of the Army." In his second year, however, de Gaulle began to question his teachers in class—the Army's faith in the effectiveness of defensive lines and mass-conscript divisions had begun to trouble him—and the reports in his dossier grew harsher. "He showed the highest qualities," one of his professors stated, but he was "arrogant. He mixed little with the other students. He came to the amphitheater almost always alone." Then, from his seat in the class, he had the gall to deliver lectures on the need for mobility in the Army's tactics—and the resentment became intense. He was "intelligent, cultivated and serious," said a report, but he was "excessively sure of himself" and beginning to act like a "king in exile." He lacked, it said, "a sense of reality." Finally, during the war games that concluded the course, Captain de Gaulle disobeyed instructions and, using his forces as if they were mobilized, managed to win the contest. He graduated with the mark of *"bien,"* a good grade.

Only a few fellow students looked past the mask of his solitude: among them was a Captain Chauvin. One evening in the late 1920's, he and de Gaulle were strolling in a meadow in Alsace after maneuvers and sat down against a beech tree for a leisurely smoke. After the sun had sunk down behind the adjacent forest, they began to chat about their futures in the Army. De Gaulle let his thoughts drift off in silence.

Chauvin had never understood de Gaulle, yet he instinctively liked this towering giant and, after a long hesitation, he decided to try out a theory. "My friend," he said, finally, "I'm going to say something to you that I'm sure will make you laugh. I have the funny feeling that you have pledged yourself to a great destiny."

Chauvin then expected a laugh of protest or an elbow in the ribs — most officers would have responded that way — but de Gaulle said nothing, nothing at all. In surprise and curiosity Chauvin looked up at his comrade. De Gaulle sat without moving, his eyes staring somewhere over the tops of the trees. Then, slowly, heavily, he turned to his friend and spoke. Chauvin would remember the words for the next thirty years.

"Yes," de Gaulle said, "I have."

Then, in 1928, a tragedy struck.

After a year in Alsace and after the birth of Elizabeth in Paris (where de Gaulle was assigned to the Superior War Council), Yvonne de Gaulle became pregnant again. Whether it was because of de Gaulle's inheritance (his father and mother had been second cousins) or whether it was because of his new assignment (the de Gaulles spent the early months of 1928 along the Rhine again where influenza ran rampant that winter) or whether it was because of some freak of nature is impossible to say. But, by the summer of 1928, after Anne, their third child was born, the de Gaulles had come to learn the awful truth. Anne could never walk or talk or live as other children: she had been born a Mongoloid.

From that moment on, many said, de Gaulle's eyes never lost their look of abstracted bitterness.

For he now faced a harsh dilemma: who was in greater need of his help; his child, who would need constant attention, or his country that he believed was pledging herself to disaster? The day would come, he felt sure, when he might have to make a choice.

For a time, in the middle 1930's, de Gaulle seemed again at peace with the world. Despite further tours of duty in Paris and the Near East, he came increasingly to think of his new stone house, la Boisserie, in the village of Colombey-les-deux-églises in eastern France, as his permanent home. There, by the den window that overlooked the fields and rolling hills, he composed his thoughts and did his writing; there, in the living room downstairs, he sang and laughed and jostled with little Anne; there, after dinner and coffee, he took long evening strolls around the barnyard or across the woods of his land. There, de Gaulle began to play the secluded country squire.

He seemed to want to settle down, to stop traipsing from post to post, to live in peace with his retiring wife, with his two older children, Philippe and Elizabeth, and with his invalid daughter, Anne, from whom only he had the gift of eliciting laughter. He seemed happy in obscurity.

(4)

But after the Treaty of Versailles, Marshal Foch had warned that the peace was not a peace but a pause, an "armistice for twenty years." Yet the French had soon forgotten his words. The Empire abroad had grown—the Allies had given France control of the Levant—and French trade was beginning to flourish across the globe; the fields at home were blooming, and the people were feeling wealthy again. "Even a young foreigner [in Paris] felt he was living in as much of a paradise as could be found on this imperfect earth." Not since Napoleon, not even perhaps since Louis XIV had the French felt so rich, so happy and so safe.

But a Frenchman wrote later,

> our victory in 1918 cost us too dearly . . . strictly speaking the French
> nation no longer [existed]. . . . We [were] living like a ruined landlord
> unwilling to seem bankrupt.

The economy showed signs of collapse. The U.S. demanded that France repay her debts from the war—"they hired the money, didn't they?" asked President Coolidge—and in 1929 France agreed to pay $6.75 billion, a sum that interest rates had raised to twice the amount of the original loan. In the late twenties, when the government tried to raise its taxes, capital fled the country, and panic spread throughout the Bourse. Then, in 1931, the Depression hit, pushing unemployment to half a million men, causing cuts in salaries and wages, and producing countless Fascist leagues that rioted in the streets of Paris and put the Republic itself in peril of its life.

The governments were always in trouble. The Right refused to pay its taxes and looked with longing toward the growth of Fascism in Italy; the Left debated and scorned and ridiculed but did nothing to save the Republic from bankruptcy. The Cabinets were notoriously unstable: sometimes they fell in the Chamber, sometimes they quit to reshuffle their members, sometimes, quite simply, they resigned out of fear of future defeats, but never did they last long enough to tackle the fiscal dilemmas of France.

Some of their members, in fact, could have solved nothing even if they had remained in office. One night after his election in 1920, the President of the Republic, Paul Deschanel,

> jumped off a presidential train steaming through the countryside and, clad only in pajamas, presented himself, after a short walk in the dark through the brush along the rails, to the guardian of a forlorn grade-crossing drawbar. When the President identified himself the guardian took him for a lunatic and called the gendarmerie. A little later the President was discovered floundering about like a wounded carp in a pond near the presidential château at Rambouillet and near to drowning. Finally . . . Deschanel was forced to resign his high office because of incapacity.

His home district of Eure-et-Loir promptly elected him to the Senate.

Worst of all was the coming of Pierre Laval. He had begun his career in 1914 as the Socialist and pacifist deputy from the working-class Parisian suburb of Aubervilliers, but, in the early twenties, he dropped the Socialists and became a conservative, for he had discovered that the Right was willing to make him rich. Between 1925 and 1930 he served as a minister in several conservative Cabinets and, on January 27, 1931, Pierre Laval himself became the Premier of France. His Cabinet lasted only a year but France had not seen the end of Laval. For Laval sought both money and power, and he would win them through betrayal and brains.

But the French took seriously neither the collapse of their budget nor the decay of their politics because, they reasoned, they had their Army, and it could keep them safe. Two of their heroes, the victors of 1918, were still in command: after his formal retirement in 1931 Marshal Pétain continued to serve on the Supreme War Council, and General Maxime Weygand, the brilliant wartime aide to Marshal Foch became Vice-President of the Council and Inspector General of Armies. Their strategy, these heroes assured the French, was theoretically sound and practically unassailable. The Army still had its horses, its barbed wire, its large infantry divisions and its artillery; and now it was building defensive fortifications all along the eastern frontier of France. In the Great War, the infantry in the trenches and the horse-drawn artillery behind coils of barbed wire had stopped the Germans twice at the Marne; therefore, the Army believed, they would assuredly do so again. They would, said the Army, ". . . suffice for everything."

Of course there were difficulties with all this: the instability of the governments made impossible a consistent diplomacy, the shrinking of the budgets reduced the number of men the Army could equip and feed, the advanced age of the High Command (in 1934, Pétain was seventy-eight, Weygand sixty-seven and his successor, Maurice Gamelin, sixty-five) produced a decided sclerosis of the brain—("after . . . 1918," Pétain later admitted, "my military mind was closed") and the arrogance of the Army

> made the defense of its prejudices and prerogatives the essence of its
> action. . . . Having retired to its own Sinai among its revealed truths
> and the vestiges of its vanished glory, [it] lives on the margin of
> events, devoting all its efforts to patch up an organization that had
> been superseded by the fact."

(5)

But in the pleasant village of Colombey, Charles de Gaulle was beginning to chafe against such passivity. At first the tip-offs were small. He grew finicky, changing his white ceremonial gloves three times a day. He grew impatient, using barracks-room language to his men and becoming sharp with his wife in public. He grew acid, making scornful remarks about his superior officers. He grew bitter, giving way to ever more frequent outbursts of temper.

What was wrong lay in his fear that France's reliance upon the Maginot Line and a mass-conscript army was making disaster inevitable, and that the leadership of the country was making the necessary changes impossible. And no one was listening to his advice.

In 1932 he had published these thoughts in his book *The Edge of the Sword*. "The times through which we are living," he cautioned," are ill-suited to the choice and formation of military leaders. The very intensity of our recent ordeal has had the effect of letting the spring of determination run down too quickly. There has been a lowering of pressure where strong character is concerned and we are now in a period of moral lassitude which had brought the profession of arms into disrepute, so that even those whose vocation is strong and determined are afflicted with doubts. What soldier has not been tempted to apply to himself the words once uttered by a famous woman: 'Why am I here? I do not know.'" France had lost faith in her Army, the Army had lost faith in itself, and, de Gaulle was afraid, they would all sit by until disaster struck.

And disaster would surely strike, for across the Rhine in Germany Adolf Hitler had come to power.

Could the leaders of France, the Premiers and the Generals, rekindle the faith of the people, restore the morale of the Army and so protect against the danger from the east? De Gaulle had the audacity to say no, in the harshest of words.

"Stuffed dummies of the hierarchy," he called them in *The Edge of the Sword*, "parasites who take everything and give nothing in return, weak-kneed creatures forever trembling in their shoes, jumping jacks who will turn their coats without scruple at the first opportunity. They often safeguard their official careers, their rank if they are soldiers, their portfolios if they are ministers. They even, on occasion, receive the deference which custom and convention accord to their office. . . . But such cold and shrewd intelligences can never command the confidence and enthusiasm of others."

Who, then could? Who could uplift the faith of the French? Who could renew the élan of the Army? What kind of man could rebuff the forces of Hitler?

What France needed, de Gaulle wrote, was the "man of character." "It is character," he said "which will constitute the new ferment—character, the virtue of hard times. . . . The man of Character has recourse to himself. His instinctive response is to leave his mark on action, to take responsibility for it, to make it *his own business*. Far from seeking shelter behind his professional superiors, taking refuge in textbooks, or making the regulations bear the responsibility for any decision he may make, he sets his shoulders, takes a firm stand, and looks the problem straight in the face. . . . He is passionately anxious to exert his own will, to make up his own mind. . . . He embraces action with the pride of a master . . .

"Nothing great has ever been achieved without that passion and that confidence which is to be found only in the man of character. Alexander would never have conquered Asia, Galileo would never have demonstrated the movement of the earth, Columbus would never have discovered America, nor Richelieu have restored the authority of the crown had they not believed in themseves and taken full control of the task in hand. . . . We can go further and say that those who have done great deeds have often had to take the risk of ignoring the merely routine aspects of discipline. . . . After the Battle of Jutland and the English failure to take the opportunity offered them of destroying the German fleet, Admiral Fisher, then First Sea Lord, exclaimed in a fury after reading Jellicoe's dispatch: "He has all Nelson's qualities but one: he doesn't know how to disobey!"

And who was this man of character? Who had the strength to act alone? Who could "embrace action with the pride of a master"? Who had the passion and the confidence and the control to disobey?

In all of France in the 1930's, *The Edge of the Sword* implied, there existed only one such man: Charles de Gaulle himself.

The High Command of France found the thought preposterous: de Gaulle, in their eyes, was a pompous ass, a mere Major obsessed with greatness, an officer thoroughly arrogant and undisciplined. Some superiors were eager to have him retire and even Marshal Pétain began to lose faith in de Gaulle.

Then, in 1935, all eyes in France began to turn toward the Rhine.

(6)

In April, 1935, the French consul in Cologne, Jean Dobler, noticed that everywhere he walked or drove, through the narrow medieval streets of the city, high along the banks of the Rhine, out into the fertile countryside, he saw swarms of men erecting barracks, building depots and laying out airfields: just what the Rhineland would need to shelter a German occupation force. Dobler fired two dispatches to Paris and settled back to hear the response.

The Rhineland was out of French control—Wilson and Lloyd George had seen to that—but during the negotiations at Versailles France had accepted a compromise: Articles 42 and 43 of the Treaty forbade the emplacement of German troops and fortifications in the Rhineland, either on the left bank or in a zone extending fifty kilometers to the east of the right bank. In theory this gave France a measure of protection against another German invasion but in practice it just created bitterness and resentment. And, in the spring of 1935, while he was publicly promising to respect the territorial provisions of the Treaty, Hitler was secretly scheming to recapture the Rhine and fill it once more with arms and troops. He called his plan OPERATION *Schulung*, to be "executed be a surprise blow at lightning speed."

In Cologne, as soon as he saw the preparations for OPERATION *Schulung*, Jean Dobler sent another warning to Paris. He received neither acknowledgement of his work nor encouragement to continue.

Then, one day that autumn, the secretaries in the French Embassy in Berlin were frowning in puzzlement. It was November 21, 1935, and their Ambassador, André François-Poncet, had just rushed in from a session with Hitler, leaving the strictest orders that he be undisturbed. Obviously, the secretaries remarked, the Ambassador was greatly alarmed. Was it something Hitler had said?

It was. Hitler had launched into a tirade against the recently signed Franco-Soviet Pact, a treaty, ironically, more threatening to France than to Germany: the French and the Russians had agreed that before they labeled any German act aggressive and went to war, they would ask for a verdict from the League of Nations, and before the League had finished meeting, discussing, debating and deciding, the Germans would easily be parading through the Arc de Triomphe. In fact, Pierre Laval, then the Foreign Minister of France who had become notorious for his dealing with Mussolini, had boasted that the Treaty was worthless. "I've extracted the most dangerous things from it," he had gloated. "I don't trust the Russians." But Hitler had denounced the Pact anyway, and Ambassador François-Poncet had realized what the Germans meant to do. Back to his Embassy he had raced, whishing past the secretaries, and locking his office doors he frantically coded a message for Paris: Hitler intends to grab the Rhineland. What will France do to stop him?

Weeks passed. François-Poncet heard no reply from Paris. On the last day of 1935, in a black and bitter mood, he repeated his message. Once again, silence.

On March 2, 1936, François-Poncet drove again to Hitler's Chancellery to plead for peace, but the S.S. guard beside the Führer's office ordered him to wait in the antechamber. The Führer, they said, was in an urgent meeting. Suddenly the door of Hitler's office flew open and through it stepped a figure familiar to the Ambassador: General Werner von Blomberg, the Nazi Minister of Defense. His face was white, his cheeks twitching; in a daze he rushed through the antechamber, wordlessly. The S.S. guards allowed the Ambassador through Hitler's door. The Führer was "nervous, excited and disturbed." France had no intention of attacking Germany, François-Poncet began to say—but Hitler cut him short. The Franco-Soviet Pact, he screamed, was criminal, a "grave menace for Germany." François-Poncet thought it useless to stay and rose from his chair. Once more he tried: France wants peace, he said, not war. He put on his coat, but then he paused, for Hitler had spoken his name. All smiles and charm now, the Führer had one small favor to ask: would the Ambassador mind keeping his visit and its purpose a secret for just a few days? François-Poncet soon learned why Hitler had made such a peculiar request. General von Blomberg had gone straight to his senior generals with the Führer's orders to mobilize the troops. Five days later, on Saturday, March 7, on the pretext that France was about to attack, the Germans were to parade into the Rhineland. The generals protested: surely, they said, the *Wehrmacht* was still too weak to risk a war. Yes, von Blomberg admitted, it was a considerable gamble, but he would send only a token force into the Rhineland, and if the French counterattacked, he would retreat immediately.

So France could have won. But on the morning of the invasion, the French Ambassador in London scurried to No. 10 Downing Street, only to find that Prime Minister Baldwin and the Cabinet had scattered for a weekend in the country. And a week later, during a dinner party, Baldwin told the new French Foreign Minister, Pierre Flandin, that "if there is even one chance in a hundred that war would follow [a counterattack in the Rhineland] I have not the right to commit England. England is simply not in a state to go to war." He was leaving the job to France, and France was reluctant to move.

The French, of course, did a great deal of talking. They conferred with each other, they negotiated with their allies and they orated in the chambers of the League of Nations. But when the three battalions of gray-uniformed German soldiers marched over the mist-shrouded bridges of the Rhine, the French failed to act. Had they budged, Hitler later admitted, "we would have had to withdraw with our tails between our legs." Said General Jodl: "Considering the situation we were in, the French covering army could have blown us to bits." But why would France have bothered to fight, her High Command reasoned, even against three small battalions? France was safe. She had the Maginot Line.

(7)

One Frenchman, at least, saw the flaw in that reasoning. The "continued unity" of the German Empire, wrote Lieutenant Colonel de Gaulle in 1936, "depends upon outside expansion and great designs, which alone in the eyes of the Germans justify the sacrifices they make for them. Bismarck understood this at first; when he seemed to forget it, a young emperor turned him out, with the approval of everyone. Today the Reich follows along the same lines. Who can doubt that a fresh crisis will once more draw the Germans toward Paris?"

"Nowadays," he observed in a new book, *The Army of the Future,* "Germany is . . . marshalling [all] the means at her disposal with a view to rapid invasion." From where would the Germans come? They would take the route they had always followed: "the adversary who strikes simultaneously in Flanders, in the Ardennes, in Lorraine, in Alsace and at the gates of Burgundy, is delivering converging blows. If he succeeds at one point he shatters the whole system of the French defense. . . . This breach in the ramparts is the age-old weakness of the country."

The *Wehrmacht* would simply sweep around the Maginot Line and race down the roads of northern France toward Paris. France had no defense, de Gaulle believed, and the Army's most urgent task in his mind was that of creating a new force, with new weapons and new tactics.

The Army, de Gaulle insisted, must abandon its most hallowed traditions: the idea that a string of fortifications and huge masses of civilian draftees could win a modern war. Too many forts lulled armies into quiescence, too many conscripts made them ponderous and slow and, unfortunately, the armies of the future would win wars only through movement and speed. For mobility was the essence of warfare. "We shall see," wrote de Gaulle, quoting the poet Valéry, "'the development of undertakings by a few chosen men, acting in crews and producing, in a few moments or in an hour, the most shattering results in the most unexpected places.' . . . Surprise, the old queen of the art of war, which was consigned to the rubbish heap so long as power lacked speed, will find a new instrument, and in consequence will recover its power." What was the new instrument? It was the tank: "A new technical progress will bring about the formation of a privileged body among the soldiers. Armor will reappear, carried by the engine." Tanks allowed an army to initiate action, to move without constraint, to deliver, unexpectedly, blows that are "both sudden and violent": tanks, in the hands of professional soldiers, would be "everready instruments for purposes of active assistance"; tanks would enable an army to launch an attach, to pierce the heart of Germany.

But the High Command was not about to change its thinking. A General Debeney said he saw no reason whatsoever to change existing defense plans; others proved beyond a doubt that the plains of Flanders and northern France were unsuitable for tank warfare; General Weygand assured the public that since the Army already had a few tanks—under strict orders to follow the infantry into battle—there was no need for a special armored corps; and one writer likened de Gaulle's proposal for a mobilized army to the medieval fantasy of a wind machine.

The Army did more than just ridicule de Gaulle. Its active campaign against him had begun in 1934, soon after the appearance of *The Army of the Future*, when Pétain changed his mind about bringing him into the Ministry of War, and it had continued in 1935 when General Maurin proposed assigning him to Corsica where people could hear his voice no more.

One other high-ranking officer, however, did take de Gaulle seriously: in Germany, Heinz Guderian, creator of the *Panzer Korps* and now a top Nazi general, read *The Army of the Future* in translation and found in it a confirmation of his own theories of mobilized war.

(8)

At four-fifteen on the afternoon of "Black Wednesday," September 28, 1938, Neville Chamberlain, the Prime Minister of England, scanned a note a page had just given him, and said to the House of Commons:

I have now been informed by Herr Hitler that he invites me to meet
him at Munich tomorrow evening. He has also invited Signor
Mussolini and Monsieur Daladier. Mussolini has accepted and I have
no doubt Monsieur Daladier will accept.

Edouard Daladier, the Premier of France, did indeed accept. After
having endured many months of Hitler's threats of war over the Sudeten
German question, Daladier welcomed this chance for a peaceful solution
to the Czechoslovakian crisis. On April 24 the leader of the Sudeten Nazi
Party had demanded that the Sudetenland, the German-speaking portion
of Czechoslovakia, be united with the "Fatherland"; on May 28 Hitler
had ordered an increase in the size of the *Luftwaffe*, the strengthening
of the Siegfried Line along the border of France, and the preparation of
plans for the invasion of Czechoslovakia by October 2; on September 15
he had told Chamberlain that he intended to incorporate the Sudetenland
into the Reich even at the risk of starting a general war; and on September
26 he had informed a British envoy that unless England and France met
all his demands on Czechoslovakia, he would invade that country within
forty-eight hours. Now, two days later, Daladier felt an immense gratitude
to the Führer simply for having offered to talk, and that night he told the
French people in a broadcast that, finally, he would have the chance "to
safeguard the peace and the vital interests of France."

When Daladier's plane put down again at Le Bourget airport outside
Paris that Sunday afternoon, he stepped to a microphone and told the
crowd gathered along the runway that "I return with the profound conviction that this accord [the pact he had signed in Munich] is indispensable
to the peace of Europe." Daladier had feared that the crowd might jeer
him but now he saw how wrong he had been. They had come not to boo
but to cheer, and as he drove back toward the center of the city, Daladier
noticed that tens of thousands of other Frenchmen were lining the rue
Lafayette and the boulevard Haussmann, and that shopgirls on the balcony
of the Galeries Lafayette were waving little tricolor flags of France. Daladier was the hero of the day because at thirty minutes after midnight that
morning at Munich, he and Chamberlain had given Hitler total control of
the Sudetenland in exchange for the Führer's pledge to honor the peace.
"There is not a woman or a man in France," Léon Blum wrote that night
in *Le Populaire,*

who will refuse MM. Chamberlain and Daladier their just tribute of
gratitude. War is spared us. The calamity recedes. Life can become
natural again. One can resume one's work and sleep again. One can
enjoy the beauty of the autumn sun.

On the following evening Daladier went to the Arc de Triomphe to rekindle the flame of the Unknown Soldier. A searchlight illuminated the tricolor hanging from the top of the Arc, and a huge crowd collected below, stopping traffic for over an hour and singing with one voice the words of the *"Marseillaise."*

But, of course, Munich was a disaster. "We have sustained a total, unmitigated defeat," Churchill warned the House of Commons:

> We are in the midst of a disaster of the first magnitude. . . . All the countries of Mittel Europa and the Danube valley, one after another, will be drawn in the vast system of Nazi politics. . . . And do not suppose that this is the end. It is only the beginning.

On March 14, 1939, Hitler threatened an aerial bombardment of Prague and this time the defenseless Czech government had to surrender its population into the vassalage of Germany. France in turn found herself shorn of allies in Eastern Europe. The Poles, the Rumanians and the Russians alike concluded that they could no longer depend upon France to help defend their soil, and they began a mad scramble to make the best deal possible with the Reich; and by her failure to stand up to Hitler at Munich, France lost any assistance she might have had from the thirty-five divisions of the Czech Army. "Munich tolled the bell for a certain France," a French diplomat stated years later, *"la grande France* of former times and even on 1914. . . . Tolling bells do not kill a sick man; they announce his death. The accord of Munich did not provoke the fall of France. It registered it."

(9)

De Gaulle eventually received some support in his fight for mobilized war. His political ally, Paul Reynaud, proposed a bill in the Chamber of Deputies that would have authorized credits for the creation of a new armored corps, and General Gamelin, the new Chief of Staff, put him in charge of a tank regiment stationed behind the Maginot Line at Metz. (De Gaulle became a full colonel in December, 1937.) But the Chamber of Deputies responded to Reynaud's bill by drastically cutting the money allotted to armored regiments, and Henri Giraud, de Gaulle's commanding General in Lorraine, informed him that "as long as I am alive, de Gaulle, you will not impose [your] theories here!"

De Gaulle's private life continued much as before. There were regular weekend trips to Colombey, songs and dances and games for Anne, and a kitchen full of de Gaulle's white gloves, drying out on wooden frames. His few friends found de Gaulle courteous, devoid of arrogance and even charming in a distant sort of way.

And once, during a review on the parade ground at the Metz garrison, a cavalry regiment drew up in close formation directly in front of de Gaulle's tanks. He was standing on the ground beside his machine and at the proper moment waved with his long right arm for his crews to start up their machines. The roar was deafening. Unfortunately for Colonel de Gaulle, it had arisen just under the horses' tails. The horses whinnied, reared and began a runaway charge upon the reviewing General and his assembled guests. For days thereafter de Gaulle mimicked the look of consternation on the General's face.

But the laughter soon came to an end. On August 31, 1939, the German Generals on the border of Poland received a "most secret" order:

Directive No. 1 for the Conduct of the War

1. Now that all the political possibilities of disposing by peaceful means of a solution on the Eastern Frontier which is intolerable for Germany are exhausted, I have determined on a solution by force.
2. The attack on Poland is to be carried out in accordance with the preparations made for Case White.
   Date of attack: September 1, 1939
   Time of attack: 4:45 A.M.

Adolf Hitler

The fall of Poland convinced de Gaulle that his ideas on mobilized war had been correct. In January, 1940, determined somehow to force a change in the course of events, he distributed a memorandum entitled *The Advent of Mechanized Force.* "If the enemy has not yet been able to build up a mechanized force sufficient to break through our lines," he wrote, "everything compels the belief that he is working toward the end. . . . A defender who should hold to static resistance with outdated forces would be pledging himself to disaster. Mechanized force is the only effective weapon with which to smash mechanized force. . . . To remain inert is to be defeated."

The French government, however, reacted as if nothing were wrong. The Inspector General of tanks repeated the earlier orders that armored units must follow the infantry into battle; the Commander-in-Chief, General Gamelin, glanced through de Gaulle's memorandum and turned to what he considered far more important matters; and the Premier of France, Edouard Daladier, declared that he was far to busy even to skim it.

Daladier was too much the product of French politics in the 1920's and 1930's to provide new leadership for the country. The large number of political parties represented in the Chamber of Deputies, interested either simply in seizing power or in opposing those already in power, had paralyzed the Chamber and produced a string of Premiers skilled not in leadership but in manipulation, wheeling and dealing and backroom political brokerage. A few politicians had tried to reform the system, but had failed, and instead, power lay in the hands of the compromisers, of whom Daladier was perhaps the most agile and expert of all.

The spring of 1940 brought the Nazi conquests of Denmark and Norway, and de Gaulle was desperate. "The events of Norway, coming after those in Poland," he wrote to Paul Reynaud, the new Premier, "have proved that there is today no longer any possible military operation except through the use of and according to the degree of mechanized strength. . . . [But] the French military system is conceived, organized, equipped and commanded contrary [to this principle]. There exists no more absolute and pressing need than that of radically reforming this system. . . . The military organism, because of the . . . traditionalism in its very nature, will not reform itself of its own accord. It is a matter for the State, a matter which takes precedence over all others. . . . You alone . . . by virtue of your position, your personality, of the stand you have taken in regard to this problem — and taken alone for the last six years — can and ought to achieve the task."

Reynaud responded favorably to this plea, ramming a massive tank-building program through the Chamber of Deputies and putting de Gaulle in charge of the newly created Fourth Armored Division, stationed behind the Maginot Line near Sedan.

But the High Command sabotaged even these measures. By May, 1940, it had dispatched one half of the five hundred freshly constructed Renault tanks it had received to Yugoslavia and Turkey and had given virtually no training to the crews of the other half; and when de Gaulle arrived in Alsace to take command of his armored division, he found that he possessed neither crews nor drivers nor tanks — his division "did not yet exist." "I am sorry," General Gamelin told him by way of explanation, "but I simply do not share your anxieties."

So the High Command had its way in the end: neither pleas from below nor commands from above, neither the theses of books nor the example of Poland could deter it from following the course it had chosen. Right up to the end, right up to the early morning hours of May 10, 1940, it continued to stake the security of France upon the infantry and the batteries of the Maginot Line.

Six days later, after the Nazis had struck, General Georges, the Army's second-in-command, spoke to Colonel de Gaulle. "Go ahead, de Gaulle," Georges told him. "You who have so long held the ideas the enemy is putting into practice—now is your chance to act."

Chapter 3

(1)

A TALL GANGLING COLONEL WITH THICK POUTING LIPS AND A LONG DROOPING NOSE WAS STANDING TRANSFIXED IN HORROR. IT WAS THE MORNING OF MAY 16, 1940, AND FROM THE DOORWAY OF A COTTAGE in Bruyères, in eastern France, Colonel de Gaulle was staring at the highway that passed through the center of the village. Far away, against the horizon, stood the citadel and the cathedral of Laon; in the middle distance, in the valley below, spread the fields of beetroot and wheat; closer still, surrounding the village, were the copses of lush green oaks that rose above the thatched roofs of the peasant cottages. But his mind was on neither the church nor the crops nor the trees of the village: it was on what he saw on the dirt road in front of his cottage.

He had been puzzled at first: why should the passersby outside, he had wondered, be wearing not shoes but string and coarse brown paper on their feet? Then the answer had become clear. Old men before him were trundling their wives in wheelbarrows; women were pushing their belongings in prams; and soldiers were limping and groaning as they struggled along. Their clothes were covered with mud, their bodies drooped with exhaustion, and their faces were distorted with fear. These were refugees, and as de Gaulle watched them from the cottage door, his incessant cigarette smoking alone betrayed the emotions that he felt within.

Then his mood hardened. "At the sight of those bewildered people and of those soldiers in rout," he wrote, "at the tale, too, of that contemptuous piece of insolence of the enemy's [the *Panzer* commanders, overtaking these soldiers, had turned them loose along the roads, saying they had no time to take them prisoner], I felt myself borne up by a limitless fury. 'Ah! It's too stupid! The war is beginning as badly as it could. Therefore it must go on. For this, the world is wide. If I live I will fight, wherever I must, as long as I must, until the enemy is defeated and the national stain washed clean.'"

Under orders to place his tank division in the path of the invading *Panzers* and to slow them long enough at least to let the troops in Belgium escape, de Gaulle began to map out his plan of attack. Roughly midway between him and the Germans, now fifty miles to the east near Sedan, lay the River Serre and parallel to it a canal that passed through the village of Montcornet. The land around the canal was swampy, too soggy for tanks, and de Gaulle knew that to cross it the *Panzers* would have to pass over the Montcornet bridge. When they reached the bridge the Germans would face a bottleneck, and there de Gaulle decided to concentrate his tanks and delay the *Panzers* for a day, or even two. But his tanks had not yet reached him.

De Gaulle glanced at the road again. Servicemen of every kind were trudging along—cavalry, artillery, aviators, service corps, infantry, marines, engineers, cuirassiers, anti-aircraft and commissariat. These men had two things in common. They were all in uniform and they were all unarmed. The civilians were varied: butchers in aprons, farmers with luggage, men with suits but no ties, mechanics in overalls covered with grease, mothers, nurslings, toddlers, brothers, sisters, fathers and grandparents. Vehicles filled the road from edge to edge, small trucks and large trucks, buses and tractors, municipal sprinklers and autos, forage wagons and field kitchens, pushcarts and wagons, forage carts and caterpillars, ambulances and hay carts, motorcycles, bicycles and tricycles. And every vehicle was packed with people—civilians had climbed into trucks and soldiers were hanging from the running boards of cars. A car was trying to push through the crowd, hitting the ditches, screeching its brakes, then starting up again in low gear. A mother was dragging a packing case on rollers; her six-year-old daughter was scrambling to keep up.

But there was no sign, yet, of Colonel de Gaulle's tanks.

Shortly after noon on May 16, de Gaulle did see an encouraging sight. At first he heard only the roar of the motor, but in a moment he saw the barrel as long as man and, finally, as he looked out toward the bend in the road, he made out the widespread treads and the ten-foot high tower of his first French-built heavy tank. A dozen or so more followed behind, rolling between the refugees who had jumped to the sides of the road and stopping in the dirt and grass in front of the cottage. One understrength tank battalion had reached his command post. But another, scheduled to come, was nowhere in view.

A junior officer showed him an intelligence report: the Germans, it said, were halfway between Sedan and the bridge at Montcornet.

Then he turned his mind again to the road through Bruyères.

From the road there came a medley of sounds. The autos were coughing, the tractors were chugging, the buses were panting, the large trucks were honking, the small trucks were wheezing, the motorcycles were spitting, the bicycles were rattling; the old people were groaning, the babies were crying, the children were whimpering, the mothers were scolding, and the fathers, each according to his makeup and his nervous condition, were shouting or screaming or walking in silence.

But there was one sound that de Gaulle could not yet hear: the sound of more tanks.

Again he checked the road outside, for, just before dusk, he heard new rumblings. Down the road was coming a smaller tank—narrower than the heavy ones, and equipped with a shorter barrel and stubbier turret. Two dozen light tanks just like the first came next, and behind them, drawn by horses, a column of 75-mm cannon. Two more tank battalions and a supporting artillery unit had reached de Gaulle, but these outfits, too, were depleted and driven by soldiers both exhausted and undertrained.

De Gaulle received more news: the Germans were setting up camp for the night near the outskirts of Montcornet.

De Gaulle set out by car to round up foot soldiers and more artillery from the nearby towns. He drove alone all night, north to Laon, where the cathedral was silhouetted black against the clear moonlit sky, southwest to Soissons, where the graveyards attested to the horrors of the First World War, and south to Rheims, where in another cathedral the Maid of Orléans had seen Charles VII crowned King of France. Here and there de Gaulle managed to round up a unit and, toward dawn, as the shadows were fading and the fields were glistening with dew, he returned to his cottage at Bruyères.

There, aligning his tanks in formation outside the cottage and reviewing them with glaring eyes and tightly compressed lips, de Gaulle got his men ready to move off to war. As they set out from Bruyères, the tankmen in the rear could see de Gaulle's skinny neck sticking out from his turret and his long dangling arms waving them on for the fight.

(2)

Shortly after noon on Sunday, May 19, a French bomber was circling over Paris in search of an unshelled airstrip. From the window of the cabin, General Maxime Weygand, France's new Commander-in-Chief, could see the River Seine winding along past all the familiar landmarks: the skirts of the Eiffel Tower, the Obélisque in the Place de la Concorde, the ponds and the flowers in the Jardin des Tuileries and the twin squarish towers of the cathedral of Notre-Dame. Soon these sights receded behind the tail of the plane and the pilot sent back word that he had seen a usable runway southwest of the city. As Weygand got ready to land, a glint of determination came over his deep-set eyes.

Premier Reynaud had finally fired General Gamelin and, after much consultation with the members of his Cabinet, had called back to Paris the two men he thought most likely to restore the morale of the French Army. From the French Ambassadorship in Spain he had recalled the eighty-four-year-old hero of Verdun and former Commander-in-Chief, Marshal Philippe Pétain, and from the command of all French forces in Syria and Lebanon (territories mandated to France by the League of Nations) he had brought in the seventy-three-year-old former aide to Marshal Foch, Maxime Weygand. Pétain was to become Vice-President of Reynaud's Cabinet and Weygand was to take charge of both the French Army and the British Expeditionary Force.

Weygand's plane was hovering over the runway of the Stampes airfield, thirty miles from Paris. Nothing had gone wrong on the long trip the day before from Beirut to Tunisia or on the flight that morning over the Mediterranean to Marseille but, now, trouble had struck. The air was clear and the runway was smooth, but as the bomber's wheels touched ground its undercarriage broke and it pancaked on its belly to the opposite end of the runway. Airport crews started out on foot to get to the damaged plane. From a distance they saw no sign of life, but as they reached the side of the fusilage, the door of the plane opened and down climbed the dapper little Weygand in a stiffly starched tunic and gleaming riding boots. He was shaken but unscathed.

A staff car whisked him immediately off to Paris.

Parisian newspapers had heaped lavish praise upon Weygand. General Weygand had been the brilliant aide to Marshal Foch during the First World War, he had persuaded Poland to adopt a defense plan that had saved it from the Bolsheviks in the 1920's and he had served intelligently and courageously as the French Commander-in-Chief during the early 1930's. Weygand had never actually commanded troops in battle, it was true, and he was notorious for his mercurial temperament, but the Parisian newspapers had failed to discuss those weaknesses. Instead, they unanimously welcomed him to Paris.

Within the hour Weygand's car reached Paris and plunged into the rue St-Dominique. It drove past a sentry, crossed over a courtyard and stopped on the tan gravel driveway that led to the steps of the Ministry of War.

Premier Reynaud was inside, waiting for his first formal talk with his new Commander-in-Chief. Weygand threw open the door of his car and dashed up the steps for the meeting.

Reynaud welcomed the General with a warm embrace, and expressed the greatest confidence in Weygand, praising his past record of brilliance and officially making him Commander-in-Chief not only of the Army in France but also of all other French services in all other theaters of operation. Reynaud did, however, neglect to say one thing. "The idea did not pass through my mind," he wrote later, "to say to this man, who was as lively as a fighting cock, . . . 'It is clearly understood that there is to be no thought of capitulation.'"

(3)

On that same morning, May 19, de Gaulle's tanks roared off to war for a second time.

His first attack had met with success. He had caught the Germans off guard, gunned down a convoy of Nazi trucks, taken one hundred and twenty prisoners and so effectively slowed Guderian's columns that, far behind the German lines, General Halder, Hitler's Chief-of-Staff, had written, "The Führer rages and screams that we are on our way to ruin the whole campaign."

But de Gaulle had had to retreat that night—his supply column was nonexistent—and far to the north and west the other *Panzer* units had gone racing on, unimpeded, in their effort to trap the Allies in Belgium. In the lead, of course, was the Seventh *Panzer* Division of Erwin Rommel.

And now, two days later, Colonel de Gaulle had his own division on the move again, starting out from St-Quentin (twenty miles northwest of Bruyères) and trying to sneak up again upon Guderian's flank. The Fourth Armored Division was still raw and undermanned. Most of the tanks had no radios, the artillery had remained ill-coordinated, and the few infantrymen who had joined the Division were exhausted from the lack of sleep. They had, furthermore, only a few rickety country buses in which to travel and so were vulnerable to attack from the air. Only a few more lightweight tanks had joined the Fourth in the two previous days and their crews, like most of the others under de Gaulle's command, were new to their jobs.

But, knowing that no other unit was in position to slow the German advance, de Gaulle determined to push on anyway. His destination was the River Serre, where the Germans were digging in along the east bank.

Pushing out from St-Quentin, de Gaulle picked his way through a nation in a state of collapse. All the roads he crossed were packed with cars—abandoned cars, towed cars, wrecked cars, cars with smoking engines, cars with mattresses on the top, cars with wheels that were stuck in the ditches, cars filled with chickens, children, soldiers, loaves of bread and bottles of wine. De Gaulle could scarcely get through. Every village and every hamlet and every junction was jammed with vehicles and, to make any progress, de Gaulle had to ford over the streams and crunch through farmers' hedgerows. Once he saw an entire family—the father, the mother and all three children—pushing their stalled automobile; and once a woman with a jug in her hand begged his crewmen for gasoline.

At last he cut through the woods that led to the Serre and reached a meadow on the west side of the river. Across the water he could see a pillar of dust the *Panzers* had kicked up, and a column of infantry singing in rhythm as they followed the tanks. At first he saw no sign that the Germans had detected his presence: then he learned differently.

Artillery began blasting at his tanks from across the Serre and, from behind the woods on the opposite bank, a wave of *Stukas* came screaming out of the sky. They fired directly into the battalion of French infantry, destroyed a good number of the 75-mm cannon, and made it impossible for de Gaulle's tanks to move up or down along the bank of the river. The barrage was merciless and, far to the right up the river, a unit of *Panzers* started to cross the stream.

Half a mile down the stream, at the bend in the river, de Gaulle saw a hamlet on fire. Flames, shimmering red, shot skyward in a pyrotechnic display; roofs, sucked upward by the heat, buckled and collapsed; walls, blazing with heat, leaned, reeled, hesitated and then toppled through the smoke. A farm dog, racing in panic, charged right into the field of battle.

Closer at hand, a French supply truck exploded in flames: smoke billowed from the turrets of nearby tanks.

Columns of *Panzers* were thundering down upon both flanks of the Fourth Armored Division. A Captain Idée, in a tank near de Gaulle's, wrote that he felt a "formidable shock." "The turret shakes, struck at the base. The traversing gear is jammed. The turret won't move anymore. I struggle furiously with it, strike the gear, and just when I am despairing, unjam it. The turret moves. I fire. Bing! A heavy shell strikes obliquely at the top of my turret, which glows red." Incendiary bullets began to ricochet off his armor. "I am blinded by sweat. I wipe myself with my sleeves—and the medallion of Ste. Thérèse that I wear on my wrist smiles at me. I kiss it." More shells struck near the treads of his tank; more bullets bounced off its steel-plated walls. Certainly now, thought Idée, "We shall never live through this attack!"

De Gaulle saw that his position was hopeless: he radioed out for help. There was no response.

His visorless helmet, padded with leather and secured by a broad chin strap, made his features stand out. Sweat began trickling from under his helmet, stinging his eyes, forming drops at the end of his nose, spreading the taste of salt throughout his pasty mouth. His eyes were red with conjunctivitis.

He looked out the slit in his turret. From the river ahead he saw only waves upon waves of *Stukas*, diving and climbing at will and unmolested by a single French fighter plane.

Finally, from the headquarters of General Frère, commander of the French reserves in the sector near St-Quentin, there came a response to de Gaulle's call for help.

General Frère was sorry, the radio said, but he could send de Gaulle neither tanks nor guns nor planes. They had already been shipped up toward Belgium.

(4)

Weygand had made a great splash in Paris.

Despite his seventy-three years, he had stunned his staff at his new headquarters at Montry—a Rothschild estate east of Paris—by racing down the main staircase, leaping over the entrance steps and performing a hundred-meter sprint across the manicured lawn. He looked tough. A British General thought he "gave the appearance of being a fighter"; a journalist enjoyed the sight of his riding crop and spurs; and a French officer wrote that his swagger, passion and fierceness of will "constrasted sharply with the pale and curdled calm of his predecessor," General Gamelin. One observer, it is true, found Weygand "wizened and dried up," but Weygand silenced all such doubts when, on May 21, he issued his General Operation No. 1. The Allied armies in Belgium, his order said, were immediately to attack the Germans and to make sure that, once "rounded up," the *Panzers* would "not escape again."

The Allied armies, Weygand told his country, were to retreat no more: "We shall have victory," he said, "or we shall have honor."

Precisely what he meant by those words would become clear a few days later.

But the Allies were beginning their counterattack in Belgium. On the morning of May 22 the 121st French Infantry Regiment, a motorized outfit, started out from Bouchain and rode over lowland canals until, that night, it had reached the town of Cambrai in France, just across the border from Belgium. At least one French unit was now in position to break the encirclement.

Weygand was delighted with the news. Late in 1939 he had told an audience in Lille that "the French Army is a more effective force than at any moment of its history. Its *matériel* is first rate, its fortifications are first class, its morale is excellent, its High Command remarkable. No one amongst us wants war, but I affirm that if we are compelled to win victory again, we will win it!" Weygand had staked his prestige on the ability of France to win and the first night's reports from Belgium implied that he had been right.

Darting around Montry that night like a minnow, an Englishman observed, Weygand fired off a new order to the front: "Offensive will continue tomorrow," it said, "supported by armored units. . . ."

On the morning of May 24, General Blanchard of the Seventh French Army and Lord Gort of the British Expeditionary Force worked out the details. Three French and two British divisions were to advance southward along the Canal du Nord and push on to Douai in France. The attack was to start on May 26: Blanchard and Dort wired these orders out to their men.

Weygand told other French generals to join the offensive and wired Blanchard that he was "highly pleased" with the "decision." If the French did not win, Weygand reasoned, at least they would have salvaged their honor.

All day long on May 24 Blanchard worked to gather his forces. He sent out orders for food, plans to the infantry, calls to the cavalry. That evening, from all across Belgium, the responses came in. Blanchard could see where he stood. He sent a Major Fauvelle to inform Weygand: late the next afternoon Fauvelle reached Paris with the news from Blanchard.

Fauvelle had driven to Dunkirk, taken a boat to Britain, flown wide over the Channel and now, taking his seat at the table in the Ministry of War, had been about to describe the offensive in Belgium.

He glanced at the faces around him: Paul Baudouin, the Foreign Minister, blue eyed, clean shaven and handsome; Jean Darlan, the Navy's top Admiral, nautical looking with a bulldog pipe in his teeth; Philippe Pétain, Vice-President of the Cabinet, white faced and sad with his eyes dropped down toward the carpet; Paul Reynaud, the Premier, with eyebrows drawn high like open umbrellas; Maxime Weygand, the Commander-in-Chief, with high cheekbones and sharply pointed chin; and General Sir Edward Spears, Prime Minister Churchill's liaison officer with Reynaud, big faced, solid and strong. Fauvelle looked around the group, and then related his story.

And as Fauvelle began, wrote General Spears, "I felt my heart turning to stone."

"The troops have no more bread," said Fauvelle. "There is still meat and wine, but all the heavy artillery has been lost. Horse-drawn transport no longer exists, as all the horses have been killed by air bombardment. There are no armored vehicles left. We have only three divisions left. There is only one day's reserve of ammunition. The men are stupified by the air bombardment."

Weygand spoke up. Despite the news he was hearing he had still managed to look quick and fresh.

Surely there must be some way, he insisted. Surely Blanchard must have some men left with whom he could fight!

Fauvelle answered him, slowly. The forces in Belgium, he said, had no hope at all of acting on Weygand's orders.

Weygand's voice came back in a tone that sounded like a saw on steel. There must be an offensive! The honor of France depends on it!

Then, in the "voice of a seasick passenger asking a passing steward for a basin," Fauvelle contradicted his Commander-in-Chief. "I believe," he said, "in a very early capitulation."

"We shall have victory," Weygand had said, "or we shall have honor." Now he had neither, and in his presence a Frenchman had used the word "capitulation."

Spears turned instinctively to study Weygand: and what he learned made him fear for the future.

(5)

"Excuse me, but where can I find General de Gaulle?"

It was just after dawn on May 28, on the plateau above Abbeville, near the mouth of the Somme, and a young Lieutenant with a packet of dispatches was asking a tank mechanic the way to de Gaulle's field headquarters.

"The General?" asked the mechanic. "He has no headquarters. He's out in the open."

"Under the open sky?"

"Yes. Go to the end of the village and cross the orchard to the right, following the hedge. You'll find him over the crest of the hill, under an apple tree."

The Lieutenant started to move away but the mechanic called him back.

"By the way," he said, "if the General has gone somewhere else, look at the ground, going from one apple tree to the next. You'll trace him by the trail of his cigarette butts."

After a harrowing escape from the Serre—some of his crews in their fright had actually fired upon each other—after receiving more artillery, motorized infantry and three battalions of tanks, and after Reynaud had promoted him temporarily to Brigadier General, Charles de Gaulle had set out for battle again.

The French had still one hope—albeit an infinitesimal one—of saving the men in Belgium. At one point on the map of France and for one brief moment in time, the *Panzers* would be vulnerable to assault.

The *Panzers* had swept northwest across the coastal plain of France until they had reached the sea near St. Valéry, right at the mouth of the Somme. At that point the shoreline of France turns up in a sharp right angle for fifty miles until, at a cape between Calais and Boulogne, it forms another right angle, extending eastward past Dunkirk and straight across to the border of Holland. Since the *Panzers* had reached the coast at the base of this rectangle, they had to swing more than ninety degrees to the right to get back to Belgium. The *Panzers*, in short, had to turn their backs upon the body of France.

They had already begun that turn by May 26 and the hinge in their line, their most vulnerable point, lay ten miles inland from St-Valery close to the town of Abbeville.

Two days later, wearing a leather tank jacket without insignia and leaning against a tree on the top of a hill, de Gaulle was watching the gunfire near Abbeville below.

The battle had started the night before. After aligning his tanks, de Gaulle had struck first at Huppy, eight miles southwest of Abbeville, then toward the east at Limeux, where he had captured several German anti-tank batteries. Then he had moved to the north, setting up camp in the trees of the hill, and looking out toward his first main objective, Mont Caubert, that controlled the access roads to Abbeville.

Now, at dawn, de Gaulle's tanks were rolling down the slopes toward the Somme and out across the valley once again in the direction of Mont Caubert. This time, however, their assignment was harder: during the night the Germans had carted more guns and ammunition and food onto the ridges of Mont Caubert.

But de Gaulle did have a large division at his command and, on the previous night, it had proved it could win. "An atmosphere of victory hovered over the battlefield on the morning of May 28," wrote de Gaulle. "Everyone held his head high. The wounded were smiling. The guns fired gaily. Before us, in pitched battle, the Germans had retired."

"What, in fact, happened on May 28," wrote a Major Gehring, an officer in the *Panzer Korps*, "was that the enemy had attacked us with powerful forces. Our anti-tank units had fought heroically. But the effect of their blows had been reduced by the strength of the [French] armor. The enemy had managed to break through with his tanks between Huppy and Caumont [between Huppy and Abbeville]. Our anti-tank defenses had been crushed, the infantry had withdrawn. . . .

"When the alarming news poured into divisional H.Q. and under the incessant fire of the French artillery, there was no means of communicating with any of the battalions in the line, the General commanding the Division went forward himself. . . . He encountered the routed troops, regrouped them, and led them to prepared defensive positions some kilometers to the rear of the first lines. . . .

"But a profound terror of the tanks had got into the bones of our soldiers. . . . Losses were heavy. . . . There was, practically speaking, nobody who had not lost beloved comrades . . ."

De Gaulle, however, had paid a price for these gains. His men on the valley floor below had suffered greatly: the troops on his right had lost a third of its men; the men in the middle had lost nearly half; and the crews on his left had lost all but ten of their tanks. None had succeeded in scaling the slopes of Mont Caubert.

Throughout the night the Germans reinforced the ridge around Mont Caubert, pouring in still more men and matériel, and before dawn, the *Panzers* were plunging toward the two gaps their planes had spotted in the lines of the French.

From his mobile headquarters in the apple orchard the next morning de Gaulle could follow the course of the battle below. At dawn he could see the two gaps in his lines where the *Panzers* had plunged through; at mid-morning he could see the columns of French supply trucks approaching his tanks for refueling; at noon he could see his units clustering around the overextended *Panzers* and forcing them back toward the Somme; at mid-afternoon he could see his tanks chasing a German infantry regiment across the valley floor toward Abbeville; and at dusk he could see his vehicles grinding up the sides of Mont Caubert, pushing on and on until no more than the narrow crest at the top remained in the hands of the Germans. Victory seemed close at hand.

Then, after a third night of reinforcement, the *Panzers* rolled down the slopes again, and this time, sensing the exhaustion of his division, de Gaulle knew that he had to withdraw.

De Gaulle had launched the strongest French attack yet upon the columns of *Panzers:* he had destroyed a large number of tanks, captured more than sixty anti-tank guns and brought back four hundred German prisoners of war. General Weygand cited him that day as "an admirable, energetic and courageous leader."

But the Battle of France was over. The Allied armies in Belgium were trapped without hope of rescue and a week later, after the Dunkirk evacuation, the *Panzers* would be free to begin their sprint toward Paris.

"One poor division," de Gaulle wrote later of the failure of his Fourth Armored, "weak, unprovided, and isolated. What results would not have been obtained during those last days of May by an elite armored corps?— for which many of the elements did, indeed, exist, though deformed and dispersed. If the State had played its part; if, while there was time, it had directed its military system towards enterprise, not passivity; if our leaders had in consequence had at their disposal the instrument for shock and maneuver which had often been suggested to the politicians and to the High Command; then our arms would have had their chance, and France would have found her soul again."

(6)

But he swore he would fight on. The Battle of France was over, yes, but France herself had not yet lost the war. Above all else, thought de Gaulle, she must avoid surrendering—for she still had a way to win.

The plan, to be sure, was a last resort, but Army regulations had forbidden surrender until "all means commanded by duty and honor have been exhausted," and therefore, de Gaulle reasoned, the French were obliged to try his scheme.

The solution had occurred, too, to other high-ranking officers in the French Army, to General Bertrand in North Africa, to General Bührer in charge of the colonial troops and to General Prételat in command of the armies on the Maginot Line. All these men, independently of each other, had reached the same conclusions as de Gaulle, but none of these men was prepared to stake his career upon the worthiness of this plan. De Gaulle was.

He was also prepared to act fast. The success of the plan depended upon whether the French could move faster than the Germans.

Chapter 4

(1)

"**D**EAREST LU,** WROTE GENERAL ROMMEL TO HIS WIFE ON THE MORN-
ING OF JUNE 5, ''TODAY THE SECOND PHASE OF THE OFFENSIVE
BEGINS, . . . I SHALL BE OBSERVING THE ATTACK FROM WELL
back in the rear. A fortnight, I hope, will see the war over on the mainland. . . . The whole world is sending its congratulations. I've opened
nowhere near all the letters yet. There hasn't been time."

After the British escape from Dunkirk, just west of the border of
Belgium, the German armies had regrouped, refueled and resumed their
drive toward Paris. General Rommel was in the lead again. His first objective was a point on the River Somme, seventy-five miles north of Paris.

A few French cavalry units threw themselves in the path of the *Panzers* on the morning of June 5 but the Germans quickly overpowered them.
"Over to our left," wrote Rommel, "a giant pillar of smoke belched up from
a burning [French gasoline truck] and numerous saddled horses stampeded
riderless across the plain."

At nine o'clock that night Rommel sent a message back to divisional
headquarters: "All quiet forward, enemy in shreds."

He was now thirty miles above the Somme.

The *Panzers* moved forward again at dawn the next morning: French
resistance was scattered and feeble. Rommel's units, forming a column two
thousand yards wide and twelve miles deep, "moved as if on an exercise.

In this formation we advanced up hill and down dale, over highways and byways straight across country."

At dusk he was fifteen miles above the Somme.

The next day's advance, wrote Rommel, "went straight across country, over roadless and trackless fields, uphill, downhill, through hedges, fences and high cornfields. . . . We met no enemy troops, apart from a few stragglers, but plenty of indications in the shape of military vehicles and horses standing in open country that they had left shortly before our arrival. . . . Sometimes we even surprised refugee trucks in open country, their occupants, men, women, and children, underneath the vehicles, where they had crawled in mortal fear."

"Dearest Lu," Rommel wrote home that night: "More and more signs of disintegration on the other side. We're all very, very well. Slept like a top."

By that evening the Germans had reached the Somme. At dawn on June 8 they spread apart to begin their encirclement of Paris.

(2)

De Gaulle's hope that the war could be continued was based on several factors. England, he thought, would probably stay in the war; Russia, he believed, was bound to enter the fight; and America, he was convinced, would soon throw the weight of her industrial might against the forces of Hitler. So France would have allies. The question, therefore, was not whether to fight but from where to fight.

The answer to that, he felt, was clear: across the Mediterranean in North Africa, France had the colonies of Algeria and Morocco. There the Army could recuperate, modernize its techniques and re-equip its men, and wait until the moment to reconquer France had come. And the Army had a way to get there. By taking the railroads westward from Paris and crossing the hills of Brittany to Brest, on the sea, it could pile into the fleet docked there at the piers and sail for Algiers or Casablanca.

On the morning of June 8, therefore, de Gaulle went to see General Weygand, in the hope of persuading the Commander to accept his idea.

De Gaulle foresaw two problems: First, Weygand was likely to reject his plan and brand him a heretic for proposing it. Second, even if Weygand did accept the idea, the French would have to move with lightening speed: the Germans would soon be around Paris, closing off the route of escape.

(3)

"We moved off at 10:30 hours [on June 9]," wrote General Rommel, "Low-flying enemy air attacks on [our] battalion had little success to show for their efforts: the [German] defense was too strong."

The *Panzers* were on the move again that morning, moving down and out from the River Somme: one column headed southeast, striking toward *the rear* of the Maginot Line; another was streaking across the flat coastal plain of Picardy toward Paris; and a third, under General Rommel, was turning westward toward the mouth of the Seine, from where it could close the pincers around Paris.

Some British units still in France had blown up a bridge midway between the Somme and the Seine and Rommel had to take time to locate a ford. But "several British soldiers had waded across to us with their hands up," Rommel wrote, "and, with their help, our motorcyclists started to improve the crossing. Great pieces of the demolished railway bridge nearby were thrown into the deepest part of the ford. Willows alongside the river were sawed down and similarly used to improve the passage. . . ."

Then Rommel resumed his push through Normandy, past dairy farms and half-timbered houses, past shrubs and hollyhocks and roses, and past avenues of elms that lined the long straight roads toward the Seine.

His advance continued well into the night. "The noise of our passage as we drove through the villages wakened people from their sleep, and brought them rushing out onto the street to welcome us—as British. We drove past an enemy anti-aircraft battery. There was still light in the guardroom and the sentries paid us honors as we passed. . . . We turned south at Les Autieux and reached the village of Sotteville at midnight. . . ."

General Rommel had reached the Seine.

(4)

General Weygand was in no mood to see de Gaulle.

Upon his return from Syria in May, Weygand had quickly urged a last-ditch resistance to the onrushing German forces: "The French Army ought to resist desperately on the Somme and Aisne positions," he had declared. "Then, if the enemy has broken this resistance, what is left of the French Army should continue to fight where it stands until it is annihilated, to save the honor of the French flag."

But few in the French Army had either resisted or fought back or saved any honor: most had fled from the front in a headlong retreat. And Weygand had undergone a collapse of morale.

He was neither stupid nor treasonous, but he was intellectually rigid and determined above all else to keep intact his personal prestige, and these qualities of mind had left him incapable of devising a flexible plan of national defense. He had already staked his reputation on his prediction that France would win, yet the *Panzers* had made mock of all such boasts. He had concluded, therefore, that France—and Weygand—had lost everything save the chance to win glory in one last apocalyptic battle. But Weygand's mind was narrow. Although he saw that the speed of the *Panzers* gave him no time to organize a resistance and so prevented his vindicating himself through martyrdom, he was unable to see that, in addition to the alternatives of last-ditch resistance and complete surrender, he had the choice of a strategic retreat. He could not leap toward the unknown.

Instead, in his humiliation, frustration and rage, he proceeded to denounce the idea as heresy and to accuse its proponents of incompetence and treachery.

"I began to understand," wrote General Spears, Churchill's representative to Reynaud, "the Weygand was living in a . . . demented dream conjured up by his vanity to rescue his self-esteem. He could find no remedy to the disaster, no solution occurred to him. This splendor of fighting to the end à la Vercingetorix [the Gallic chieftain who had unsuccessfully defended France against Caesar and who was later executed in the streets of Rome] was a vision not vouchsafed to him. As neither he nor the General Staff could be at fault, as the French Army could only be the best in the world, then the explanation must be that France was betrayed . . . tripped up by her allies, let down by her odious politicians. And so he spared himself the labor of seeking solutions of which his mind was denuded. Like an empty wrinkled toothpaste tube, there was nothing to be squeezed out of it, so he turned savagely on others to avoid looking inwards and reckoning up his past responsibilities."

Then, on the morning of June 8, the embittered Weygand had looked up from his desk in the spacious nineteenth-century Montry mansion to see the challenging eyes and tight-pressed lips of General de Gaulle.

(5)

"Dearest Lu," wrote General Rommel on the morning of June 10: "I'm in fine form although I'm on the go the whole time. Our successes are tremendous and it looks to me inevitable that the other side will soon collapse. We never imagined that war in the west would be like this . . ."

Rommel now veered away from his comrades, directing the 7th *Panzer* Division to cut off the British 51st Highland that was trying to escape to the coast. Two days later, at the small Channel port of St-Valéry-en-Caux, he caught that Division, imprisoning 40,000 men and capturing the commander, Major General Victor Fortune.

The French had called his *Panzers* the "Phantom Division." In six weeks of fighting he had captured 277 heavy guns, 458 armored vehicles, more than 4,000 Allied trucks and 97,648 prisoners of war. He had also spread panic and terror throughout every level of the French chain of command.

On the morning of June 10, meanwhile, other *Panzer* units began pushing up the Seine toward Vernon, a small, tree-shaded town just twenty miles above the main railroad line from Paris to Brittany.

The pincers were closing around Paris.

(6)

On the morning of June 8, General de Gaulle, newly appointed by Premier Reynaud as Undersecretary of Defense in the War Cabinet, stood towering over the desk of Maxime Weygand in the Army headquarters at Montry. He was bent on persuading Weygand to accept his plan for a strategic retreat through Brittany.

De Gaulle had little hope of securing Weygand's agreement. "As he [Weygand] had never considered the real possibilities of mechanized force," de Gaulle wrote later, "the immense and sudden effects produced by the enemy's resources had stupified him. To face the disaster effectively he would have had to renew himself; to break, from one day to the next, with ideas, a rate of action, a set of methods which no longer applied; to wrench his strategy out of the narrow frame of the French mainland, to turn the deadly weapon back against the enemy who had launched it, and to take into his own hand the trump card of great spaces, great resources and great speeds. . . . He was not the man to do it. His age, no doubt, was against it as well as his turn of mind — but, above all, his temperament."

But de Gaulle was determined to try, at least, to rally Weygand: this was scarcely the time for being a yes-man. De Gaulle outlined his plan: if Weygand would order the troops to Paris and load them on the trains to Brittany, enough could escape through Brest to re-establish themselves in Africa and from there they could one day help in the invasion of France. Upon this step rested the honor of France. But time was fleeting away, said de Gaulle: Weygand would have to issue the order immediately.

Weygand's mind seemed to be somewhere else. He reminded de Gaulle that he had already predicted "the German attack on the Somme." "They are in fact attacking," Weygand went on. "At this moment they are crossing the river. I can do nothing to stop them."

Weygand gestured toward the large wall map behind his desk to illustrate his point.

De Gaulle retorted, being unwilling to shrink even before a Supreme Commander: "All right," he shot back, "they're crossing the Somme. And then?"

"Then?" Weygand looked wizened and dried up. "Then the Seine and the Marne."

"Yes," de Gaulle responded. "And then?"

"But that's the end," answered Weygand. His patience was beginning to snap.

"What do you mean, 'the end'?" de Gaulle crackled. "Why is this the end. What about the world? What about the Empire?"

General Weygand, de Gaulle wrote, gave a "despairing laugh."

"The Empire," sneered Weygand. "But that's childish! As for the world, when I'm beaten here, England won't wait a week before negotiating with the Reich."

The interview was over: Weygand had no intention of retreating through Brittany to Africa.

As de Gaulle's car drove him through the gate of Montry and out along the road back to Paris, he began to chain-smoke his gold-tipped cigarettes. For he had realized that Weygand, "carried away by a current he was no longer trying to master, was bound to seek the issue within his reach: capitulation. But as he did not intend to assume responsibility for this, his action would consist in steering the Government towards it." Weygand would try to force the French to surrender—by any means at his disposal.

De Gaulle knew what his own next step must be: He knew he had to warn Paul Reynaud, and ask the Premier to get rid of Weygand.

(7)

War came to Vernon on the Seine with a sudden brutality. At midday on June 10, a huge, limping column of refugees reached the bridge that led to the town. Slowly, with babies in wheelbarrows, grandparents in pushcarts, youngsters on bicycles, soldiers in army cars, women and children in horse-drawn carts, the procession plodded toward the center of town. Some had spent days on the road, some had been bombed, some had been strafed, and all bore the dust and grass on their clothes that told of the nights they had slept in the fields. But now, as they shambled over the bridge that crossed the Seine, their cares seemed over: the last of the stragglers had passed into Vernon. There, under the arch of the elms that crossed over the streets, they felt safe from attack.

The *Luftwaffe* hit the town with shattering blows. Trees toppled, houses caved in, shopkeepers shutters banged shut, the refugees sought safety under the crumbling walls, and the old Norman church began to blaze in an inferno of flames.

The Germans had reached Vernon.

(8)

The morning of June 9 found de Gaulle in the War Ministry in Paris, standing this time opposite the desk of Paul Reynaud. The Premier was starting to look gray about the eyes. He motioned de Gaulle into a chair.

"In the higher ranks of the command," de Gaulle said he told Reynaud, "the game was considered lost and that everyone, while carrying out his duties mechanically, was suggesting in whispers, and would soon be proposing out loud, that an end be put, somehow or other, to the Battle of France. To steer men's minds and their courage toward the continuation of the war in the Empire, a categorical intervention by the Government was immediately necessary."

And, de Gaulle insisted, it was up to Reynaud to do the intervening. Reynaud's eyebrows were snapping up and down. He was quick to agree and, with his customary briskness, he assured de Gaulle that he would do anything he possibly could to save the nation. But, Reynaud wanted to know, what precisely did de Gaulle have in mind?

De Gaulle spelled out his idea of a retreat through Brittany: if the Army could get on the trains in Paris and head out to Brest on the coast, it could sail to North Africa and there, trading space for time, prepare itself one day to reconquer France. But the Germans were swinging fast around the west side of Paris and so the Army would have to move out immediately. Here, de Gaulle said with a glare, was where Reynaud came in.

Reynaud seemed grayer than ever but again, in his clipped manner of speech, he expressed his agreement with de Gaulle—he, Reynaud, had espoused exactly the same idea himself. But just what did de Gaulle want him to do about it?

De Gaulle came straight to the point: "I urged [Reynaud]," he tells us, "to take away the command from General Weygand, who had given up trying to win," and to order the retreat himself.

Reynaud's neck twisted in his high starched collar. He had recently complained, out of Weygand's earshot, that the Commander-in-Chief was devoid of ideas, but now, confronted with de Gaulle's demand, he seemed to be evading the issue.

"We must think of a successor," said Reynaud, trying to postpone his decision. "What's your view?"

De Gaulle would not let Reynaud wriggle free. Honor demanded a strategic retreat, he said, and if Reynaud had any courage left, he would know what he must do.

Reynaud looked away for many minutes, and, when he turned back to face de Gaulle, the corner of his mouth had begun to twitch.

Then Reynaud gave his answer.

(9)

In the middle of the afternoon on June 10, the day after Reynaud had made his decision, the German units at Vernon began to plunge southward again, bearing down upon the main rail line that stretched across Normandy to Brest.

(10)

The American diplomat, Robert Murphy, walked out of his Embassy on the afternoon of June 13, 1940, and crossed the Obélisque in the Place de la Concorde. He looked up the broad expanse of the Champs Elysées past the chestnut trees and toward the Arc de Triomphe.

"As every visitor to Paris knows," he wrote, "this is one of the world's greatest traffic hazards. But now the only living creatures in sight were three abandoned dogs cavorting beneath the large French flags which still hung at each corner of the great concourse."

Three days before, the government and most of the people of Paris had fled the city. Premier Reynaud had finally agreed to retreat: not to the west, however, not out to Brest and not to North Africa. He had decided to flee to the south.

On June 14 the French flags were hauled down throughout Paris and a swastika began to flutter from the top of the Eiffel tower.

Chapter 5

(1)

THE CONTROLLER IN THE AIRPORT TOWER OUTSIDE LONDON WAS HAVING A BUSY TIME AT MID-AFTERNOON ON JUNE 11. HE HAD ALREADY ORDERED SIX HURRICANE FIGHTERS INTO THE AIR AND FROM THE CORNER OF HIS eye he could see six more lining up along the runway for takeoff. But he was more concerned with the big Flamingo passenger plane revving up its propellers on the strip just below.

Inside its cabin, the controller knew, were a number of top British officials: Captain Berkeley (a translator), Brigadier Lund, General Dill, General Ismay and General Spears, who had represented Churchill to Reynaud. The Minister of War, Anthony Eden, was also aboard, cool as always and elegantly dressed. But the controller knew that someone else, too, was sitting in that plane: the stooped, potbellied, black-suited, balding figure of Winston Churchill.

The controller gave a signal and the Flamingo roared down the runway, lifting into the clouds behind the first six Hurricanes. The other six followed immediately behind.

Churchill's destination was General Weygand's château near Briare, seventy miles southwest of Paris, where the Commander-in-Chief had established his new headquarters. Churchill's purpose was to meet there with the French Cabinet and persuade them to set up a defensive line behind which the Army could escape, through Bordeaux or Marseille, to North Africa. He had little hope of success but, being Churchill, he was determined to try anyway.

The planes skirted westward over the white cottages and rocky fields of Brittany, then, crossing square fields of wheat and the broad ribbon that was the Loire River, they angled down toward Briare.

They touched down on the grassy runway late that afternoon. "Airports," wrote General Spears, "seldom give the impression of being over-populated, but this one seemed particularly flat and deserted." Four cars drove up to greet the Flamingo and in the lead car was a French colonel who, "from his expression, might have been welcoming poor relations at a funeral reception."

As Churchill started down the landing ramp, he wrote, he "realized immediately how very far things had fallen."

The Britishers became more depressed when their motorcade stopped in front of Weygand's Château du Muguet—the "Lily of the Valley Castle." It was a "monstrosity," wrote Spears, "of red lobster-colored brick and stone the hue of ripe Camembert." Things grew even worse inside: "It was like walking into a house thinking one was expected," Spears went on, "to find one had been invited for the following week. Our presence was not really desired."

But Churchill was insistent on pleading his case: thrusting out his broad lower lip and leaning forward on his walking stick, he barged into the long dining room where the French Cabinet was waiting to hear him out.

Reynaud was there, and Pétain, Weygand and the civilian members of the Government. Sitting against a tall French window was General de Gaulle, with a formidable, bitter and distant look about his eyes.

It was seven o'clock in the evening and the room was gloomy and dark. The conference was about to start.

(2)

Some of the men in the room, and a few others close to the Government, had already voiced their support for Weygand. Paul Baudouin, the Minister of Foreign Affairs, Jean Prouvost, the Minister of Information, and Admiral Darlan, the top man in the Navy, had all quietly begun to favor an armistice.

Weygand's most solid support, however, had come from Philippe Pétain. The Marshal had begun to show his great age. For years he had looked dour and sad but now his face seemed blank and dead, and his moustache had turned to white; for years he had been thought conserva-tive but now such "realism" had hardened to pessimism; for years he had seemed unapproachable but now this remoteness had changed to indifference. For Pétain, the fall of France would have seemed a "tiresome, very sordid, almost boring drama taking place in a distant branch of the family" had it not been for one thing: it gave him the opportunity of a lifetime.

And someone else, too, in the dining room of the château had sided with Weygand: but this man had kept his defeatism a secret from Premier Reynaud.

(3)

After coughing slightly Reynaud invited Churchill to start the discussion.

Churchill did. His words came slowly and carefully selected. He lisped as he talked.

He had come to France, he explained, to discuss with Monsieur Reynaud and the rest of the Cabinet the means by which England and France could continue the struggle together. The Germans would soon stop pushing down into France, he thought, and turn their attentions toward Britain. And when they did that, he was certain the Royal Air Force would be able eventually to neutralize their air power. So France would shortly have a respite, and if her Cabinet would agree to stay in the war, the British would soon be able to place fresh men and equipment at her disposal.

Reynaud gave another cough—the weeks of pressure had given him a touch of laryngitis—and he thanked Churchill for his comments. Then he asked Weygand to report of the military situation.

Weygand spoke in high, sibilant notes.

Churchill's talk of continuing the fight, he snapped, was sheer insanity, for the French had nothing left with which to fight—neither arms nor reserves nor any hope at all. "The men had neither food nor rest," he said. "They collapse into sleep when halted and have to be shaken in the morning to open fire. . . . There is nothing to prevent the enemy reaching Paris. We are fighting on our last line and it has been breached."

Then Weygand concluded his report: "I am helpless. I have no reserves, there are no reserves. *C'est la dislocation!*"—the breakup.

The Frenchmen around the table sat with "set white faces," wrote Spears. "They looked for all the world like prisoners hauled up from some deep dungeon to hear an inevitable verdict." Only one Frenchman, Spears said, "matched the calm, healthy phlegm of the British"—de Gaulle—and his thoughts seemed far away, as if he were trying to reach a painful decision.

Churchill puffed at the stump of his cigar, and then went on. His voice was warm and deep.

He wished, he said, to express his admiration for the heroic resistance of the French, and he was bitterly sorry that the British had been unable to help more effectively in the defense of France. But neither the British nor the French, he insisted, "must be hypnotized by their defeats or blind to the Germans' difficulties." The German armies must be exhausted, he said, and "feeling the strain of their immensely long lines of communication. It would be months or years before the Germans could threaten North Africa, and by then the French there could be retrained and re-equipped. So if Weygand could set up a temporary line of defense, the French could start their retreat to the sea.

All the Frenchmen, including Reynaud, looked frightened—all, that is, except de Gaulle. He had been chain-smoking again but nothing had caused him to change expression. His thoughts seemed somewhere else, far into the future.

Weygand spoke up again. His voice was rasping now, slipping out of control.

"I cannot guarantee," he said, "that our troops will hold out another hour . . . I cannot see how a co-ordinated defense will be possible. . . . To say anything else would be untrue."

Churchill was sitting hunched over the table. His expression was malevolent, and crossly, he gestured as if he were brushing away a fly.

He "found wonderful flashing words with which to express his fiery eloquence," wrote Spears. "They came in torrents, French and English phrases tumbling over each other like waves racing for the shore when driven by a storm. . . . He wanted the French to fight in Paris, describing how a great city, if stubbornly defended, absorbed great armies. And the pageant of history, the lurid glow of burning cities, some as beautiful as Paris, collapsing on the garrisons who refused to accept defeat, arose before our eyes. The French perceptibly froze at this.

"But Churchill, if he had noticed the perceptible movement which had led all the French to sit back in their chairs with the tension of a motorist pressing hard on the brakes save de Gaulle . . . did not heed it, or if he did, it merely spurred him on . . ."

Churchill's voice rose in oratorical splendor. Today, he said, the Allies had lost the Battle of France, but tomorrow they would face the Battle of Britain, and it was on *that* field that they would win or lose. And if they won tomorrow they would redeem all that they had lost today.

But whatever happened, the British would "fight on and on and on, *toujours*, all the time, everywhere, *partout, pas de grâce*, no mercy. *Puis la victoire!*"

Spears looked around the table: Reynaud was easing his neck in his collar and Pétain sat straight and pale, staring at his hands spread flat on the table.

Weygand's turn had come again.

To fight on was tantamount to treason, he screamed. The army was in chaos, he said: he had no way, no means, no time to organize a retreat. The Germans already held bridgeheads across the Seine, and the *Panzers* were about to complete their encirclement of Paris. He had no hope of slowing them down. Once the Germans were beyond Paris, there would be "nothing to prevent the total invasion of France . . .!"

Churchill was scowling, waiting for what came next. And what came next was scarcely a surprise to him.

No doubt the French could fight on, Weygand admitted as he started up again, but that "would be unco-ordinated warfare," and he, himself, as Commander-in-Chief, would have become "completely powerless."

So that was it. "There was," wrote Spears, "no mistaking [his] meaning."

Weygand was afraid of losing power.

He had finished, and under his tight parchment skin his jaw worked up and down in silence.

Churchill's big face was ruddy with anger. He had had enough and he threw back his chair to leave. But as he rose he looked directly across at de Gaulle.

He was "searching for something he had failed to find in the other French faces," wrote Spears. "I thought he had detected [in de Gaulle] the thing he was looking for."

The next day the Cabinet resumed its flight, this time toward Tours, in the valley of the Loire.

(4)

As the Cabinet left Briare the list of defeatists continued to grow. Paul Baudouin, Jean Prouvost and Jean Darlan were still in that camp, and so was Marshal Pétain. Even before his return to France, in fact, he had believed that France was about to fall. "My country has been beaten," he had said to his friend Franco in Spain, "and they are calling me back to make peace and to sign an armistice. . . . They're calling me back to take charge of the nation." And now, Pétain was certain, events were proving him right.

But the desire to surrender had spread: a General Laure had succumbed; so had Jean Ybarnégaray, the Minister of State, and Yves Bouthillier, the Minister of Finance.

Another Minister, too, belonged to the defeatist camp: he was also a trusted member of Reynaud's entourage.

This group of men was growing not only in number but also in strength. The chaos they found in Tours helped them push France closer to armistice.

(5)

The city of Tours was a mess. It was far too small and far too old to be the seat of government. Its streets were narrow, its phones were few, and its hotels were wholly inadequate for the floods of persons pouring in from the north. "Much of the time in the new capital," a journalist wrote, "was spent in a sort of furious hide-and-seek, trying to find the functionaries with whom one had business. The ministers themselves arriving . . . with their flustered and indignant mistresses who put the blame for the whole inconvenience upon them, were unable to find their ministries in some cases. The mistresses occasioned a great deal of trouble; there were not enough suites at the Hôtel de l'Univers to go around. Some of the women had to choose between putting up with a room and a bath or going to a second-rate hotel. Naturally they made things unpleasant for their protectors who had subjected them to such humiliation."

When Reynaud reached Tours on June 12, he installed himself outside town in the Château de Chissay, high on a bluff above the River Cher. Things there were as bad as in Tours.

Innumerable cars that evening were racing up and down the long narrow drive to the château and in the inner courtyard at the top of the hill, Madame des Portes, Reynaud's mistress, wearing a bathrobe and red pajama trousers, was shouting directions at drivers and telling them where to park. The confusion was even greater inside. At the end of the gallery was a small room that once had been the owner's den. "Everything there," noted an observer, "was dusty and rather dirty. The walls were hung with pictures which had long lost all meaning, together with small antlers. . . . Hooked onto these were a couple of French hunting horns, black with grime. From another stag's point hung a depressed and ancient fez, grey with the same dust that lay thick on the table. On this, a pile of ancient bills and letters were held in position by hideous Victorian bronze paper weights, a dog that looked like a sheep, and a shepherdess that might have been fashioned out of melting chocolate."

Two of Reynaud's people were there: Roland de Margerie, his aide, and a pretty, plump girl named Leca, his secretary. These two kept busy: the phone was continually ringing, telegrams were constantly flooding in, and visitors were milling about the gallery without cease. De Margerie and Leca alone had the job of trying to make sense of it all.

Beyond the secretary's little office was a larger space, a big drawing room filled with Victorian sofas and French officials of every description. The men were all in that room for the same reason—Reynaud had stationed himself in an adjoining office—and most of them had come there for the same purpose: to beg Reynaud to put a stop to the war.

One official, however, had something else on his mind. "Only one man showed any hope in Tours," a journalist wrote, "the long-nosed, storklegged Brigadier General Charles de Gaulle." Throughout most of the day on June 13, de Gaulle lurked in the antechamber outside Reynaud's office, sitting on a circular couch "with his long legs stretched out before him and his nose and the visor of his kepi nearly parallel, pointed at a spot on the floor just in advance of his big right toe." Whenever the defeatist ministers and officers would leave Reynaud's office for a moment, "de Gaulle would squeeze in" and insist that *now* was the time to order the retreat to North Africa.

Feeling the pressure of de Gaulle's repeated wheedlings, in fact, Reynaud cried out at one point: "This de Gaulle certainly does have character! He's got too Goddamned much character!"

But Reynaud was still unwilling to commit himself either to surrendering or to continuing the war: certain defeatist Ministers had resolved that, at that afternoon's Cabinet meeting, they would force him to make up his mind.

(6)

The defeatist Ministers were becoming brazen. As the Cabinet assembled in the garden of the Château de Cangé, where now the Government was scheduled to hold a late afternoon meeting, Pétain and Weygand openly pressed their case. Strolling on the lawn together, Weygand in polished boots and brass spurs and Pétain with a cane, a straw hat and a gray flannel suit, they would drop a word here, giving a knowing smile there, then corner a Minister and give him dark warnings about how close the *Panzers* were to Tours.

They were successful, too: a sense of panic spread across the garden; more and more Ministers believed they had no choice but to accept surrender.

One of these Ministers, ostensibly on Reynaud's side, was about to join the effort to unseat the Premier.

(7)

At six o'clock that afternoon all the Cabinet except de Gaulle, who had not been invited to attend, trooped up to the sitting room, and the meeting began; Paul Reynaud opened the session: he looked gray and worn, and his facial tic had grown pronounced.

Weygand spoke first.

"When I became Commander-in-Chief," he began, sitting straight in his armchair, "I found that the Meuse front had been broken through and that our armies were retreating in disorder . . ." In vigorous language and in great detail he refought the Battle of France, and then, after having recited his long litany of defeat, he came to the point. "From now on, I am obliged to say clearly that a cessation of hostilities is compulsory. . . . The war is definitely lost. . . . I do not want France to run the risk of anarchy that follows a military defeat. That is why, I repeat, as much as it hurts me as a soldier to say so, an armistice is imperative."

The Ministers sat up rigid and silent. For the first time in public, Weygand had used the word "armistice."

Then the storm broke loose.

César Campinchi, the Minister of Navy, Yves Delbos, the Minister of Education, Raoul Dautry, the Minister of Armaments, and Georges Monnet, the Minister of Blockade, all fought back with energy. Georges Mandel, the Minister of Interior, fisheyed, arrogant, friendless and one of the few politicians who had consistently opposed Pétain and Weygand, helped out by passing them cryptic notes.

Weygand's concern with anarchy, they said, was irrelevant and ridiculous, for the Nazis would permit no disorder wherever they were in control. The real question, they insisted, was whether the Cabinet and what remained of the Army could escape through Bordeaux or Marseille to North Africa. Such a move was conceivable—for Churchill had pledged his support.

Weygand snarled back in anger: "In three weeks," he snorted, "England's neck will be wrung like a chicken!

"Paris has been abandoned," he snapped out, "but at least the Government must have the courage to remain in France. . . . First, it is at this price only that the French will accept the heavy sacrifices demanded of them. You may say that it is a greater sacrifice for the Ministers to abandon the soil of the country. No one will accept that. The people will say that the Ministers are continuing to insist that the population be killed, bombed and burned after having taken care to put themselves tranquilly in the shelter of Africa . . .

"Secondly,"—and now Weygand began to pour out his scorn in the darkening room:

"Secondly, in admitting that they will be well received in our colonies —which is by no means certain—what authority do they think they will conserve in France? How long would they remain outside it? The time necessary for the American factories to turn out the planes and tanks permitting them to reconquer it? That would take several years. . . . And then how will they reconquer France? By bombing and bombarding our towns, our compatriots? That is an absurd and odious program!"

Then Weygand fired off his shot of contempt: he would, pointing his forefinger at Reynaud, Weygand declared, "refuse to leave the soil of France even if put in irons."

The Commander-in-Chief was serving notice that, if need be, he would disobey the orders of the constitutionally elected Government of France.

Premier Reynaud said nothing: he merely twisted his neck in his collar.

The mood of the meeting had changed. Campinchi and Delbos raised their voices again in argument, pointing out that help from America and an eventual invasion of France were precisely what they had in mind, but they sensed their support was beginning to dwindle. At this moment, one of the Ministers said, "My resistance [to Weygand] completely collapsed. From then on I was for an armistice."

One man sitting there in the gloom, however, seemed quite unmoved. Georges Mandel, cold and calculating, was staring through Weygand as if the Commander-in-Chief did not exist.

Then, as sometimes happened, the left side of Mandel's mouth twitched involuntarily. Weygand was on his feet in a flash.

"He's laughing at me," Weygand screamed and, as Mandel described it later, "gathered up his skirts like a furious prima donna and, without even a bow before the curtain, flounced out."

"We could then hear him shouting," said Georges Monnet, the Minister of Blockade," . . . before the ministerial secretaries in the vestibule of the Château. [Weygand] said: 'They sit with their asses in their chairs and they don't give a damn that all this time the French Army is being massacred. They choose not to get it through their heads that it is time to make an armistice.'"

The Cabinet could hear Weygand shouting something else, too: the Ministers back there, he was screaming, were "mad and ought to be arrested."

The next morning the Cabinet fled further south, to Bordeaux. And as he fled with them General de Gaulle struggled to reach a decision.

(8)

On the night June 13, 1940, several of the defeatist Ministers were sitting in the chairs and on the double bed in Pétain's hotel room in Tours. Pétain had been observing the Cabinet, he told his companions, and he was sure that the Ministers would never accept surrender unanimously. Therefore, he advised, in his quavering thin voice, they would have to "make an end of it" in Bordeaux, legally if possible, illegally if necessary.

Chapter 6

(1)

CHARLES DE GAULLE AND WINSTON CHURCHILL STEPPED OUT OF A CAR ON ST. JAMES'S STREET IN LONDON EARLY IN THE AFTERNOON OF JUNE 16, PASSED THROUGH A BLACK IRON GATE AND WALKED UP THE STEPS OF the Carlton Club to its brass-handled glass front door. De Gaulle had begun his trip two days before. He had driven a staff car to Brittany, seen his wife, Yvonne, in Carantec (where he had sent his family for safety), taken a fishing boat from Brest to Plymouth and then ridden a train up to London where, now, he was about to propose an idea to Prime Minister Churchill.

A heavy old six-sided lamp lighted the narrow corridor inside the Carlton Club. On one side of the passageway stood a massive coatrack that for over a century had held the coats and cloaks of England's greats; on the other side of the hall was a doorman's office and an ancient grayhaired man who nodded in deference through the windowpanes on his door. Churchill nodded back and then led de Gaulle through the gloom to the musty dining room in the back. Huge portraits of England's titled nobility covered the wall behind their table. A waiter in a frock coat filled their glasses from a bottle of wine. Churchill smiled across the table at the frigid, humorless de Gaulle and, lifting his glass, offered a toast to victory.

De Gaulle talked throughout their lunch. Weygand's hold over the French Cabinet, he explained quietly, was now so strong that Reynaud might last as Premier for only a few more hours. Therefore, de Gaulle argued, only a drastic, extraordinary and dramatic step could persuade the Cabinet to oppose Weygand. And that, de Gaulle explained, was why he had come to London. He laid out a proposal that he and other Frenchmen then in London had favored. He would like to see the British and the French create joint organs for defense, foreign and financial policies, associate the House of Commons and the Chamber of Deputies and formally unify their two War Cabinets. De Gaulle was proposing nothing less than Anglo-Franco Union.

He stopped again to let his meaning sink in.

Churchill was silent. He cut a cigar and lit it. A cloud of blue smoke enveloped his face. Then he put the cigar down and looked across at de Gaulle.

He would have to obtain the consent of his Cabinet, he said, before he could dare take such a step.

But, he promised, he would call the Cabinet together that same afternoon.

(2)

At six-thirty on the afternoon of June 14, an exhausted and bedraggled Premier Reynaud drove into Bordeaux with his middled-aged mistress, Hélène des Portes, who chattered and twitched in fear at his side. Over the Pont de Pierre they inched—the harbor below was packed with ships and cranes—pushing on through the refugee-jammed streets in search of the district Army headquarters on the rue Vital-Charles where Reynaud was going to set up residence.

"There was a smell of death in Bordeaux," an observer wrote, ". . . [the] piano player from Harry's New York bar in Paris slept at a table on the terrace of a café, his head cradled in his arms. He typified all uprooted Paris packed into this city of indecision. . . . The famous restaurants like the Chapon Fin had never known such business." While the less fortunate refugees slept in their cars outside or simply slumped in the gutters, the men of wealth, "heavy-jowled, waxy-faced . . . were ordering sequences of famous claret vintages as if they were on a *tour gastronomique* instead of being parties to a catastrophe."

Reynaud drove on through the streets past the Tour St-Michel and the city's business district until he found the rue Vital-Charles. He eased his Citroen into the gravel driveway of the Army headquarters, then, with Hélène at his side, climbed the steps to the large hallway inside. There he found his office—and sat down to work with a new determination.

Reynaud had changed. As tired as he was, and as worn down by the pressures of the previous month, he was now ready to fight back against Weygand. Gone was his indecisiveness, gone was his fear of making enemies, gone was his desire to appease all factions. Upon becoming Premier he had given way to these temptations, for these were the ways, he had thought, to remain in power. But now he knew better, for his earlier methods had led to disaster, and he sensed that the only way to hang on to his job—and to rally his country—was by defeating Weygand. Once again Paul Reynaud had become a combative gamecock.

(3)

De Gaulle's long legs stretched out before him as he tried to get comfortable on the narrow petit-point sofa. The room around him was filled with expensive Chippendale furniture and dark oil portraits of Disraeli, Gladstone, Ramsay MacDonald and other Prime Ministers of a bygone age. The place reeked of stale cigars. It was mid-afternoon on June 16, and de Gaulle was sitting, chain-smoking, in the antechamber of the Cabinet Room at No. 10 Downing Street. Through the thick, polished, oaken doors in front of him, the War Cabinet was meeting and debating his proposal for an Anglo-French Union.

Once or twice the oaken doors swung open and a British Minister, bustling and preoccupied, would come out, and once or twice a male secretary in a black morning coat passed silently in front of de Gaulle to deliver a telegram inside. But no one appeared to tell de Gaulle the results of the meeting.

He was beginning to feel the pressure of time. Only if he could fly back to France that same afternoon with a British offer of Union, he felt sure, could he have any chance of keeping Reynaud in power. He paced to the window. Beyond Churchill's garden at the rear of the house were the trees and shrubs of St. James's Park and, farther away, the top-heavy red buses and the scuttling black taxicabs streaming along the Mall, moving to and from the Memorial in front of Buckingham Palace.

De Gaulle stopped pacing to look at his watch: it was four o'clock, and the Cabinet had been consulting for more than an hour; he had no more time to lose.

At the moment the doors swung open again and the British Cabinet began to file out: first came Herbert Morrison, the Minister of Supply, Lord Lloyd, Secretary of State for the Colonies, and A. V. Alexander, First Lord of the Admiralty; then came the nervous little Clement Attlee, Lord Privy Seal, the beefy, powerful Ernest Bevin, the Minister of Labor, and the handsome, elegant Anthony Eden, the Minister of War. Finally, through the doorway, came the paunchy, stoop-shouldered, black-suited Winston Churchill, with the ever-present cigar in his mouth.

Churchill rushed up to de Gaulle, took the cigar out of his mouth, put his hand on his hip, then rumbled: "We agree."

De Gaulle raced off immediately to the Hendon airport outside London for his flight to Bordeaux—but as he boarded the plane he debated with himself what he should do if he reached France too late.

(4)

A long row of cars pulled into a gravel courtyard off the rue Vital-Charles in Bordeaux. Out of the cars climbed the Ministers of France: the handsome Baudouin, the bespectacled Bouthillier, the ruddy-cheeked Darlan, the white-faced Pétain and the parchment-skinned Weygand. With them walked the Minister who was bent upon betraying Reynaud.

It was the afternoon of June 16 and the meeting for which they had come had promised to be stormy: Weygand was hoping to get rid of Reynaud, and Reynaud was intent upon fighting back, upon making France stay in the war.

As they entered the hallway of Reynaud's new residence, they passed the large pillars inside and stopped at the foot of the staircase. An office door on the left had opened and into the hall had walked Reynaud. He moved up to the staircase and spoke to Weygand.

He had a suggestion, Reynaud said: rather than seeking a truce, perhaps France could follow the Dutch example of allowing the Army to surrender and the Commander-in-Chief to stay at home, while the Head of State, Queen Wilhelmina, fled abroad as a symbol of Dutch resistance.

Reynaud said this quietly, but firmly.

Weygand, however, began immediately to raise his voice. Reynaud was trying to start a conspiracy against him, he shouted to the Ministers on the staircase, Reynaud was plotting to transfer the onus of defeat onto the shoulders of the Commander-in-Chief.

Reynaud snapped right back: Weygand's talk of conspiracy was utterly absurd! Weygand could do as he pleased but he, Reynaud, would urge the Cabinet to go abroad.

Weygand was flying into a rage: "The Government," he screamed, "simply cannot leave France!"

"But what is North Africa," Reynaud came back, "but two departments of France?"

"That's not the same thing at all," Weygand barked. Then he yelled on: he had no intention of assuming responsibility for a flight overseas.

"If that's what's bothering you," said Reynaud, "I myself will take the responsibility. I will give you a written order."

Weygand glared back with his arms crossed. Then he gave out a cackle of a laugh.

With that the Cabinet walked on up the stairs to the conference room on the second floor.

(5)

The English landscape spread out beneath the two-engined De Havilland Dragon Rapide. It was late afternoon on June 16, and the plane was carrying its sole passenger, General de Gaulle, back to Bordeaux. Dark hedgerows below marked off yellow and green patchwork fields, and toy cars and trucks were crawling along the narrow roads. A farmer stacking sheaves of wheat looked like a tiny animated doll. De Gaulle's thoughts, however, were neither on the fields nor the roads nor the tiny farmer below. They were on the hands of his wristwatch, the speed of the plane and what might be happening to Reynaud, far ahead in Bordeaux.

The plane was shortly over France. Eight thousand feet below, on the left, was Le Havre, burning. Anti-aircraft shells trailed black and scarlet puffs in the cloudless, twilight sky. Night was falling. As the plane crossed Brittany, de Gaulle could see the shimmer and brilliance of flames: entire villages seemed on fire. He shuddered. Somewhere down there was Paimpont, where his elderly mother, Jeanne, lay dying in the home of his older brother, Xavier; somewhere else down there, he trusted, his wife and children had followed his instructions and were racing to Brest to catch the last boat to England.

But deGaulle had another, more immediate, worry. The sky was now black and he still had not reached Bordeaux. Could the plane go no faster?

Soon after the plane passed La Rochelle in the dark de Gaulle looked down from the window again: below him were innumerable lights, two long rows of lights on either side of a long straight strip of darkness. The plane was over a runway; it had reached the Mérignac airport outside Bordeaux. De Gaulle felt the pilot cut the engines and begin the long descent.

Then the plane touched ground, and de Gaulle thought again of what he might have to do if he was too late to save Reynaud.

(6)

"I demand the signing of an armistice," Weygand was shouting, "which has already been delayed too long!"

The French Cabinet had begun its session: the Ministers were seated around a long table in Reynaud's residence in Bordeaux, and the conspirators were about to spring their trap.

Reynaud was angry now; his eyebrows were snapping up and down, and he was gesturing violently as he spoke.

"No," he insisted, "France must fight on to the end!"

The Ministers were dead quiet: no one had expected Reynaud to be this resolute.

Weygand was out of control: his voice was rasping, his manners were gone, and he glared accusingly at everyone around the table as he repeated his demand for an immediate armistice.

Reynaud argued back, and Georges Mandel came to his aid. Dark and cold, Mandel began spitting out hatred and contempt for the defeatists. Of all the men in the Cabinet, he, being Jewish, had the most to lose in case of surrender. He saw through the defeatists, he said. They were after power, personal power, and nothing else—and he would denounce them, in private and public, as long as he had words to speak.

For a moment the mood of the Cabinet swung toward Reynaud and Mandel. Then came the trick.

Camille Chautemps, a suave and brilliant lawyer, a former Premier and, like Pétain, a Vice-Premier on the Cabinet, had seemed a loyal Reynaud supporter in the month and a half since the outbreak of hostilities. And so, when first he heard Chautemps' soft voice from across the table, Reynaud thought he was going to receive more support.

Perhaps, Chautemps began, as he steepled his fingers, to justify continuing the fight from abroad to the French, who would think the government was betraying them, Reynaud should ask Germany, not for an armistice, but for its *conditions* for an armistice.

Chautemps paused. Reynaud was silent, looking puzzled.

Chautemps continued in his soft and persuasive voice. "If, contrary to what we expect," he said, "the conditions appear moderate, our British friends will no doubt agree that we should study them."

Reynaud was sitting straight and alert.

"If, on the other hand," Chautemps went on, "as you and I expect, the conditions are catastrophic or dishonorable, I hope the Marshal, cured of his illusions, will agree with us that we must continue the war. . . .

And the French people, when they learn that an honorable peace is impossible, will be ready to support the supreme sacrifice which we will have to ask of them."

In this moment, Reynaud wrote later, "I learned . . . that the man had already passed over to Pétain's camp."

For Chautemps' proposal was the trick. It appealed to the defeatists because it meant a decisive step forward for them—beginning negotiations with Germany; it appealed to the resisters because it meant that, while France was talking to Germany, the government itself would have the time to sail to North Africa.

Reynaud stood up in an immediate protest. To ask for the *terms of* armistice, he insisted, was no different than asking *for* an armistice. Either way he would break what remained of the Army's morale and so make it impossible to rally the troops to Africa.

"Gentlemen," he said, "this motion is incompatible with the pledge of solidarity which we gave to England."

But the majority of the Cabinet had swung against him.

Paul Reynaud took one more step to win back the Cabinet. He used the last weapon in his arsenal, his trump card, his last resource, and he knew that if it failed he would have to step down as Premier.

He asked the Cabinet to vote on Chautemps' proposal.

(7)

De Gaulle got out of his car at the gate of Reynaud's residence and dashed toward the steps of the building. Now, with Churchill's promise of union in his briefcase, de Gaulle had something concrete with which to persuade the Cabinet to fight on. But when he reached the doorway of the residence, de Gaulle stopped walking.

Roland de Margerie, an aide to Reynaud and one of the few friends de Gaulle had left in France, was standing in the half-opened door. He told de Gaulle the news.

Reynaud had resigned and Pétain would become the new Premier.

De Gaulle knew then what he would have to do: go into exile, create a French Army abroad, prove to the world that it could, and would, fight, and so give the French a banner to which they could rally, and do all this before Pétain's new government and the German Army destroyed the Resistance once and for all.

De Margerie passed along something else as well: Weygand had apparently issued orders for the arrest of several obstreperous French officials. One of these was General de Gaulle.

General Spears has given an eyewitness account of what happened to de Gaulle during the next two days.

Chapter 7

(1)

Two ENGLISHMEN CRUNCHED ACROSS THE GRAVEL COURTYARD OF REY-
NAUD'S RESIDENCE LATER THAT NIGHT: ONE WAS GENERAL EDWARD
SPEARS, TALL, BURLY, IN UNIFORM, AND CARRYING THE SWAGGER
stick of the British officer; the other was Sir Ronald Campbell, the British
Ambassador to France, shorter, slender, and elegantly dressed in striped
pants and a tailcoat. They, too, had just learned the news of Reynaud's
resignation. "So this was the end," Spears says he thought when he heard
the news. "Reynaud was beaten, he had not made the grade; France was
leaving us to fight alone. I felt stunned and suffocated." Spears had controlled himself, however, and with Ambassador Campbell had gone to the
rue Vital-Charles to see if Reynaud might lead the resistance.

Now they were inside the residence, trying to locate Reynaud's office
in the dark. The hallway was gloomy and the columns and wide staircase
threw deep shadows across the floorboards. The place seemed deserted:
no sentries were on duty, no lamps in the hall were lit. Ambassador Campbell stayed in the hall while Spears climbed the stairs to look around.
Finding no one, he groped his way back down but, through the darkness,
he could now see that Campbell was talking with a man by the door of the
study. Spears walked over to join them. Then he stood perfectly still.

Someone else was in the hall, calling out his name in a loud whisper.
Spears looked around. Through the gloom he became aware of a tall

figure wedged straight and stiff behind one of the large columns. Spears could now see who it was: it was General de Gaulle.

"I must speak to you," de Gaulle whispered, "it's extremely urgent."

"But I can't now," Spears whispered back. "The Ambassador and I are trying to find Reynaud."

"You must," de Gaulle insisted. "I have very good reason to believe Weygand intends arresting me."

Spears glanced around the hall. The man Campbell had found was de Margerie who was in the process of opening the door to the study. Campbell had turned, beckoning Spears to come along.

"We shan't be long, I think," Spears told de Gaulle. "Stay exactly where you are until we come out. It should be all right."

A light was on in the study and behind the desk sat the once fastidious Reynaud, slumped in his chair with his collar unbuttoned and his hair disheveled, his eyebrows were lowered and still. Spears had hoped that Reynaud might still go abroad and somehow rally France to renewed resistance, but now, inside the study and watching Reynaud, Spears saw there was no hope of that. Reynaud no longer cared about the fall of France: he felt only a great relief that now he could stop running, stop begging the Army to fight on, stop worrying about the endless lines of refugees limping along the roadways of France. No words could win him back. Reynaud now seemed a broken old man. Spears could bear no more and walked to the door.

Was there no one left in Bordeaux, he wondered, who had sufficient stature to lead the resistance?

When the Englishmen left the study Spears checked the hall at once. De Gaulle was in the same spot, still backed up against the column where no one could see him from the entrance. He was tense; even in the darkness he looked ashen. He told Spears again of Weygand's ordering his arrest, and said that he had to slip out of Bordeaux at once to get to England. Could Spears help him?

Ambassador Campbell had moved a few steps away, tactfully, but when Spears motioned to him he came back. The three men decided they must talk somewhere else. The soldiers in the streets outside might already have received Weygand's order, and anyone entering might become suspicious at seeing two Englishmen whispering upward at the stone column. Spears' room in the Hôtel Montré, a five-minute walk from the rue Vital-Charles, might be safer—but how was de Gaulle to get there?

The Ambassador's Rolls Royce, parked in the courtyard outside, would be conspicuous: with its pointed grill and long sweeping lines, the crowds in the streets would know it immediately.

That was not the solution: de Gaulle would have to go to the hotel alone, in the dark and on foot.

(2)

When, in the years to come, Charles de Gaulle looked through the windows of his study at Colombey-les-deux-églises he could see the sweep of the hills of eastern France, the hills of a land at peace, the hills of a France free at last of Nazis and goose-stepped parades. His memories were rich with heroism, with the Frenchmen who had shot, bled and conspired for their country, with the citizens of Paris the day he led the triumphal procession down the Champs-Elysées. Gazing through his windows de Gaulle remembered the salvation of France. He also remembered Bordeaux.

There, too, he had dreamed of a France without the swastika, a France whose leader could talk as an equal to the greats of the world, of a France strong, free and proud. But how slender this hope had seemed in the alleys and doorways of Bordeaux. For on the night of June 16, 1940, the future President of France who would one day march in glory through the Arc de Triomphe was stealing from house to house, shadow to shadow, trying to make his way unseen to two Englishmen in a small hotel room in Bordeaux.

De Gaulle reached the room in the Hôtel Montré. Spears let him in and locked the door. Now, what was going on, Spears and the Ambassador wanted to know? Why was de Gaulle so insistent upon getting their help in fleeing to England? Were there no French who could help him out?

Spears was sitting with his chin in his right palm.

De Gaulle, wrote Spears, "was plainly overwrought" and pacing about the room. His words came so fast that they spilled together. He was all alone now: there were so few left in France he could trust. So he had had to turn to the English for aid.

If he could get to London, he explained, he could appeal to the French and to France's Empire to keep on fighting: if he could get to London he could gather together any Frenchmen who might oppose the armistice; if he could get to London he could train and equip such men and one day lead them back to the fields of France. But delay would be fatal. Weygand's supporters were everywhere in Bordeaux, and the last thing they wanted was a defiant de Gaulle in London and out of their reach.

So de Gaulle had two specific requests: first, would Spears send an order to the pilot of the Dragon Rapide that had flown de Gaulle to Bordeaux to fly him back to England? Second, would Spears help de Gaulle get back to the plane in the morning?

Spears thought he had better clear the matter with Churchill first, and slipped across the corridor to an English diplomat's room where there was a wall telephone above the bed. Spears placed the call to London and then lay down on the bed the "better to manipulate the ear-trumpet" on its short wire. In a moment he heard Churchill's voice on the other end of the line. Spears explained de Gaulle's fears of being arrested and informed Churchill that de Gaulle might be just the man to keep alive the spirit of resistance in France.

"Winston understood perfectly," wrote Spears. "The line was good, he only asked me to repeat one or two words. I could feel him hesitate." Then Churchill gave his answer to de Gaulle's plea, and the receiver clicked down at the London end of the line.

Spears went back to his own room and told de Gaulle, who in his tension had been chain-smoking, that Churchill had at last agreed. De Gaulle would come to the Hôtel Montré at dawn, they agreed, and then Spears would drive with him out to the airport.

But where was de Gaulle to hide until then? The police might search Spears' hotel room and de Gaulle had no place of his own to go. Spears stroked his square chin as he voiced his opinion: de Gaulle would have to step out again into the night, trusting his safety to the shadows till dawn.

(3)

While Spears and Campbell were asleep in their beds that night, de Gaulle was in the streets outside, hearing, for a time, the voice of temptation. Seek out Weygand, it pleaded, and give yourself up. Ask for amnesty and perhaps, a post in the new Government. What does France matter anyway? You have a wife and three children to support, and one of those children desperately needs your care. What if you get to England and they are unable to join you?

You are committing yourself to a life of unceasing self-discipline, taking of risks and inner struggle against loneliness. You are weary and your personal security is what counts most. Besides, if you leave, the French will call you a coward.

Temptation spoke, and throughout most of the night de Gaulle struggled to make up his mind. We know now that, on that night in Bordeaux, he seriously considered going into retirement. When morning came he did the only thing he could.

(4)

Spears climbed out of bed at six o'clock on the morning of June 17 and rode the elevator down to the lobby to meet de Gaulle. The place was packed: refugees were still sprawled sleeping in the armchairs and those with cars outside were crowding into the *lavabo* to wash and shave. But de Gaulle was missing.

Spears passed the time chatting with two British officers who walked in as he sat watching the door. Then they moved off. Seven o'clock had come, but de Gaulle had not yet appeared in the lobby.

Spears sat back in his armchair uneasily. Seven-fifteen came, and he began to pace. Then it was seven-thirty, and still he could see no de Gaulle.

Spears phoned from the lobby to the British Air Attaché upstairs. He hoped, Spears wrote, "we could concoct some scheme to find out if de Gaulle had been arrested. If he had we should have to find some means of releasing him for long enough to get him to the aerodrome and on to the plane."

Moments later, Spears saw the Air Attaché coming down the stairs, and, in the same instant, high over all the other heads in the lobby, he saw two golden oak leaves above the visor of a French kepi, and beneath it, the elephantine nose and the tightly pressed lips of General de Gaulle.

De Gaulle had gone to find an aide he knew to be loyal, a Lieutenant Geoffroy de Courcel, and a trunk full of documents he had hidden before his first flight to London, but the search had taken time and before he and de Courcel could get to the trunk, the sun had started to rise. Finally, hoisting the trunk through the back alleys and across the sidewalks filled with sleeping refugees, they had reached the Hôtel Montré.

General Spears helped them store the trunk in the back seat of his car, and then they set off through the city, inching their way past the abandoned cars and the refugees sprawled in the gutters, hoping that no one would notice the trunk and become curious about their destination.

They were lucky. Not till the airport gate were they stopped.

(5)

The guard at the gate was peering into the car. He was alert and sus-picious, wondering why an Englishman was seated with two French of-ficers in a car headed for the runway. Fortunately de Gaulle's profile — the elephantine nose, the clipped moustache, the pouting mouth and the receding chin — was not yet famous, and so the guard failed to recognize him. Nor did he notice the trunk in the back hidden under a woolen blanket.

Spears drove on through the gate, and after a few minutes of searching among the planes, he found the twin-engined De Havilland. The pilot was waving at them from beside the tail of the plane. He came over to the car to work out plans for departure.

Immediately the pilot spotted a problem. He would have to lash the trunk inside the fusilage, for otherwise its weight would shift in flight and cause the plane to crash. And nowhere did he have a rope. So couldn't they simply leave the trunk behind?

No, said de Gaulle. The trunk contained papers from the War Ministry in Paris, papers that would help him organize the resistance but that, falling into Weygand's hands, would kill the resistance before it was born. Someone, he said, would simply have to find a rope. Brusquely he gave de Courcel the order, and the Lieutenant set off on the double to find one.

This, wrote Spears, rated "high among the unpleasant periods of waiting I have experienced." As soon as de Courcel had run off, the pilot had tried to release the ropes from the wooden blocks that held the plane in place, but the ropes were too stiff for him to budge them. Time was slipping away: "The possibility of de Gaulle's departure from Bordeaux being detected," Spears wrote, "was increasing. Somebody was sure to think of him in the course of the morning; then steps would be taken to locate him."

Beside Spears in the car, de Gaulle sat chain-smoking gold-tipped cigarettes. He seemed to have changed overnight: during the previous evening he had paced and fidgeted, but now he was cold, silent and distant as Olympus. His legs and his arms were crossed; he seemed oblivious to his danger.

But Spears was not, for de Courcel had not yet returned and "if it occurred to anyone that [de Gaulle] had gone, the aerodrome would be the natural place to look for him." And in this bright sunshine, someone would sooner or later be able to spot him. Yet there was still no de Courcel.

Spears was frightened. He looked first out of the windshield of the car, then he climbed aboard the plane to search for any sign of de Courcel. "Someone would remember having seen me in the car with [de Gaulle]," he wrote, "that would be the clue. Then there would be a telephone call." Spears looked over the tops of all the parked airplanes. Nothing.

He was in despair. He looked this way and that across the airport, then started to clamber down again from the fusilage. Then something caught his eye.

From under the wing of the next plane came someone running. It was de Courcel. As fast as his "stilt-like legs" were going, Spears thought de Courcel "appeared to be moving in slow motion." But he was dashing for the plane, and in his hand he was clutching a ball of twine.

(6)

All his life de Gaulle had had a certain idea of France, a France "like the princess in the fairy stories or the Madonna in the Frescoes," a maiden for whom solitary knights in armor fought and died. He had clung to that dream as a boy marching lead soldiers, as an adolescent reading French history in his father's study, as a cadet towering above his classmates on the parade ground at Saint-Cyr. Nor had he forgotten in adulthood. His dream of being that solitary knight had always marked him apart from others, but his hell at the moment was that the dream, at last, had become a reality. For as the vineyards and pine trees around the airport swayed beneath his climbing airplane, he felt, he wrote, "like a man on the shore of an ocean, proposing to swim across."

PART TWO
The Birth of Free France

Chapter 8

(1)

THE NEXT DAY AT NOON, THICK, BLACKENING, RAIN-FILLED CLOUDS BEGAN TO GATHER OVER BORDEAUX, THROWING A SHADOW OVER THE RAMROD FIGURE OF MARSHAL PÉTAIN WHO WAS STARTING UP THE STEPS of the city's radio station. Pétain had come to the radio station to make an announcement to the people of France. With his stiff carriage and curt nod to the officer who opened the door for him, Pétain looked as much the military man as he had when, on the Day of Victory in 1918, he had ridden his white horse through the Arc de Triomphe and past the cheering crowds along the Champs-Elysées. Even now, as he marched to the microphone on the studio floor, his gait seemed dignified and portentous.

Pétain extracted a piece of paper from the pocket of his tunic, unfolded it, and held it at arm's length to focus his eyes on the script. Outside the window the branches began to shake and sway with the approaching storm. Pétain inched closer to the microphone to begin his speech. His hand trembled slightly as he spoke.

"It is with a broken heart," he said, in his quavering thin voice, "that I tell you today it is necessary to stop the fighting." He went on to explain that France's military position was beyond redemption, and that he had taken over as Premier. He was offering France, he said, the "gift" of his person to "assuage her misfortune."

In that moment, an observer noted, "the sky exploded in a violent thunderstorm, sheets of water lashed the windows, and sparks crackled out of the radio panels."

The British newspapers carried reports of Pétain's speech that afternoon, and when General de Gaulle, having just landed in London, saw the headlines, he understood immediately that the Marshal was asking for an armistice. De Gaulle understood something else as well: he would have to find a way of striking back at Pétain, and fast.

(2)

A little before six o'clock on the afternoon of June 18, General de Gaulle, wearing two bronze stars on his kepi and carrying his ceremonial white gloves in his left hand, mounted the steps of the British Broadcasting Corporation off Oxford Street in London. Just behind him and trying to keep pace with de Gaulle's long stride scurried his only aide, Lieutenant Geoffroy de Courcel. A British secretary inside expressed her amazement that a man so pale and tight lipped as the General could at the same time seem so calm and determined. Then de Gaulle pushed through the doors of a soundproofed underground studio.

De Gaulle's airplane had landed early the previous afternoon outside London and General Spears had treated him to lunch at the Royal Auto Club.

London that day had been "quiet as a village," for with Pétain's asking for an armistice, the British had lost an ally whom they had expected to fight on to the end. "You could have heard a pin drop in the curious, watchful hush," Mollie Panter-Downes wrote to *The New Yorker.* "At places where normally there is a noisy bustle of comings and goings, such as the big railway stations, there was the same extraordinarily preoccupied silence. People stood about reading the papers: when a man finished one, he would hand it over to anybody who hadn't been lucky enough to get a copy, and walk soberly away. For once the cheerful Cockney comeback of the average Londoner simply wasn't there. The boy who sold you the fateful paper did it in silence; the bus conductor punched your ticket in silence. The public seemed to react to the staggering news like people in a dream, who go through the most fantastic actions without a sound."

It was through a shocked and stupefied London that General Spears drove de Gaulle after lunch to No. 10 Downing Street to see Prime Minister Churchill.

As de Gaulle ducked his head to get through the back door of Churchill's residence, he blinked his eyes slightly in the bright sunshine. Then he saw Churchill sitting in a wicker chair and sunning himself by a corner of the garden.

Churchill rose to greet his guest: his walk was heavy and his big ruddy face was flecked with the splotches of age. He gave de Gaulle a quick smile of welcome, then thrust out his broad lower lip and grumbled, glowering at the two men. Was there no one else, he muttered at Spears, whom they could have smuggled out of France? Surely, somehow, somewhere, some prominent Frenchman must have been willing to lend his prestige to the cause of resistance? But even as he spoke he knew the answer to these questions.

Churchill's eyebrows knotted together at the thought of having to work with de Gaulle. He respected the strength of de Gaulle's will, to be sure, but he also sensed that de Gaulle lacked the suppleness to be a member of the team. De Gaulle was a loner, and for his tactlessness his fellow officers had long ago dubbed him *"le maître gaffeur."* Churchill feared that such rigidity would prevent de Gaulle's being an effective leader for France—and from accepting British priorities in the conduct of the war. So Churchill had his doubts. But de Gaulle was all he had, and, with a shrug of his heavy, stooped shoulders, Churchill offered him financial assistance and a chance to speak the following evening over the B.B.C.

Soon after the B.B.C. studio doors had closed behind de Gaulle, red lights began to flash in the control booth and the hands of the clock on the wall pointed exactly to six o'clock. Gibson Parker, the B.B.C.'s broadcast supervisor, leaned closer to the microphone before him on the table and began to speak. Talking in French, he presented to his audience "the man whom you all know and admire, General de Gaulle."

Sitting on folding chairs along the back wall of the studio, Jean Oberlé and Jean Marin, two French broadcasters already working with the B.B.C., frowned in puzzlement: they had never heard of General de Gaulle.

De Gaulle took his place before the microphone. His black hair was pasted back sweatily from his forehead. He placed his white gloves on the table beside him and then laid out the two pieces of typing paper he had extracted from the inner pocket of his tunic. He began to speak:

"The leaders who," he started, "for many years past, have been at the head of the French armed forces, have set up a Government."

He stopped to catch his breath. His voice had been firm at first but then it had grown unsteady. Looking across at the skeptical eyes of Oberlé and Marin, he continued.

"Alleging the defeat of our armies," he said, "this Government has entered into negotiations with the enemy with a view to bringing about a cessation of hostilities. It is quite true that we were, and still are, overwhelmed by enemy mechanized forces, both on the ground and in the air. It was the tanks, the planes and the tactics of the Germans, far more than the fact that we were outnumbered, that forced our armies to retreat. It was the German tanks, planes and tactics that provided the element of surprise which brought our leaders to their present plight.

"But has the last word been said? Must we abandon all hope? Is our defeat final and irremediable? To these questions I answer—No!"

De Gaulle glanced again at Oberlé and Marin: they were following him this time with close attention.

"Speaking in full knowledge of the facts," de Gaulle went on, "I ask you to believe me that the cause of France is not lost. The very factors that brought about our defeat may one day lead us to victory.

"For, remember this, France does not stand alone. She is not isolated. Behind her is a vast Empire, and she can make common cause with the British Empire, which commands the seas and is continuing the struggle. Like England, she can draw unreservedly on the immense industrial resources of the United States.

"This war is not limited to our unfortunate country. The outcome of the struggle has not been decided by the Battle of France. This is a world war. Mistakes have been made, there have been delays and untold suffering, but the fact remains that there still exists in the world everything we need to crush our enemies some day. Today we are crushed by the sheer weight of mechanized force hurled against us, but we can still look to a future in which even greater mechanized force will bring us victory. The destiny of the world is at stake.

"I, General de Gaulle, now in London, call on all French officers and men who are at present on British soil, or may be in the future, with or without their arms; I call on all engineers and skilled workmen from the armaments factories who are at present on British soil, or may be in the future, to get in touch with me."

De Gaulle paused again: Oberlé and Marin were transfixed. Then, in his hollow, jarring voice, de Gaulle read out his last sentence: "Whatever happens," he proclaimed, "the flame of French resistance must not and shall not die!"

As his words flew out over the Channel to France, de Gaulle found himself wondering what effect, if any, they might have. The French had ignored him before: Would they begin to listen now?

To that question de Gaulle had no immediate answer, but that night, Jean Oberlé and Jean Marin came to the apartment he had taken at No. 8 Seymour Place, to become the first members in de Gaulle's new organization, Free France.

A few others too, already in London, joined up the next day. One of these, a diplomat named Robert Mengin, went with a reporter, Pierre Maillaud, to Seymour Place to meet de Gaulle.

In the antechamber of de Gaulle's flat, Mengin said, "We were met by Lieutenant de Courcel, the General's aide-de-camp, tall, blond, rosy cheeked, and very polite. He told us that the General had people with him but would see us shortly. It was not long before the General's callers emerged from the *salon*. We recognized them as prominent members of the French colony in England. They seemed already to have that preoccupied look, that kindly and protective smile of men who felt themselves weighted down by ministerial responsibilities to come."

De Courcel motioned for Mengin and Maillaud to go in.

"The room was vast," Mengin went on, "and flooded with sunlight. At the far end, his back to a window, stood General de Gaulle, immobile and statuesque. After we had been introduced, Pierre Maillaud led off in a complimentary vein, saying that he had come to place himself at the General's disposition in response to his magnificent appeal of the night before. In what way could he be useful?"

"'What exactly is your profession,'" de Gaulle asked.

A newsman, answered Maillaud.

"'Very well, then,' said the General, 'tell me the news.'"

"This reply," commented Mengin, "was hardly expected, but Maillaud did as ordered. He gave the General the latest news . . . [then], doing his professional duty, Maillaud asked the General if he had any statement to make about his immediate plans. The General's answer was that he would speak again over the B.B.C. that evening, addressing himself to all Frenchmen everywhere but especially to those in North Africa, to tell them where their duty lay. He felt in his heart, he said, that he was speaking in the name of France."

"I looked," said Mengin. "I listened. I had come with a great store of admiration. But I felt it was beginning to ebb away, giving place to a sense of constraint, due in part, I think, to the General's appearance. He was seated in an armchair facing the two chairs to which he had motioned us, and as he talked to Pierre Maillaud, I could see only three quarters of his face. The one eye visible to me somehow suggested the eye of an elephant, quite round when the heavy eyelid was raised. . . . He had very little chin, so little that I found myself wondering whether it wasn't the result of a war wound. Yet it gave no impression of weakness, but rather of smugness, of self-sufficiency, as did also the mouth under the little brush of a moustache, really a very small moustache. . . . There was also something that suggested a very tall Boy Scout, too tall, really to be still a Scout."

The General suddenly turned to Mengin.

"'And you, monsieur?' asked de Gaulle."

Taken by surprise, Mengin said simply that he wanted to go to sea as soon as possible since he had resigned from the French Embassy the day before.

"'Just yesterday?' de Gaulle asked, "with a quick glance that seemed not quite friendly. He then got to his feet and we took our leave most ceremoniously. In the street, Pierre Maillaud asked what my impression had been. I answered that the General seemed inflated."

"'No, not that,' said Maillaud. 'That isn't quite the word.'"

"'But *I* think it is the right word. You haven't had to do your military service, so you have had no experience with that kind of officer—inflated with the concept they have of themselves. If you stuck a pin into them, you'd hear it—their idea of themselves—come out whistling like the air from an inner tube.'"

Mengin and Maillaud resolved to stay with Free France, but they did so with the gravest of reservations: could de Gaulle, they wondered, with his coldness of appearance and ungainliness of manner, possibly appeal to anyone in the French side of the Channel now? Could he possibly persuade the French to forsake their new leaders? Could this obscure general gain an audience of any kind?

(3)

In the middle of the afternoon two days later in France, General Charles Huntziger, the former commander of the Ninth French Army at Sedan and now the ranking emissary of the new French government, stepped forth from his car, noticed the warmth of the sunshine in the chestnut trees around him—and then stood erect with shock. In the clearing of the Forest of Compiègne before him stood a railway coach draped with swastikas and the military flags of the Third Reich. Huntziger and his two French companions knew that coach: it had once been the railway car of Marshal Ferdinand Foch. German engineers had hacked away the museum that housed it and had towed it onto the rusty tracks where, on November 18, 1918, German representatives had signed the papers that signaled their surrender. Now, in that same coach and on those same tracks, it would be Huntziger's turn to sign. As he walked toward the coach from his car he noticed three men standing together in the clearing. On the left was the deputy Nazi Party Leader, Rudolph Hess; on the right was the German Foreign Minister, Joachim von Ribbentrop; and in the center, his face ablaze with hatred, scorn and anger, stood the vengeful figure of Adolf Hitler.

The Führer snapped his hands onto his hips, arched his shoulders, planted his boots wide apart. "It was a magnificient gesture of defiance," a journalist wrote, "of burning contempt for this place now and all that it had stood for in the twenty-two years since it witnessed the humbling of the German Empire." Hitler then turned away to lead the way to Marshal Foch's coach.

The Frenchmen walked with their eyes staring straight ahead: their faces were solemn and drawn. They marched stiffly to the steps of the car where two German officers, Lieutenant General Tippelskirch, the Quartermaster General, and Colonel Thomas, chief of Hitler's headquarters, extended their arms in the Nazi salute. The Frenchmen saluted back, and passed into the interior of the coach.

The cluster of reporters some fifty feet away could see through the dusty windows of the old railway car. As the French entered the drawing room, Hitler and the other Nazi leaders rose. The Führer gave the Nazi salute. He was not at all talkative and he simply nodded to General Keitel at his side. Keitel shuffled his papers and started to read. The French, their faces marble colored, sat at the table listening attentively. Hitler was restless. At 3:42 P.M., just twelve minutes after the French arrival, he stood up, saluted again, and marched out of the drawing room. The French stayed seated by the green-topped table, concentrating on the voice of the General Keitel.

Hitler and his aides climbed down the steps of the coach and marched toward their waiting staff cars. A German band struck up the "Horst Wessel" song and the national anthem *"Deutschland, Deutschland über Alles."*

The terms of the Armistice were hard: the French would retain control of only the southeastern two-fifths of their country and would turn over to German command the entire stretch of the Channel and Atlantic coastline; they would demobilize their fleet and dock it securely out of the reach of the British; they would pledge to turn over to the Germans all anti-Nazi refugees who had escaped into France; and they would try to arrest and shoot any of their own countrymen continuing the fight against Germany.

General Huntziger affixed his signature to those terms, and soon the French learned that their new government meant to uphold the agreement to the very last letter.

(4)

Only a handful of Frenchmen had set out to join de Gaulle.

One French solider swam naked two miles into the Mediterranean to reach a tramp steamer bound for London, and another soldier arrived in

England hidden under the deck of a Breton fishing boat. A tourist-plane pilot took off from the courtyard of his house in Brittany and, with almost no gas, flew off into the face of a storm so severe that even the German pursuit planes refused to fly: the pilot reached Cornwall in safety. Two workmen in an aviation factory near Paris stole a plane, taxied it down the plant's runway, roared off and landed on an England beach just a yard short of a British landmine. A student pilot with only fifteen hours' flying experience patched together a plane from the remnants of three smashed machines lying in a field, flew to Oran on the coast of Algeria, which he thought had gone over to de Gaulle, found it had not, hopped off again and landed on the racetrack in British-controlled Gibraltar.

Three French sailors pushed a dinghy into the surf of the English Channel and rowed it off to sea: a German plane machine-gunned them and missed; a storm hit them and they disappeared into a fog, bailing out their boat with a cooking pot; hours later they hailed a British speedboat and managed to drag themselves aboard. A group of five teenagers stole a pleasure launch in Bordeaux and steered out toward the Atlantic Ocean. They ran out of gas and drifted across the waves for ten chilly days; an English cargo boat picked them up, but a German plane bombed the ship and sank it; a second freighter rescued them again, but a magnetic mine sank this boat too; finally, the crew of a British speedboat plucked them out of the water and hauled them back to the coast of England.

Three French enlisted men, captured in mid-May, 1940, landed in a German prison camp in Poland and started immediately to plan their escape. The chief obstacle facing them was a fence ten feet high and wired to deliver electric shocks to anyone who touched it. But beyond the fence was a clearing, and then a forest, and this was what inspired them to act. For three weeks, working mainly at night, they clawed out a tunnel beneath the fence, stuffing the loose earth into their pockets and casually scattering it all over the camp. Before dawn one morning in June, they finished their work and, crawling out of the tunnel's exit and dodging across the clearing, they dived into the trees beyond and lay still under a clump of bushes until night had fallen again. A Polish peasant who stumbled over them at dawn gave them some money, and with this they bought tickets on a train headed for the Russian frontier. They tried to cross the frontier wire at night, but this set off a clanging alarm system, and a German border patrol began to fire red flares over their heads. As soon as gunshots began, the Frenchmen stretched flat on the ground in the darkness. Eventually the Germans tired of shooting into empty space, and the escaped Frenchmen made it safely to Russia. Soon they started their trek toward the Mediterranean to join Free France.

Another Frenchman, Raoul Aglion, an officer in the Army stationed in a small Arab town near the Suez Canal, was sitting at a marble-topped café table drinking Turkish coffee with a group of Australian soldiers. His companion, a French sergeant, had gone off in search of a radio to get the latest news. Suddenly, Aglion heard some shouting in a back room of the café and, above the racket, he heard the voice of his Sergeant yelling at him: "Come here! Hurry up! Hurry up!" Aglion bumped past other customers at the bar, British soldiers in khaki and Egyptains in big red fezzes, and pushed his way into the little room in the rear. The sergeant was bent over a small wooden radio on a table, twisting the dials this way and that. His face was glistening with sweat. The static was heavy and sometimes the hollow, jarring voice from the radio faded out altogether. But a few sentences did come through clearly:

"But has the last word been said? Must we abandon all hope? Is our defeat final and irremediable? To those questions I answer—No!"

The voice faded out again and only at the end of the broadcast did it come ringing through once more.

"Whatever happens," it said through the static, "the flame of French resistance must not and shall not die!"

"Who was that talking?" Aglion asked.

"I was turning the dial for news," the sergeant said, "and I tuned in on a broadcast from London, but I couldn't get the name. That damned station in Bari always gets in the way. It was some French general, I think."

They went to work on the dials again but all they could get this time were reports from Radio Cairo about Pétain's asking the Germans for an armistice.

Aglion later boarded a big, flat-bottomed ferryboat that meandered up the Suez Canal, and only in Cairo, a week later, did he learn the answer to his question: he had been listening to the B.B.C. and to the voice of General de Gaulle.

Aglion set out immediately for London.

Others, too, tried to reach England, and failed, and drowned or were shot in the process. Mary Borden, the wife of General Spears, called them all the "magnificent madmen."

(5)

A curtain of darkness was falling on France. The first of the German troops to reach Paris had appeared at the outskirts of the city before dawn on June 14. They encountered no hostile gunfire, and at ten o'clock that morning, detachments from the *Wehrmacht* divisions toured the boulevards of the city, hauling down the tricolor and running up the swastika. Soon the city was packed with Nazis: a triumphal procession passed down the Champs-Elysées, and Adolf Hitler posed in front of the Eiffel Tower. Enlisted men and officers, tankmen from the *Panzer* divisions, navigators from the *Luftwaffe*, infantrymen from the *Wehrmacht*, all milled about Paris like country boys come to the big city for the first time. They clambered up the Eiffel Tower, gazed in awe at the tomb of Napoleon, climbed the steps of the Sacré-Coeur, ogled the nearly naked chorus girls in the Folies Bergères and, precisely at noon on each day of the week, they lined up in their perfect formations to parade past the Arc de Triomphe.

About twenty thousand uniformed Germans were stationed in Paris, and although they swarmed through the reopened shops as tourists had done for centuries, they actually helped impoverish the city: France had to pay the staggering occupation bill—which included the unusually high pay given to the German soldiers stationed in Paris. Such paychecks, however, were scarcely enough to satisfy the Germans. With all their renowned passion for detail and organization, they proceeded systematically to loot the homes and museums of the city. Anything—linen, Gobelin tapestries, milk, champagne, furniture, paintings—anything of value that they could lift they carried with them through the front doors of Paris and into the backs of their waiting trucks.

General Stülpnagel, the military commander in Paris, supported his men by suppressing all but the most pro-Nazi and anti-Semitic French newspapers, and on his list of indexed materials he placed the books and speeches of General de Gaulle. And because a little boy in Fontainebleau, just south of Paris, stuck out his foot and tripped a German soldier, the Nazis announced that whenever the residents of the town saw Germans approaching on the sidewalks, they themselves had to move out of the way by stepping down into the gutter. The Nazis forbade all but the most necessary travel across the Demarcation Line between Occupied and Un-occupied France, and to enforce security in their Occupied zone they imported the men with the civilian clothes, gray felt hats and closely shaved skulls. These agents' official title was the *Geheimestaatspolizei*, or secret police. Throughout Europe they were known, more simply, as Gestapo.

Here and there, of course, signs of resistance did appear: French soldiers who had had the nerve to escape from German stockades and found their way home again could never feel completely secure, since their own friends might inadvertently betray them, and so from the very start they were no-compromise men; and in the hamlet of Champagne-sur-loue, close to the Demarcation Line in central France, a network began to help escaped prisoners, Jews and other refugees escape southward to

Spain. In Lyons a Captain Henri Frenay founded a secret society called Combat.

But such instances of resistance were rare: most of the French seemed to think them suicidal and even treasonous. "You are committing treason," Frenay's mother wrote to her son, "and I ask myself the appalling question whether I should not tell where you are, for you are doing wrong."

At this point neither the resisters at home nor the Gaullists abroad seemed the answer to the nation's prayers. Despite the great numbers who were beginning to help their countrymen escape, most of the French at this time seemed to be looking rather to the old Marshal Pétain in the resort town of Vichy: it was he who would rescue them from their plight; it was he who would exorcise all the terrors that surrounded them; it was he, and he alone, who would save France.

(6)

The French community in London seemed equally impressed with Pétain. Late in June, 1940, an English writer Mrs. Robert Henrey went to have lunch in the restaurant of the Savoy Hotel—the grill room was closed because, to protect it against air raids, workmen were busily bricking in its windows. The restaurant upstairs was still open, but its usual atmosphere of gaiety was gone. It looked, she wrote, "like the dining room of a temperance hotel. . . . There was not the slightest glamour about this international crowd. It was sober and depressed. There were no champagne and cigars, no laughter, no long discussions over coffee, no pretty women to show off their hats. . . . The city folk who normally patronized it at lunchtime, spending their money lavishly on brandy and cigars, seemed to have faded away. In place of them one met groups of Poles, Dutchmen, Belgians, Norwegians, and a few American newspapermen who had just crossed over from France. General de Gaulle, almost unknown as yet, held court at a large round table. French diplomats from the Embassy, and members of the various naval, military and economic missions who nearly all intended to obey the instructions of the Pétain government, kept as far from the new leader as possible, and even glared at him with undiplomatic rudeness."

De Gaulle, nevertheless, was managing to attract more volunteers.

The first stop in London for those who wanted to join Free France was Olympia Hall, a huge gray armory in Kensington, where Englishwomen working in the Red Cross helped the Frenchmen adjust to their life in Britain. "One of them," wrote Romain Gary, the novelist who was a

Free French aviator, "a ravishing blonde in military uniform, played innumerable games of chess with me. She seemed determined to bolster up the morale of the poor little French airmen, and we spent many hours with a chessboard between us. She was a very good player and beat me hollow every time, and then at once suggested another game. For a French volunteer dying to do some fighting, to have to play chess with an extremely pretty girl, after seventeen days at sea, is one of the most nerve-wracking experiences I know. Matters reached such a point that I found it preferable to avoid her altogether and to watch her from a distance trying *rocades* against an artillery sergeant who, after a bit, began to look as melancholy and dejected as I. There she was, blonde and desirable, pushing her chessmen over a board with a slightly sadistic gleam in her blue eyes. She was a truly vicious number if there ever was one. Never, never, have I seen a girl from a good family do more to demoralize an army."

After such days of recuperation the Free Frenchmen-to-be would move on to St. Stephen's House on the Thames Embankment, where de Gaulle had wangled the loan of a suite of third-floor offices for his Free French headquarters.

As a volunteer passed between Westminster Abbey and the Houses of Parliament, or trooped through the long stone canyon of official buildings along Whitehall and turned the corner at Big Ben, he came across the blackened-stone facade of a tall commercial building that gave onto the River Thames. A French sailor with a red pompon on his navy-blue cap was doing sentry duty at the doorway. This was St. Stephen's House, the home of Free France.

If the volunteer who walked up the stoop past the sentry and pushed open the glass-paneled door expected to find inside the Persian rugs and the oil portraits of French nobility that adorned the offices in Parisian Ministries, he was in for a rude surprise.

The elevator usually refused to work, and after trudging up the three flights of echoing stone stairs, a volunteer came to an office door whose bell was also out of order. In a dark alcove just inside the door, he saw a stocky French soldier in shirtsleeves trying to repair a telephone switchboard, and in a second antechamber, so small that it could barely contain a desk and half a dozen rickety folding chairs, the visitor saw the welcoming grin of Geoffroy de Courcel. A small road map of France was pasted on the wall above the fireplace just to the right of de Courcel. The caller then sat down, delicately, on one of the wobbling chairs and awaited his turn for an interview with General de Gaulle.

When the big moment came, the volunteer entered a larger office with wallpaper that was curling and peeling with age, and uncertain light bulbs that seemed likely to blow out at any moment. Then, as he looked at the desk beneath the two windows, in the back, he saw the General himself, uncoiling his great length and extending his arm for a handshake of welcome.

"I saw a man from another age," a Free Frenchman later remarked. "Very tall, he was wearing a uniform and leggings and held himself extremely straight. But his erectness, accentuated by his thrown-back head and by his arms, which followed exactly the line of his body, seemed a natural and comfortable position for him. . . . The bearing of his head, so remote, and the expression of his face showed his intransigence. At first his features reminded me of a medieval drawing. I felt like framing them in a visor and a chin-piece. There was something aquiline and unchanging about the eyes and the shape of the eyelids. But a touch of awkwardness was added to the face by the very long and bulbous nose. . . . The chief characteristic of his eyes was that they were oblivious of the outer world. Their expression could not change to suit the mood of the people around him. Their look seemed preordained."

The recruits kept trickling into St. Stephen's House until some four hundred men had joined up with de Gaulle. Then, on July 3, the British took a step that nearly destroyed Free France.

(7)

According to Article Eight of the Franco-German Armistice, the new French Government was to let its ships be "demobilized and disarmed under German . . . control," and the Nazis, in turn, were to abstain from using the French fleet to further their own war aims. But Churchill did not trust the Germans. At some point, he knew, while these ships were fully armed, they would pass under German control, and at that moment the Nazis could commandeer the boats and decimate Britain's coastal defenses. "There was no security for us at all," wrote Churchill. "At all costs, at all risks, in one way or another, we [had to] make sure that the Navy of France did not fall into the wrong hands, and then perhaps bring us and others to ruin. . . . There was one step to take. It was obvious, and it was dire."

Part of the French fleet was docked at Toulon, on France's Mediterranean coast, where it was well beyond the reach of British guns. But a few French ships had sailed over to Portsmouth and Plymouth before the Armistice, and many more, including the *Dunquerque* and the *Bretagne*, the fastest battleships of the French Atlantic Fleet, lay in the small, curving—and accessible—harbor of Mers-el-Kébir in Algeria.

Churchill wanted both sets of ships: he called his plan "Operation Catapult."

On July 2 everything was ready. British admirals received their top-secret orders and prepared to move at dawn on the following morning. The pattern was the same everywhere, in both of the British ports.

At four o'clock in the morning of July 3, British officers climbed the gangplanks of the French ships nestled against the docks of Plymouth and Portsmouth. No one was stirring aboard the ships save the lone sentries. They were sleepy and unsuspecting.

"An ugent message for the commanding officer," the Britishers announced. "It must be delivered into his own hands."

"Very well," the sentries said, and left the decks to awaken their Captains.

This, wrote a French observer, "was exactly what the British had planned for. Groups of armed English soldiers were waiting nearby, hiding behind a building, or a hangar, or a pile of coal or under the canopy of a boat. With one leap they were on board and in command of every hatch and passage. Meanwhile the officer, gun in hand, had followed close on the sentry's heels, and his silhouette was framed in the doorway before the commanding officer, abruptly awakened, knew what had happened. Ten armed men crowded around him while he was handed a memorandum from Admiral James or Admiral Dunbar-Nasmith stating that he must hand over his ship. It was a grotesque and humiliating experience which the French officers would have difficulty in ever forgetting."

The surprise at Mers-el-Kébir was equally complete.

The morning of July 3, 1940, was clear and hot along the Algerian coast. When they bothered to raise their heads, the French sailors lolling about the decks of their sun-drenched ships could look through the entrance of the harbor at Mers-el-Kébir and see the bright blue of the Mediterranean and the clear, cloudless sky beyond. Only a faint mist rose above the horizon, and along the shoreline of the harbor itself, the *Dunquerque* and the *Bretagne* rolled gently at dockside, no longer ready to fight. Canvas hoods covered their smokestacks, the fires in their engine rooms were burning low, and their big sixteen-inch guns pointed in toward the shore as if danger could never come again from the sea. Even the lookouts high in the crow's nests above dozed away or dreamed of their upcoming leave-times on shore, feeling the torpor of a Mediterranean day that was so hot, so languid and so peaceful.

The shells hit with a tremendous roar: for the British fleet, that had crept up along the coastline, it was as easy as "shooting rabbits in a pen." Shells bored deep into the *Dunquerque*, ripping through her generators, paralyzing her electrical system and forcing her to crash on the beach.

Another salvo hit the *Bretagne*. She staggered, caught fire, exploded, broke the ropes that held her to the pier and, with a great sound of sucking, sank to the bottom of the harbor. Within seconds her entire crew of 131 men had drowned. Six small French destroyers struggled to escape through the white columns of water that the shells were spraying into the air, and headed out toward the open sea. Only one, the *Strasbourg*, made it. At Mers-el-Kébir that day, 1,297 French sailors died, 351 were wounded, and most of the ships were destroyed.

"No act," Churchill told the House of Commons, with great sadness, "was ever more necessary for the life of Britain and for all that depended upon it." That was probably true—but no act more nearly destroyed Free France.

As far as France herself was concerned, England was now an enemy, and any Frenchman who worked in conjunction with the British was committing treason against his own people. General Noguès in Morocco had considered joining forces with de Gaulle, but now he openly refused to do so; and the Free French efforts to win recruits among the hundreds of sailors whom the British had interned were greeted with hoots, catcalls and curses. (The British soon offered these men safe conduct back to France.) And Commander Thierry d'Argenlieu, a former monk who had come to St. Stephen's House, asked several days leave to enter a monastery for prayer: he had given his word that he would fight for de Gaulle, and he did, valiantly, but he refused ever again to don his French uniform while still on British soil.

The seizure of the French ships and the British attack at Mers-el-Kébir, de Gaulle said simply, was a "hatchet blow to our hopes."

Chapter 9

A FEW, HOWEVER, HELPED HOLD FREE FRANCE TOGETHER: ONE SUCH MAN WAS ANDRÉ DEWAVRIN.

AS DEWAVRIN'S SHIP, THE S.S. MEKNES, SLID SILENTLY PAST THE stone fortress that guarded the harbor at Brest, he looked up at the white flashes of the German guns above St.-Thégonnec, twenty-five miles in from the Atlantic coast. Hours before, on June 17, he had seen the fishermen's wives in black shawls weepingly openly on the quays while their husbands, sprawled drunk behind nearby bistro doors, bowed their heads in resignation upon the barroom tables. The news had been flashing from cottage to cottage: "The war's over . . . it's over . . . Pétain himself has said so . . . the war's over!" As Dewavrin leaned on the railing along the *Meknes'* deck, and watched the great square battlements of the fortress recede into the night, he swore to himself that, somehow, he would erase the shame of that defeat.

André Dewavrin was twenty-eight years old: before the war he had been a professor of fortifications at Saint-Cyr, but when the Germans invaded Norway, he had joined up with a detachment of Foreign Legionnaires who tried, unsuccessfully, to stop the Nazi *blitz* at Narvik, in a fjord far above the Arctic Circle. He had stayed with the Legionnaires through the Battle of France, and now, as he left his railing and headed down into the bow of the ship, he believed he was going with them to a port in North Africa. From there, he was sure, they would continue the war.

At dawn four days later, however, a voice shouted down "Land!" and the Legionnaires, still in their underwear, clustered as closely as they could to the wet wooden railing. Several began to sneeze. The water beneath the side of the ship looked gray and chilly, and across the harbor they could see brick smokestacks, rectangular customs sheds and unending rows of wet, gray slate roofs.

"Name of God," someone muttered. "This isn't Africa. This is England."

It began to rain: André Dewavrin had arrived at the docks of Southampton. In a few days, after reaching London, he went off to join Free France.

Opposite the sidewalk where Dewavrin was walking on the morning of July 1, the hands of Big Ben were striking ten o'clock. The traffic in the street was thick with red double-decker buses, black, old-fashioned taxicabs and olive-drab trucks loaded down with helmeted soldiers and big, wooden, stenciled boxes. He assumed the vehicles were heading for the Channel coast. Dewavrin turned off the sidewalk and turned the handle of a glass-paneled front door. He had reached St. Stephen's House.

A man in a faded uniform took him up to the third floor in the creaking elevator—it had decided to work that day—and he sat down in a tiny antechamber with several other French soldiers, most of them unshaven and with bloodshot eyes. Half an hour later his turn had come. He followed Lieutenant de Courcel into an inner office through whose windows he could see tugboats and barges on the gray waters of the Thames. Then he had his first glimpse of General de Gaulle.

The General was rising from behind his desk to shake the young Captain's hand; Dewavrin saluted and gave his name and rank. He remembered later that de Gaulle was smoking heavily.

De Gaulle wasted no time on the amenities.

"Regular or temporary?" he barked.

"Regular, *mon Général.*"

"Any decorations?"

"None, *mon Général.*"

"Do you speak English?"

"Yes, quite well, *mon Général.*"

"Have you done any fighting yet?"

"Yes, at Narvik, *mon Général.*"

De Gaulle paused a moment to crush out his cigarette in an ashtray. Then he continued.

"All right, you can start my intelligence service, the *Deuxième Bureau.** Lieutenant de Courcel outside will find you an office."

---

* The *Deuxième Bureau,* part of the Ministry of Defense in Paris, had long been in charge of all security matters of the French state, including espionage and counterespionage.

Dewavrin saluted in response, but de Gaulle no longer even saw him, so furiously was he absorbed again in the papers before him on his desk. Dewavrin glanced at his watch: in exactly one minute and twenty-five seconds, General de Gaulle had settled his fate.

De Courcel led Dewavrin to a small, sparsely furnished office at the end of the hall, and staring out the window at the tugs plowing along the Thames, André Dewavrin began to ponder. All he knew of the *Deuxième Bureau* was from a popular movie he had once seen in Paris: his training had been not in intelligence but in engineering, and he had only the barest idea of what spies really did.

Within a few days he did manage to recruit a few fellow workers: Jacques Mansion, a young man from Brittany; Naval Lieutenant Henri Louis Honoré—the Comte d'Estienne d'Orves; Maurice Duclos, the son of a Parisian stockbroker; and Alex Beresnikoff, a lean-faced young man whose passion for hiking and sleeping outdoors equipped him superbly for the months that lay ahead.

But, for the moment, what were they to do? As Dewavrin paced a narrow circle around his office, banging his shins against the two wooden benches in front of his desk, he finally confessed to himself that he had not the slightest idea how to do the job de Gaulle had given him. And so he and his companions began to let their imaginations roam.

As they huddled around the desk in Dewavrin's cramped office, they dreamed that instead of staring at the depressingly gray Thames outside, they were sitting at a marble-topped table along the Champs-Elysées, turning their heads to watch the behinds of the girls passing by. Someone would conjure up a ravishing blonde, a Mata Hari, outlining her form with the palms of his hands; someone else would mention truth drugs, or hobble over to the door to show that he could simulate a clubfoot. And one day at lunchtime, they went to Moss Bros., in Covent Gardens, to disguise themselves as proper Englishmen.

The sentry on duty at the door downstairs that afternoon had to compress his lips together in a thin white line to keep from giggling: three Frenchmen, whom he knew well and had seen every day, Dewavrin, Duclos and Beresnikoff, were marching side-by-side down the sidewalk in striped trousers, black coats, stiff white collars and impeccably shaped, black bowler hats. Almost in unison the three Frenchmen were tapping the ends of their tightly rolled umbrellas like canes on the pavement.

Their disguise, they thought, was perfect: who could guess, they asked, that under the sea of bowler hats flooding past the door of St. Stephen's House each morning and night there lurked three fearsome agents of the *Deuxième Bureau,* ready to stab, steal and spy for the greater glory of France?

One morning the young Frenchmen got their answer.

Each morning a battered black taxicab stood by the curb outside 69 Cromwell Row, Kensington, where Dewavrin and his men had bed and breakfast (they called the boarding house *"le grand 69"*), and each morning Dewavrin, Duclos and Beresnikoff took this cab to work. They would elegantly step down the porch steps, graciously bow to each other as they got into the back of the cab, gingerly place their bowlers on their laps and, speaking with the best Oxford accent they could manage, ask the driver to take them to St. Stephen's House.

On the fourth morning of this, the cabbie refused to accept their money at the end of the ride. He was withered and scrunched, and as Dewavrin extended the correct change, the man shook his head and crossed his arms.

"'S all right, mates," he said gruffly. "Nothing to pay."

"Nothing to pay?" Dewavrin wrinkling his balding scalp in puzzlement.

"That's what I said, guv'nor."

"Mais pourquoi pas?" Dewavrin had forgotten to be English.

The cabbie looked at him with a crooked smile: "You're General de Gaulle's young men, ain't you?"

Three jaws dropped.

"No need for fear," the driver went on, as he pressed his forefinger to his lips. "Mum's the word. I like the French, see—I was in the last lot myself—so this is on the 'ouse, as we say."

After that, the men of the *Deuxième Bureau* began more realistically to define their task. To protect their families back home in France, they chose false identities from the station names of the Paris Metro: Duclos became "St-Jacques," Beresnikoff became "Corvisart," and Dewavrin took for himself the pseudonym of "Colonel Passy." They also worked out specific plans for the penetration of France.

Dewavrin learned that the French section of British Intelligence would soon be dropping high-skilled solo agents, such as the famous spy, Peter Churchill, into Brittany and Normandy, and he realized that he would be foolish, given the amateur flavor of the *Deuxième Bureau*, to try to compete with London's efforts. The British would probably refuse to finance any such competition. But what could he do instead? What special contribution could Free France bring to the Allied Intelligence efforts?

Someday, he knew, if the Germans failed to invade England, the Allies would try to land in France, and for that effort they would have to plumb the secrets of the German coastal defenses—what war materials were flowing along the rails, what military traffic was moving toward the Channel, where the German fortifications seemed to be the most vulnerable. But how could Free France help in gathering such information? Day after day Dewavrin and his men met in his tiny office above the Thames, tracing their fingers along the wall map of France and trying to state precisely what it was they were trying to do. One day, however, Dewavrin snapped his fingers and said, "I've got it!"

Who could better obtain the needed intelligence, asked Dewavrin, than the little people of France? Who better than the laborers along the highways of Normandy, or the stationmasters and engineers at the rail junctions in Paris, or the farmers' wives from the countryside pedaling their eggs to market? Who could do the job better than any of these? No one. And who could better work with them than native Frenchmen? No one. If teams of French agents would organize these people into cells, collect and evaluate their findings and them smuggle the data out to London —that, Dewavrin thought, could be the special mission of Free France. That could be the purpose of the *Deuxième Bureau.*

British Intelligence scoffed at the idea. It was romantic and amateurish, said the experts, because the people of France were pro-Pétain and notoriously unable to keep their mouths shut. Besides, no intelligence service had ever tried the idea before. But one official in British Intelligence, Sir Claude Dansey, sympathized with Dewavrin and agreed to find ways to finance Dewavrin's project.

The first of the Free French agents, Jacques Mansion, using the cover name "Jack," set sail in a fishing boat from Plymouth on July 17, but Dewavrin did not hear a word from him for the rest of the summer. After two months of wandering through the fields and towns of Brittany "Jack" managed to recruit one lone fisherman, his boat and his dog to the Gaullist cause.

The next two agents, Duclos and Beresnikoff, set off during the night of August 4. After a British speedboat had whisked them across the Channel, they transferred into a rubber dinghy three miles off the coast of Normandy, but as they paddled toward the fishing village of St-Aubin, a finger of light probed out across the water toward them. They lay flat on the bottom of their boat. Finally, the light blotted out and they beached the dinghy at the foot of the dunes, deflating it and burying it beneath the sand. They had just reached the top of the bluffs, thinking they were safely at home at last, when they again had to drop hurriedly to their stomachs.

A German sentry was waving his flashlight across the top of the dunes. They managed to avoid him and escape into the interior of France, but since they had no radio they could relay no information across the Channel, and neither man returned to London until well into the winter of 1941.

Another agent, the Comte d'Estienne d'Orves, made it into France in December 1940. The Gestapo caught him almost immediately, and the following summer, he died at the hands of a German firing squad in a prison courtyard outside Paris.

By mid-August, in short, Dewavrin's plans had produced no results. His agents had neither established any cell groups in France nor relayed any information back to England. British Intelligence, sceptical from the beginning, was declaring openly that the *Deuxième Bureau* was worth no further funding, and even Sir Claude Dansey, Dewavrin's supporter, was beginning to have his doubts about Free France.

Dewavrin's blue eyes were now growing cold and implacable, and he began again to search for just the right man to send into France. The man had to be experienced, courageous and determined. He should be young and in top physical condition. He should be willing to follow orders. He should be a career officer in the French military.

He should have been everything, in fact, that the man Dewavrin finally had to pick was not.

Chapter 10

(1)

ON BASTILLE DAY, JULY 14, 1940, FREE FRANCE DELIVERED A SYMBOLIC CHALLENGE TO VICHY FRANCE. DE GAULLE MARCHED ALONG WHITEHALL BETWEEN THE ROWS OF GOVERNMENT BUILDINGS, LEADING HIS LITTLE band of men: the sailors with red pompons flaming above their navy-blue caps, the Foreign Legionnaires with their bayonets fixed and their eyes straight ahead, the soldiers with "France" written across their sleeves, the pilots with red scarves flashing above their collars, even a hospital bus filled with wounded Frenchmen, waving and shouting through the open windows. They were all wearing the badge de Gaulle had used when he had commanded the Fourth Armored Division in France, the two-barred Cross of Lorraine.

A proud family stood on the curb that day. Yvonne de Gaulle and their children had arrived safely from Brest and all around them on the sidewalks they heard crowds of Londoners shouting *"Vive de Gaulle"* and *"Vive la France."* The procession reached the Cenotaph, the monument to the Allied dead of the First World War, and there the crowds grew silent.

The Free Frenchmen faced the monument, presented arms, and with their left elbows thrust forward and their bayonets pointing toward the sky, they stood without a quiver and without a sound. De Gaulle reviewed his tiny army, then ordered the trumpeters to play *"Salut aux Morts."* Two soldiers stepped sharply from the ranks and gave de Gaulle a laurel wreath bound with a tricolor ribbon. He laid it at the foot of the Cenotaph. With one voice the English and the French joined together in singing the

"Marseillaise," then de Gaulle led his men down Victoria Street to Grosvenor Square where he laid a second wreath on the statue of Marshal Foch. Eric Sevareid, the American commentator, witnessed the scene. "I had been a spectator at hundreds of parades of military might," he wrote, "and they were all the same: merely a perfunctory display of organized faceless bodies. Now I saw a couple of lines of French sailors, airmen and soldiers, stretching for no more than a city block. Just a handful—but one was aware of every face. It would have been a familiar, French thing to see the inspecting officer smile benignly into their faces, pat one or two, and address them with *tu* and *toi*. But the towering general with the improbable nose, whose name was only then becoming a standard, strode stiffly among the ranks, never opening his tightly compressed lips, glaring, almost, into each pair of rigid eyes. He had the portentous air of a general surveying a great army. Somehow you could not feel sentimental, nor could you smile. You had the impulse to remove your hat and stand stiffly at attention yourself. This was impressive; it gave one to think. Every man there bore the conviction of confidence. There was a sense of strength in this handful that I had never felt in a demonstration by a hundred times their number."

Only three hundred marchers had started the parade, but by the time the procession had reached the statue of Foch, it had grown into the thousands. Hope had begun, said a Frenchman, there that day: for Free France was declaring in public its willingness to fight a war that Vichy had refused to fight.

And that meant doing battle against Vichy.

(2)

Vichy stood on the banks of the Allier, a little stream that meandered through the hills of central France, and had long been renowned for its restorative waters that would supposedly cure the traditional French disorder of the liver. In Vichy, nearly everyone took the cure.

In the center of the town was a shaded park equipped with wooden benches and glass-enclosed pavilions where the warm mineral waters bubbled up from their underground springs. On the streets near the park were restaurants, cafés and bathing establishments for those advised to immerse themselves in the waters; at the one end of the park was a fashionable place called the Hôtel du Parc; and at the other end was a large casino with gaming tables and roulette wheels—and a high-priced operatic theater.

It was in that auditorium, on July 10, that the delegates to the Chamber of Deputies were deciding whether to preserve the vestiges of old Third Republic or to create a new political system for France, a new régime the leadership of Marshal Pétain.

The sun over Vichy that morning was bright and the flowers around the park were brilliantly red and gold and purple; the wives, and the mistresses, of the Deputies were out in full regalia, dressed in their summer finery and strolling in groups of twos and threes in the shade of the trees. Paul Baudouin, who had belonged to Reynaud's Cabinet, was watching the ladies and thought that they looked "too elegant, too happy," too bejeweled for such a somber occasion.

As they sauntered from the Hôtel du Parc toward the casino, the ladies could see a cordon of gendarmes and *gardes mobile* with fixed bayonets preventing a cluster of newsmen from entering the theater. Then, at noontime, they saw the Deputies come through the front door of the casino, and headed down the steps for lunch.

"A great many ladies, beautifully gotten up and shining," a journalist noted, were sipping champagne that afternoon in the Restaurant Chantecler in Vichy. But from a table in the corner of the restaurant where he was sitting with Mme. and M. Guy La Chambre, the former Minister of Aviation, Robert Murphy witnessed a "very human incident." At "a nearby table," he wrote, "sat M. and Mme. Paul Reynaud, he swathed in bandages after his close call with death on the highway [Hélène des Portes, Reynaud's mistress, had died in the crash], but grimly determined to participate in the historic parliamentary session . . . Mme. Reynaud . . . came over to our table and recounted to Mme. La Chambre the pungent details of the [accident]. As she rose to rejoin M. Reynaud, she exclaimed with some emotion, 'And now, *chérie*, for my revenge.'"

The Deputies reconvened at two o'clock; three hours later word reached the journalists standing on the open grass outside that the assembly was taking another recess. It would gather together again in a moment to vote upon the motion on the floor.

A few moments later the reporters could hear sounds of shouting coming out the windows. "Vote!" came the cries, "*Clôture!* Vote! Vote!" Hundreds of voices appeared to be chanting in unison: "Vote! Vote! Vote!" Suddenly everything went silent and for a long moment the reporters could hear nothing at all. Then they heard one voice, belonging to an elderly man, cry out: "*Vive la Republic* just the same!" His challenge brought no audible response.

The twin doors of the casino then burst open and the Deputies began filing down the steps on to the grass below. In the lead came a wizened General with parchment skin and deep-set dark eyes: General Weygand.

He stopped before a group of reporters, looked briefly around the circle, and then said:

"I didn't get the *Boches*, but I did get the regime."

The Deputies had voted the Third Republic, that had existed since 1870, out of existence, and in its place had created what they called the "State of France." As its President they had chosen Marshal Philippe Pétain.

"The French leaders," William Bullitt, the U.S. Ambassador to France, cabled to Washington, "desire to cut loose from all that France has represented during the past two generations. . . . Their physical and moral defeat has been so absolute that they have accepted for France the fate of becoming a province of Nazi Germany. Moreover, in order that they may have as many companions in misery as possible they hope that England will be rapidly and completely defeated by Germany. . . . Their hope is that France may become Germany's favorite province—a new *Gau* [a province of the Third Reich] which will develop into a new Gaul."

For the new regime in France was eager to destroy all traces of opposition to its rule.

(3)

Yet the opposition from London did continue.

"*Ici Londres*," the B.B.C. French program began each evening. "Today is the ____th day of the struggle of the French people for its liberty!" The contents of that half hour would vary: Maurice Shumann might deliver a commentary entitled "*Honneur et Patrie*"; Pierre Bourdan and Jean Marin might discuss the news events of the day; Jean Oberlé might sing a satirical song to the tune of "*Deutschland, Deutschland uber Alles*"; or a small brass band might play the "*Marseillaise*," forbidden in both Occupied and Unoccupied France. Twenty times before the end of August, General de Gaulle himself spoke through the B.B.C. to France. One listener called his voice "a dominating icy complaint," another described it as series of "short studied bursts of sound," and a third thought it a "strange unknown voice with awkward modulations." But de Gaulle's manner of delivery did have one redeeming quality: it worked. Prominent Frenchmen were now beginning to join Free France.

Admiral Emile Muselier had long had enemies within the French military establishment. With his large black eyes and his thick black moustache, he looked like a pirate, which some thought he was, and his brilliance and flamboyance had won him the undying hatred of his superior officers. In the late 1920's he had competed with Admiral Darlan for the top job in the Navy—no one could deny Muselier's abilities—but he had been too contemptuous of others to woo highly placed political allies and, instead of ending his career as a four-star admiral, he had found himself drummed out of the service and living on a small government pension. He lost no opportunity to spread malicious rumors about the Navy.

When the Nazis invaded Poland, Muselier went back to work, this time in the Ministry of Armaments to oversee the operations of certain munitions factories. But he had continued to rebel. After the Armistice he had ordered the destruction of the machinery in his plants and, in a stolen government truck, had driven at night from Paris to Marseilles to engineer his escape from France. After some days in the port of Marseilles he had boarded a collier, taken command, and despite an Italian torpedo that tore a hole in the side of the boat, he kept on going across the Mediterranean. A coal-blackened and half-starving Emile Muselier reached the cliffs at the foot of Gibraltar.

Docked at Gibraltar was the French cargo ship, *Rhin*, whose radio officer, Claude Péri, was a buccaneer with pockets stuffed with hand grenades. He immediately warmed to Muselier and helped the Admiral put a small flotilla at the disposal of Free France. After Péri had stirred up a lively brawl aboard the *Rhin* in which he and six other Gaullist sailors drove the rest of the crew overboard, he commandeered the boat and three other French cargo ships, and set sail from Gibraltar to London.

As the ships rounded the coast of Portugal, the crew members looked up at an R.A.F. Spitfire roaring past them overhead. Muselier had swiped it from a runway atop the Rock, and as he overflew his tiny fleet, he let loose several bursts of machine-gun fire toward the horizon. That was his way of saying, "Come on! Hurry the hell up!"

In London, Muselier learned of de Gaulle, and joined Free France.

General Edgard de Larminat, stocky, square jawed and so military in bearing that, according to rumor, he wore his Army boots even in the boudoir, wanted nothing to do with the Armistice. He had been cited for bravery four times in the First World War and by the outbreak of hostilities in 1939, had risen to the post of Chief-of-Staff for General Mittelhauser in Syria. But when he learned of the signing of the Armistice in June, 1940, de Larminat issued an appeal to all officers in the French Empire to continue the war from abroad. Mittelhauser promptly threw him into jail.

His cell was in an old stone fortress in the desert outside Damascus. Iron bars guarded his high, narrow window, and Algerian sentries were posted around the clock outside the massive oak door. For several days de Larminat was content to snooze away on his cot. The tensions of the preceding weeks had left him exhausted, and he needed time to recuperate. But, on June 30, another officer, a Colonel Taguet, was allowed to visit his cell and warned him that the Syrian High Command was planning summarily to execute de Larminat.

This got him off his cot.

"In order to escape," wrote de Larminat, "I would have to get past the door of my cell, walk several meters to the corner of the fortress, cross a courtyard about ten meters wide, and climb over a wall with iron gratings on the top. After that I would be in the street." He arranged with Colonel Taguet to have two Foreign Legionnaires meet him as he jumped down again from the wall. But first, he had to get past the Algerian sentry outside his door. And de Larminat thought he knew how to do just that.

On the night of July 1, just after ten o'clock, he listened through his window and heard a low soft whistle. The Legionnaires had arrived.

De Larminat called through the oaken door to the sentry and asked the boy to mail a letter for him. "It's extremely urgent," de Larminat said, and he meaningfully jingled the change in his pocket. The sentry was torn between duty and greed. Greed won out. Then the sentry made his only mistake: he opened the door to take the envelope.

De Larminat had served for years with the Foreign Legion and was a skilled practitioner and instructor of the arts of hand-to-hand combat. The struggle lasted for only a brief moment. When the door slammed shut again the sentry was locked inside, gagging for breath, and de Larminat was slithering through the shadows of the darkened courtyard outside.

A battered Model-A Ford took him into British-controlled Palestine. A few days later, after he heard tales of de Gaulle, he was en route to join Free France.

A third French officer, Jacques Philippe de Hauteclocque, was only a captain when he escaped from France. He was a small and frail-looking, but de Larminat later called him the "roughest and most merciless man I have ever seen." In June, 1940, de Hauteclocque fled from the Germans by bicycle across the fields of northeastern France, but no sooner had he evaded a *Panzer* patrol than he ran into trouble with his own people. "Get the hell out of here!" a farmer screamed at him as de Hauteclocque was pedaling across the furrows, and in the village of Ostricourt, a little old man, trembling with fear, turned him away from the door of his cottage. Finally, after hiding behind a hedgerow to escape a German motorcyclist, he reached the Château de Belloy, his ancestral estate near Paris. There, early in July, he heard for the first time of General de Gaulle. Leaving his wife and six children behind he cycled next through the Unoccupied Zone to the Mediterranean coast, and down to Perpignan, just next to the border of Spain. Then he ran into trouble.

Spanish border officials at Port-Bou, under orders from France to incarcerate French refugees with anti-Axis leanings, suspected that his passport was forged, which it was, and a local judge ordered him shipped by rail to Madrid for trial.

High in the Pyrenees, however, de Hauteclocque leaped from his train and spent the next week scrambling along the ancient smuggler trails that wound up and down through the mountainous snowfields. On July 21, seven weeks after his flight had begun, he walked across a Lisbon pier to the S.S. *Hilary*, a British steamer bound for the docks at Southampton.

Others, too, joined Free France: General Legentilhomme from Djibouti at the base of the Red Sea, and General Catroux from Indochina, a four-star General who nevertheless insisted on putting himself under the command of Brigadier General de Gaulle.

And when these men joined Free France, they went no longer to St. Stephen's House, but to the new headquarters at 4 Carlton Gardens, a huge stucco-columned mansion just off the Mall in an elegant row of houses where once Lord Palmerston, Lord Kitchener and Lord Curzon had lived. Carlton Gardens had carpets and mahogany paneling, and an elevator that worked every day. Through its windows the Free Frenchmen could look up from their typewriters to see the trees of St. James's Park and, from the roof, wrote a Free Frenchman, "which was stepped back in terraces, one looked out over the Mall, with St. James's Park in front; to the left, the Admiralty Arch; and to the right, Buckingham Palace. A splendid view."

But not even Carlton Gardens gave the Free French much sense of security. "Very far off," the same Frenchman noted one August afternoon as he was standing on the roof, "to the left, down the Thames, clouds of black smoke rose from the docks which had been hit and above which, high in the sky, little silver butterflies turned, dived, chased each other, leaving behind them vapor trails of white against the blue. A fascinating spectacle that seemed some sort of game . . ."

But it was no game: the Battle of Britain had begun in earnest, and everyone in Carlton Gardens came to realize that if England fell, so would Free France. Everyone there also knew that Marshal Pétain and his advisers were predicting a British defeat.

(4)

At first, to the people of France, it seemed inconceivable that Pétain would knuckle under to the Nazis. After all, he held the baton of a Marshal. For eight centuries a Marshal had symbolized the greatness of France:

not only had he commanded the King's armies but he had also interpreted the code of chivalry and had been the spiritual leader of the men in arms. In the eyes of the French, a halo surrounded a Marshal, a luster springing not just from his own deeds but also from all the exploits of a glorious past. The red and gold kepi that Pétain wore and the seven stars emblazoned on his sky-blue sleeves shined with a radiance that attached itself to no one else in France.

In their craving for protection, in fact, many French had begun to worship Pétain. There grew up around Pétain a cult that has no parallel in twentieth-century France. Many thought Pétain could do no wrong. He was a man of experience, a wise old soldier, a stern but kindly patron who, someday, surely, would magically whisk the Germans away. His splendid military bearing mesmerized his people; his seven stars inspired the hagiography of religious veneration, songs, childrens' coloring books and even paraphrases of the Lord's Prayer. Pétain contributed to all this by putting on a spectacular show. Twice a day, at eight in the morning and five-thirty in the afternoon, the residents of Vichy could sit in their amphitheater and watch the ceremony of colors, complete with plumed headgear, resplendent harnesses, precise movements and bugle calls that commanded a silent prayer from every Frenchman in the stands. The Marshal himself would appear in public at night, standing in the floodlights on a balcony of the Hôtel du Parc, clasping a tiny tricolored French flag to his breast.

His effect on people was electric. Crowds in the dining room of the Hôtel du Parc—the Marshal lived and worked in a suite of rooms upstairs—would rise respectfully to their feet when Pétain arrived. "Wearing a lounge suit, his head held high, he [would advance] slowly with that peculiar gait of his which seemed to carry him so majestically. His blue eyes took in the whole room while he affably acknowledged with an inclination of his head or that gesture of the hand, which was his alone, the deferential salutations that greeted him."

Church bells would greet his arrival in the towns of the Unoccupied Zone, and peasants would line the railway tracks in the hope of catching glimpses of him through the windows of his carriage. During a parade in Toulouse, a woman threw herself down on the pavement before his open motorcar and took advantage of the halt by reaching out to touch him. Pétain, however, did not notice her. He was sound asleep.

But Pétain was quickly slipping into the role of a collaborationist, to a great extent because of the men around him. Swarming around the halls and suites of the Hôtel du Parc were his Ministers, advisors, lobbyists, hangers-on and officers, men who saw no chance of Germany's ever losing the war and who therefore insisted upon full military cooperation with the Third Reich. Declare war on England, they said, turn the

French fleet over to Germany, become an eager participant in Hitler's New Order, do anything that would ingratiate France with the Reich and so lessen the brutality of the occupation. The Marshal sometimes tried to resist such pressure, for he still had his pride, but he was old and tired and the collaborators were skillful and persistent. The most skillful and persistent of them all was the Vice-President of the French state, Pierre Laval.

"Black Peter" was the American code name for Laval; he hung, wrote an observer, "like an evil shadow over Vichy." He had wheedled and flattered his way into Pétain's trust, convincing the old man that the old Third Republic was worthless and that he, Laval, should play a major role in the new state.

The contrast between Laval and Pétain was stark and immediate: the Marshal stood straight and Laval slouched; the Marshall was neat and Laval was sloppy; the Marshal's hair had gone to white and Laval's was black and oily. Laval was famous throughout Vichy for the rich sauce stains on the white neckties he habitually wore, and General Weygand was said to have told him to his face, "You roll in defeat like a dog in filth!"

Laval, in short, was everything that old soldiers despised, but he was energetic, and he was seductive, and he persuaded old Philippe Pétain that France could not survive without Laval.

Laval had been born in 1883 near Vichy, in the village of Châteldon, and he kept a home there until the end of his life. "It's an old village," he once said of Châteldon, "with medieval houses. In the valley there's a knoll with an old castle on it. That's where I live."

Laval had not always lived in that castle: his father had been an inn-keeper and a butcher, a moderately prosperous peasant, and he had hoped that young Pierre would grow up to take over the family business. But young Laval was too bright and too restless for that. He wanted money and power, and he went off to Paris in relentless pursuit of both. After becoming a lawyer and a prominent politician he came back to Châteldon a rich man, and there he bought the dilapidated castle that towered above his father's inn. Then, in the late thirties, he settled back to wait, certain that the time of his ultimate triumph would come.

In his restless opportunism Laval had skipped from doctrine to doctrine and from party to party, yet whatever cause he espoused for the moment he embraced with enthusiasm and even frenzy. Laval had an enduring trust in three things only: his wife, himself and his ability as a trickster.

That was the quality he thought made him indispensable to France.

But something more was eating at Laval, and Robert Murphy, posted to the new American Embassy in Vichy, thought he discovered what it was: "Laval's château was the pride of the village, and one aspect of this many-sided self-made man was revealed when he invited me there for lunch. Explaining how he had taken pains to restore the château to its original form, Laval took me out on his private hill overlooking a beautiful valley, and told me I was seeing the place where a battle had been fought in the days when Jeanne d'Arc was saving France from the rapacious British. Then he led me into the great drawing room, one wall of which was covered with an enormous oil painting, showing British soldiers storming this very hill and being repulsed by French defenders. . . . Obviously he had staged for my benefit this little lesson in Anglo-French historical conflicts and then, it seemed to me, had let his emotions run away from him."

Murphy asked why Laval felt so bitter about the British.

"During World War I, [Laval] declared, the British had let France bear the brunt of the bloodletting, so that France had lost 1,500,000 killed, from which the nation had never recovered. This time the British had tried the same trick again, he cried, but this time the British and not the French would pay for the war."

Murphy detected in Laval's words a "curious thread of chauvinism, a fierce, earthy sort of patriotism," the kind of patriotism that made Laval want to get revenge upon "perfidious Albion" and all her allies.

But Laval was more than merely anti-British: just as he had seduced Pétain, so he sincerely believed he could seduce the Nazis, winning concessions from them in return for a policy of collaboration.

Under Laval's vigorous prodding the Vichy regime quickly showed its bent. Its new slogan, *Travail, Famille, Patrie,* replaced the traditional *Liberté, Egalité, Fraternité,* and the government pounced upon its enemies, Paul Reynaud, Pierre Mendès-France and George Mandel, shipping them off to jail and, for months at a time, to solitary confinement. Mandel eventually landed in Buchenwald, was released, then died at the hands of the French police. Domestic affairs, however, were not Laval's passion. Collaboration was.

The lobbies and bathhouses of Vichy buzzed with excitement on July 19: Pierre Laval had just flown off to Paris. That in itself did not seem extraordinary but the fact that he had apparently packed a shiny silk top hat did. Why, the people wondered, had Laval, notorious for his sloppiness, bothered to take a top hat to Paris? To the gossips of Vichy there appeared only one reasonable answer. Laval was off to meet with someone of very high rank.

The rumors were correct. Laval was off to cultivate the friendship of none other than the Nazi Ambassador in Paris, the blond-haired and stony-faced Otto Abetz.

And as proof of its friendship to the Reich, Laval's government was letting it be known what it wanted to do with "traitors" like General de Gaulle.

(5)

The morning after his first address over the B.B.C., de Gaulle had gone to the French Embassy in London to seek the support of his own Ambassador. But a secretary there handed him a telegram from General Weygand. "Inform de Gaulle," Weygand had wired, "that he is placed at the disposal of the General Commander-in-Chief once more and that he is to return [to France] without delay."

De Gaulle sent back a letter of refusal, begging Weygand to join him in England. "I wish, for the sake of France and for yours, *mon Général,*" de Gaulle wrote, "that you may be willing and able to escape disaster, reach overseas France and continue the war. There is at present no possible armistice with honor."

On June 30, de Gaulle received his response from France: "By the order of the *Juge d'Instruction* of the Permanent Military Tribunal of the 17th Region, temporary Brigadier General de Gaulle (Charles, André, Joseph, Marie) has been summoned before the Military Tribunal of the 17th Region for the crime of refusal to obey orders in the presence of the enemy and of inciting members of the armed forces to disobedience. . . . Warrant of arrest has been issued against him. . . . The President of the Tribunal has signed an ordinance, dated June 28, enjoining him to present himself under arrest at the Saint Michel *Maison d'Arrêt* at Toulouse within five days beginning 29 June, 1940, failing which he will be judged by default."

De Gaulle's reply was short: "In my eyes," he informed the French Embassy in London, "[this] communication has no interest whatsoever."

On August 2, 1940, a tribunal of seven French Generals met in Clermont-Ferrand, a city in the Auvergne Mountains close to Vichy, for the purpose of trying de Gaulle's case *in absentia.* After a few moments of deliberation, the Generals read their decision to the packed courtroom. They found de Gaulle guilty of the crimes of insubordination and incitement to disobedience, and they announced that the sentence they had decided upon was that of death.

Chapter 11

OTHER FREE FRENCHMEN, TOO, WERE OPERATING UNDER A SENTENCE OF DEATH. ANY SECRET AGENT WHO ENTERED FRANCE, SAID A CLAUSE IN THE FRANCO-GERMAN ARMISTICE, WAS TO BE TREATED AS A *franctireur*, liable upon capture to immediate execution without trial. Both the Germans and the Vichy government meant to uphold that clause, and any Free Frenchman who slipped back into France did so at the risk of his life.

The spies chosen by André Dewavrin's *Deuxième Bureau*, therefore, should have been of the highest caliber: experienced, highly disciplined and well versed in the methods of intelligence and counterespionage. Such men, however, had failed to knock at the door of Dewavrin's office, and by mid-August he was reduced to picking Gilbert Renault, who seemed totally unfit for the job.

Since his birth in Brittany some thirty-six years before, the chunky and ebullient Renault had risen in the hectic world of the Parisian cinema industry, the smart, soft, world of cocktail parties, nightclubs and expense-account dinners. But when the Nazis swept down from Dunkirk, Renault resolved to toughen up. He took his wife and their three children to his mother's home in Vannes, on the south coast of Brittany, and arranged with his young brother, Claude, to escape together to England. Yet at the last moment Renault almost gave up his plans.

Barely two weeks before, his wife, Edith, had told him that she was expecting another baby and, on the evening of June 18, as Renault was packing his bags to leave, she came into the bedroom holding Manuel, who was then one year old.

"The Germans may be coming here today," Renault said as he put a folded shirt down in his suitcase. "We don't have the right to let ourselves be taken. The war must go on. If we give in, if Germany becomes mistress of Europe, life won't be worth living. You will be sent into a factory. I shall be given work in a mine or in a German dockyard. Or we may be given jobs, you and I, as guides or servants to the German tourists. Our children will be torn from us, and their German masters will bring them up in the teachings of National Socialism. Wouldn't it be better to die?"

Edith said nothing. She rocked back and forth in the rocking chair, by the window, holding Manuel's head against her shoulder.

"Don't you agree?" asked Renault.

Edith turned her face away from him, burying her lips in Manuel's cheek.

"I'm sure," Renault went on, "that we won't give in. It's not possible that Pétain, that Weygand, won't order all Frenchmen capable of bearing arms to withdraw out of the reach of the enemy. Even if France is completely overrun, all is not lost."

"What do you intend to do?" Edith spoke for the first time, but her blue eyes still avoided Renault's. She was staring out the window into the night beyond.

"We are lucky to be on the coast," Renault explained. "It's only a question of getting to Lorient. We shall certainly find a boat there going to England or North Africa. I have asked Claude to go with me. What do you say?"

Edith's blue eyes turned finally toward her husband. They were glistening with tears. Then she spoke to him.

"Go."

That was all she said.

Renault walked past the four-poster bed to the rocking chair where she sat. He knelt and took her in his arms.

Very softly, she whispered, "I am so tired."

Renault felt his resolve weakening.

"If you tell me to stay," he said, "I will."

"No," she answered, "go."

Later that night Renault and his brother, Claude, found themselves aboard a rusty fishing trawler, *La Barbue*, whose skipper they had bribed to sail them toward the English Channel; as the lights on the coast receded, Renault realized that his right hand, thrust into his jacket pocket, was fiddling with a piece of folded paper. By crouching up against the trawler's funnel, he was able to light a match and make out what the paper said. It was a sheet torn from a pad on his desk at home, and on it Edith had scribbled a message: "I believe in you," she had written, "and I shall wait as long as it takes."

As their boat came into the harbor at Falmouth Roads, on the English Channel coast, Renault and his brother looked up at the cloudy sky: it was filled with silver barrage balloons, nearly invisible in the haze. They rode a bus to a girls' club being used as a refugee center and there, as they read a copy of a British newspaper, they experienced both a feeling of shock and a deep sense of shame.

Marshal Pétain, the hero of Verdun, the headline said, had asked the Germans for an armistice.

"Claude read the paper over my shoulder," said Renault. "He was crushed as the rest of us. We retired into a corner of the room, without saying a word, and there we wept. A sergeant in the Belgian army had joined us, and he cried too. We had our backs turned to the English people who were going about with great trays piled with tea, coffee, toast and sandwiches. We could no longer look them in the face. An Armistice, after we had given our word. We were betrayed, dishonored!"

Renault felt a hand on his shoulder. He turned to see a little old Englishwoman who might have just stepped forth from a cartoon in *Punch:* underneath her broadbrimmed hat with a large violet-colored flower on it, she wore a piece of white silk ribbon around the sagging wrinkles on her neck, and she had attached a pince-nez on a golden chain to the front of her blouse.

Her creaking voice was soft: "Don't worry, dear boy," she said, "everything will be all right."

Then she stood erect, cleared her throat and, in the tones of one who was accustomed to giving commands, said: "Have a cup of tea."

For some days Renault gave way to a feeling of hopelessness. He lived with refugees from all over Europe in the Camberwell Institute in London, sleeping on a mattress provided by the London County Council. Iron bars barricaded the windows; armed sentries prevented the departure of the Frenchmen who, in British eyes, might be enemy agents in disguise. "The days dragged on miserably," Renault wrote. "Walking about courtyards surrounded by high walls of dirty brick was by no means attractive. We ate and we tried to sleep as much as we could. I reread every letter of Edith's ten times. Then I discovered a little iron staircase for use in case of fire and was able to get away a little from the grumbling of all the unknown people who wandered about the courtyards. But I couldn't bring myself to read again the little message that had been put in my pocket just before I left; it would have upset me too much. In fact I was still not very sure of myself, and the feeling that we all had, of being abandoned, didn't help to give me courage."

One day in early July, however, Renault remembered an old British friend, Kay Harrison, a director of Technicolor in London. Renault telephoned Harrison's secretary, identified himself and explained where he was. A London County Council official came up to Renault's mattress that afternoon, where the Frenchman was lying staring into space, looked down, and announced that a British friend had come for a visit.

Renault stood up stiffly from his mattress, and began to walk to the door. The official barred his way.

"How did he know you were here?" the Englishman demanded.

"Why, I telephoned him."

"You telephoned to him? Where did you get hold of a telephone?"

"In that booth just there," Renault pointed. There was a phone booth in the far corner of the dormitory.

"Don't you know that you aren't allowed to use the telephone?" The official's face was red with indignation.

"I had no idea," said Renault, with a nervous smile.

This apparently disarmed the Englishman, because, suddenly, he turned brusquely and led Renault down a dingy corridor into a windowless little office. There stood Kay Harrison. He shook hands with Renault and pointed to a parcel lying open on the table. "It might have been the treasure of Golconda," Renault said, "magnificient bunches of grapes, glorious peaches, chocolate, cigarettes, and biscuits."

"That's for the family," Harrison announced, "and this is for you." He shoved a wad of pound notes into Renault's hand. "How is your wife?" Harrison went on. "And the children?"

Renault had to explain that he and his brother had come alone. Harrison showed his astonishment: "You mean," he exclaimed, "that you left your wife and children with those damned Germans?"

This was too much for Renault. He could not bear his loneliness for another moment: standing in front of his old friend, Kay Harrison, Renault burst into tears.

Harrison's face went red with embarrassment.

Renault recovered slightly after a while. "If you only knew, Kay," he said.

"Well, I understand," Harrison sympathized. "It's terrible for you. But it'll be all right!"

The conversation did sharpen Renault's resolve. He was homesick, and although he did not feel in the least like a hero, he knew that the only way he could do his patriotic duty and still get to see his family again was by entering France as a secret agent. With Harrison's help, he got out of the Camberwell Institute in early July and started across London to join Free France, of which he had recently learned.

Two French naval officers walking past the sandbags in Whitehall gave him directions to St. Stephen's House: "Just beyond the Houses of Parliament," one of them said, "You can't miss it." The young sailor doing guard duty at the door told him where to find the *Deuxième Bureau.*

A handwritten notice on a scrap of paper tacked to the door said "Colonel Passy." Renault knocked. A voice from inside told him to come in, and screwing his mouth into a nervous grin, he turned the brass knob and peeked into the room. The place was tiny, he wrote, "entirely filled by a table and two benches. An extremely young looking officer, prematurely bald, clean-shaven, dressed in riding breeches and white leggings, was reading a document." This was André Dewavrin.

Renault kept his hand on the door handle and kept looking into the room without saying a word. The garrulousness that had served him so well in the fast-talking Parisian cinema world seemed to have deserted him. He saw Dewavrin look up with a glare.

"What do you want?" Dewavrin snapped.

"I want to see Colonel Passy," Renault gulped as he sidled into the room. "I should like to enlist with the *Deuxième Bureau.*"

"I am Passy," Dewavrin snapped again. "Could I have your rank, m'sieu?"

"I have no rank," Renault confessed. "I'm a civilian."

Passy gave him a quizzical look: "Then give me your papers."

Renault fumbled in his breast pocket for a moment, then handed his passport and identity card across the desk.

"Why all the Spanish visas?" Passy demanded. His tone showed his suspicion that Renault might be pro-Franco and, thus, pro-Axis.

"I was working there on a movie about Christopher Columbus," Renault explained.

"A movie?" Passy's blue eyes were incredulous. "I really don't see . . ." He looked down at Renault's identity card. "It says here that you worked for the Eagle Star Insurance Company in Paris."

"I did," Renault tried to explain. "You see, we invested often in the motion picture industry."

Passy looked up again. "Look," he said to Renault, "do you have any experience in intelligence work?"

"No," said Renault, then he went on quickly, "but I thought . . ."

Passy's patience broke: "We are extremely busy here," he said. "What on earth gave you the idea of going on a mission to France?"

Renault shifted his weight from his left foot to his right; Dewavrin had not invited him to sit. Renault was sure he could get a new visa to

Spain, he said, and from there he could cross into Vichy France and on into the Occupied Zone. "I've been in business," he said, "I know a great many people. Some of them might be helpful."

At this moment the door behind Renault burst open and in strode a tall, handsome French Lieutenant with a pipe between his teeth. It was Maurice Duclos, "St.-Jacques," one of Passy's earliest recruits. He had a swagger stick under his left arm.

"Who's this?" he asked Passy, as if Renault were an inanimate object.

Passy shoved the passport and identity card across the desk and turned back to Renault. "Go on," he said.

"I know lots of people who sing or speak on the radio," Renault continued. "We could work up a code and I could ask them to put it in their scripts."

"It sounds plausible," said Duclos, "but can this guy survive?"

Passy was rubbing his bald pate in dismay. "Look," he said finally to Renault, "go back where you're staying and I'll have the British check you out. Leave these papers and your address with me and if we need you I'll call you."

For weeks Renault heard nothing from the *Deuxième Bureau*, and then, early in August, when he felt he could stand his loneliness and the separation from his family no longer (his brother, Claude, was now at a Free French training base), he sought out Passy again. Free France had moved by this time out of St. Stephen's House, and the *Deuxième Bureau* itself was leasing space in a large modern office building at 10 Duke Street, near Selfridge's department store. Renault walked into the new office and this time Passy rose from his desk with a greeting that was almost friendly.

"We like your idea," Passy said. "I've spoken about you with our British friends and they approve of your entering France through Spain."

"But," Passy went on, and his forehead wrinkled up for once with genuine concern, "are you sure you want to do this? Do you know what risks you'll be running?"

Renault looked at him squarely and said, simply, "Yes."

Late in August Renault had paid a farewell visit to some friends in Carlton Gardens. As he walked down the carpeted corridor toward the elevator to leave, he looked down the stairwell to his left. He saw General de Gaulle, with two stars on his kepi, trudging up the stairs. The General's step was heavy and unwieldy, his hand gripped the bannister tightly, his shoulders seemed bent with the weight of an invisible burden. Renault stood back to let him pass, and, instinctively, saluted. Absent-mindedly de Gaulle returned the salute. Renault ventured to speak.

"*Mon Général,*" he said.

De Gaulle stopped.

"*Mon Général*," Renault said again. "I am one of your men, Gilbert Renault, and tomorrow I leave on a mission to France. I should like the honor of shaking your hand."

"Follow me," de Gaulle replied. "Come over here to my office."

De Gaulle hung his kepi on a hook and sat behind his mahogany desk, his back to the window. Dusk was falling, and the heavy velvet curtains on either side of the window increased the darkness. Renault could barely make out the General's features; de Gaulle motioned him to an armchair and crossed his own hands on top of the desk. De Gaulle seemed less imposing sitting down than standing up because his chest and shoulders were narrow and the part of him that Renault could see above the desk looked small boned and frail.

At last de Gaulle spoke. "Did you come by yourself?" he asked.

In spite of his nervousness Renault felt strangely at ease. "My brother, Claude, came with me, *mon Général.* He's at a training camp now. He's twenty."

"We must make an officer of him," de Gaulle said.

De Gaulle lit up a cigarette, took a puff or two, then crushed it out in a wide glass ashtray by the corner of his desk. He rose from his swivel chair and walked toward Renault, holding out his hand. Renault got up from his chair, too, but the General was so tall that Renault had to crane his neck violently to see the General's face.

De Gaulle smiled and held Renault's hand for a moment in his own.

"*Au revoir*, Renault," he said at last, "I rely on you."

Chapter 12

(1)

THE TWO FRENCH SENTRIES FACING EACH OTHER IN FRONT OF THE BARRACKS DOORWAY SNAPPED SHARPLY TO ATTENTION, THEIR LEFT ELBOWS EXTENDING FORWARD AT RIGHT ANGLES WITH THEIR BODIES AND their rifles, cupped in the palms of their right hands, pointing straight up toward the sky. It was late in the morning of August 24, 1940, at the Aldershot training center south of London. Two men in officers' uniforms were walking down the two concrete steps below the barracks doorway and passing along the brick sidewalk between the two sentries: one was General de Gaulle, tall, with shortly clipped moustache, and elephantine nose, and a gold-braided kepi; the other was King George VI, shorter, slim, with brightly polished riding boots and four rows of military ribbons on the left side of his single-breasted belted Army jacket. As the King stepped between the sentries he gave them a smart British salute, with his right palm turned rigidly forward so that it nearly touched the shiny leather visor of his Army cap: he had come to pay his respects to the troops of Free France who were soon to sail for Africa.

For several weeks now the thousand-odd Free French troops (all told, the Free French Forces now numbered seven thousand), housed in barracks the British called "spiders," and outfitted with polished black boots, green leggings and shallow steel helmets, had been undergoing the most demanding physical training they had experienced in months, for de Gaulle had decided that Free France needed action. Only through action

could they preserve their morale, only through action could they keep up
their hopes, only through action could they challenge Vichy. Free France
needed a victory, he believed, and fast. Even though the men did not yet
know where they would be fighting, the British sovereign had come to bid
them farewell.

George VI paced in front of the rows of Foreign Legionnaires, who
were wearing their customary white silk neckbands. He smiled at one or
two of them. French horns sounded out, playing the slow measured strains
of *"Le Boudin,"* the traditional anthem of the Foreign Legion. After taking
a *vin d'honneur* with de Gaulle, the King left the parade grounds and the
Free French columns. As he marched away he heard the tune that bands
had once played for Napoleon Bonaparte, *"Salut à l'Empereur."*

"We French, who witnessed the ceremony," wrote the journalist Eve
Curie, "remembered the magnificent, endless parade of 50,000 French
troops that had been given for King George only two years before, in
Versailles, amidst the enthusiasm of our people. The contrast between
Versailles and Aldershot was something difficult for us to bear. But not for
de Gaulle. The tall, somewhat awkward leader behaved as proudly on the
Aldershot field as if he had been inspecting the mightiest military force in
the world. He well knew that he was reviewing one of the most important
armies our country ever had—an army which, all alone, was saving the
good name of France. People said: 'De Gaulle is difficult.' He was. He had
a defiant, even an arrogant way of being right. But what of it? He *was*
right. Moreover, when one came to think of it, what he had done in June,
1940, could perhaps only have been attempted by a man with a temper."

De Gaulle spoke soon thereafter on the B.B.C.: "Frenchmen," he
declared, "once more you have a fighting army! . . . Since those whose
duty it was to hold high the sword of France have let it fall broken, I have
snatched up the bloody stump!"

"But, my God," he wrote later, "how short it was!"

(2)

De Gaulle was gambling, and he knew it. If he won a victory, he and
Free France could become famous, and the Cross of Lorraine would appear
on stone walls and park benches all across France. A Free French victory
now could spark the flame of resistance wherever Frenchmen stood face
to face with the Germans. But if he lost—no one might hear of him again.
He had, therefore, to pick precisely the right spot to do battle: fighting for

a place without value would do nothing to enhance his prestige; trying to capture a place that was well defended, and losing, could destroy his reputation forever.

As he studied the large-scale map of the world pasted to the wall beside his desk in Carlton Gardens, de Gaulle had decided where he must strike. It had to be somewhere in the French Empire, for there de Gaulle could show that a geographical part of France was still in the war. There Free France could have a territorial home of its own. But where?

Indochina was out of the question since it was in immediate danger of invasion from Japan; the New Hebrides had declared themselves Free French but they were too remote and vulnerable to be of use; Martinique in the Caribbean, and St. Pierre and Miquelon, off the coast of Newfoundland, were possibilities but they were also small islands and far away; and the French territories along the Mediterranean, Syria, Algeria, and Morocco, lay in the solid grip of Vichy. That left Africa, the immense French colonies below the Sahara, ranging from Senegal on the westernmost tip of the continent to Chad, the Cameroon and the Middle Congo in French Equatorial Africa, far enough from France to make Vichy's grip unsteady but close enough to the Mediterranean to provide a base from which the Free French could someday rejoin the war.

The first part of de Gaulle's operation was aimed at the Equator: it had begun in utter secrecy.

Early in August a British seaplane heading for Léopoldville in the Belgian Congo carried three of de Gaulle's most trusted men: a Lieutenant Hettier de Boislambert; the former financier, René Pleven; and the man who had pedaled a bicycle across France, Captain Philippe de Hauteclocque, now going by the code name of "Leclerc." Two more men were scheduled to meet them in Léopoldville: Major Jean Colonna d'Ornano, who had just quarreled with his chief, General Husson, the Vichyist Governor of French Equatorial Africa; and General Edgard de Larminat, who had escaped from prison in Syria to join up with Free France. The five men met in the shade of a giant tree near the government buildings in Léopoldville to work out their plans.

Their first concern was the huge landlocked central African colony of Chad. Whoever held Chad, a French General had said in the 1930's, held the key to Africa: the airplanes of the day could not cross central Africa without refueling at one of Chad's three modern airports, and directly above its northern border lay the immense, Italian-controlled territory of Libya. The African Governor of Chad, Félix Eboué, had privately declared his support for Free France, and the men under the tree in Léopoldville believed they could persuade him to express his views in public.

On August 23, Pleven and d'Ornano flew to see him in Fort-Lamy,

the capital of Chad, but as their airplane descended over the white houses
and straw huts of the town, and approached the runway, they saw two
lines of African troops standing beside the landing strip. D'Ornano knew
that his ex-chief, General Husson, would have wired Fort-Lamy about his
desertion and that Vichyist officials were due at any time to be passing
through Chad. Were the troops standing below the plane, he wondered,
under orders to arrest Pleven and him? The plane jolted down onto the
runway and stopped at the terminal gate. Pleven and d'Ornano climbed
cautiously down from the plane and looked around. They fully expected
to hear a command ordering their arrest. Then the troops lined up beside
the plane presented arms, and the two Free Frenchmen understood what
was going on.

They were receiving military honors, and as they rode through the
dusty marketplace by Fort-Lamy and heard the chanting of prayers from a
minaret, they realized that Free France had won its first victory. Governor
Eboué welcomed them onto the porch of his white stucco residence; a
great crowd of blacks in the street below burst forth with the forbidden
"*Marseillaise.*" "The sun, the desert, and alcohol," a Frenchman wrote
later, "aided secession." A telegram from de Gaulle the next day cited Chad
for the Order of the Empire.

The French Cameroon was next: it held deposits of tungsten, tin and
oil, and its largest city, the port of Douala, was Chad's only outlet to the
sea. On the night of August 23, two other Free Frenchmen from the shade
tree in Léopoldville, Lieutenant de Boislambert and Captain de Hauteclocque (or "Leclerc," as his men came to call him), embarked on their
mission of seizing Cameroon. In three motorized dugout canoes, containing twenty-one other Free Frenchmen, they set out from Tiko harbor in
the British Cameroon and headed across the ocean for Douala. After
battling throughout the night against the wind and the high waves, the
dugouts reached calmer waters in the mouth of the Wouri River just before
dawn; the long canoes slid silently through the warm, wet fog toward the
piers at Douala. A few resident French and African soldiers joined them
and, by noon, without having fired a shot, the little Free French band had
seized the radio station and the principal administration buildings of the
city.

Now in complete charge, Captain de Hauteclocque—Leclerc—tore
the silver braid off his left sleeve and pinned it to the right. On one side
he was still a captain, but on the other, "as by enchantment," de Gaulle
wrote, he was now Colonel Leclerc. Without waiting for anyone to approve
his promotion, he signed a document, as Colonel Leclerc, proclaiming
Cameroon's freedom from Vichy. Three days later the garrison in Yaundé,
Cameroon's capital, declared itself Free French, and Leclerc received a

wire from de Gaulle saying: "My warmest congratulations. . . . Hang the tricolor everywhere!"

That left the ,Middle Congo, whose largest city, Brazzaville, lay directly across the Congo from Léopoldville, and served as the capital of all French Equatorial Africa.

Brazzaville had once been a small trading settlement of mud huts and primitive shacks, but by 1940 it had grown into a modern town with wide paved avenues and European bungalows covered with bougainvillea on the bluff at the center of the city. Below these homes, on the slopes that ran down to the banks of the Congo, were the conical huts of the native Africans. Giant palm trees lined the streets and, occasionally, pythons would wander in from the surrounding equatorial forests.

In was at Brazzaville that the Free Frenchmen made their next move. From Léopoldville, General de Larminat had sent to General Husson, in Brazzaville, an ultimatum that gave him the choice of resigning his post or of having to fight the Free French. Husson was furious when he received this message, and in response to it set up machine-gun nests throughout the native quarter and around the government building.

De Larminat saw that he had to move fast. On August 28, while he himself waited on the Belgian bank of the Congo, his men surrounded the military camp just outside Brazzaville and, without having to fire a shot, persuaded it to surrender.

But a greater trial lay ahead. General Husson had retreated to the Government House in the principal square of Brazzaville and had stationed his soldiers in formation around the long, double-winged building. The Free Frenchmen arrived in trucks from the military camp outside town and pulled up around the iron fence that guarded Husson's official residence. The Free French shouted at Husson's men to surrender. There followed a long moment of silence. The broiling sun was directly overhead and tempers were beginning to flare. A great crowd of African onlookers wondered if Husson's men would fire upon their fellow Frenchmen. With a sudden clatter they had their answer.

The General's men had dropped their rifles.

Only Husson, rushing down from the porch, fought back. He swung his fists, lost his glasses and managed to tear a hole in his tunic, but he inflicted no damage on anyone. Two Gaullist officers proceeded to roll him up snugly in a blanket, and Husson left his command as "nothing more than a gesticulating bundle." A little boat then carried General de Larminat across the Stanley Pool in the Congo to Brazzaville: from the prow of his vessel fluttered a flag bearing the Cross of Lorraine. "I reached Brazzaville at 14:00 today," he wired to de Gaulle, "and have assumed full control."

Free France now had a home in Equatorial Africa, a center in the sweltering heat where it could assemble equipment and train its men on their own imperial soil. "The events of the past months," said the London *Times,* early in September, "have steadily justified the lead taken by General de Gaulle. He has worked in a spirit of patriotic devotion, with no ambition of his own to serve, for a vision of the honor and glory of France that has been obscured to most Frenchmen by the cloud of defeat. . . . His example has lit a flame from which many other torches have been kindled, as the doubters in Africa and Asia take courage from a dauntless example."

In a few weeks, however, the press would present a much different picture of de Gaulle.

(3)

For de Gaulle's design for Africa had still one more phase: the seizure of the Senegalese port city of Dakar. "No world strategy," said the Free Frenchman, Jacques Soustelle, "could neglect Dakar." Because its harbor, the largest between Europe and Capetown, had quays, dry docks, fueling facilities and a tonnage equal to those of Le Havre in France, Dakar dominated the shipping routes between the Atlantic and Indian oceans. Its large fortresses and four nearby airfields made it both defensible and capable of launching strikes against passing Allied convoys, and since it was a potential U-boat station 1,700 miles from South America, it seemed "like a loaded pistol pointing across the Atlantic toward the heart of the New World." But Dakar was in the hands of the Vichy regime and soon, according to the rumors flying about London, the city would play host to numerous Nazi agents who were planning to seize it for themselves.

If the Free French could capture Dakar they would have earned their greatest prize yet in Africa; but if they fought there, and lost, they and de Gaulle could have forfeited all the prestige they had won since the invasion of France.

Both the rewards and the risks were great: de Gaulle decided to take up the gamble. But he did so knowing that a serious obstacle stood in his way. The pro-Vichy Governor General at Dakar, Pierre Boisson, had recently made quite clear where his sympathies lay. "I have been charged with the defense of Dakar against all comers," he had declared, "and I will obey my orders."

Late in July, de Gaulle had asked Churchill what he thought about the idea of trying to take the city. Churchill was noncommittal at first but on August 6 he invited de Gaulle to No. 10 Downing Street to discuss the scheme in greater detail. De Gaulle entered the long chamber in Churchill's home that served as both the Prime Minister's office and the Cabinet's boardroom. Churchill was pacing up and down along the huge mahogony table that filled the center of the room. The place smelled of cigar smoke.

Churchill began immediately. "We must together gain control of Dakar," he said. "For if the business goes well, it means that large French forces are brought back into the war. Having conferred with the Admiralty and the Chiefs of Staff, I am in a position to tell you that we are ready to assist in the operation. I have something to propose to you."

Churchill began to gnaw on his cigar. Then he went on, savoring (in de Gaulle's version of the incident) the sound of his own words.

"Dakar wakes up on morning, sad and uncertain," said Churchill as he gesticulated with the hand that held the cigar. "But behold . . ."—and here Churchill paused to let de Gaulle behold—"by the light of the rising sun, its inhabitants perceive the sea, covered with ships. An immense fleet. A hundred vessels! Some of them are flying the tricolor. Others are sailing under British colors. From this Allied force there breaks away an inoffensive small ship bearing the white flag. It enters the port and disembarks the envoys of General de Gaulle. Their job is to convince Governor Boisson that, if he lets you land, the Allied fleet retires. On the contrary, if he wants a fight . . ."

Churchill stopped again to drop the wet stub of his cigar into a shiny brass jar of sand. He lit a fresh cigar. Then he continued.

"If Boisson wants a fight, he has every chance of being crushed. The Governor feels that, if he resists, the ground will give way under his feet. He will go on with the talks until they reach a satisfactory conclusion. Perhaps meanwhile he will wish, 'for honor's sake,' to fire a few shots. But he will not go further. And that evening he will dine with you and drink a toast to the final victory of France."

Throughout the month of August, Churchill and de Gaulle worked secretly in an underground staff room of the Admiralty building, listening to the faint crump of the bombs outside, and sorting out the details of their plan for Dakar. By the end of the month they were ready.

Soon the wharves of Liverpool were bustling with preparation for "Operation Menace." Unmarked crates appeared on the wharves, and young French sailors were busy finding the cheapest bars and most available girls of the city. The fleet that assembled at Liverpool was small: two Free French sloops, an aircraft carrier, a supply ship, a liner carrying a brigade of British Royal Marines, the troopships *Pennland* and *Westernland* carrying 1,200 Foreign Legionnaires, a few destroyers and the flagship *Barham*, under the command of Admiral J. H. D. Cunningham. General de Gaulle would spend most of his time aboard the *Westernland*.

On the night of August 31, the time for departure had come. One by one the ships of the fleet slipped out of the Liverpool harbor, divided themselves into two columns, and slid silently across the sea for Dakar.

One Free French midshipman, a lad named Robert Cremel, recounted his feelings in his diary that night. "August 31. At last, the big moment. It is not without a certain emotion that we leave England at seven o'clock at night. And the emotion was reflected in a rather abnormal amount of drinking. That's because we're so happy. We're leaving on a long and exciting trip. As the Commandant had just explained, the war has begun again for us. At last we can work to free France and all those who are suffering there. I think of my parents, of my friends, surrounded by our worst enemies; of my pal Pierre, who died or was taken prisoner; of all those families I knew so well and who are perhaps scattered, living painfully and miserably. Where are my own parents? I hope they are not too unhappy. I know they worry most about me and I would so much like for them to know what I am doing. They would be happy and proud of their son."

They would also have been alarmed had they realized what had occurred during the preceding week.

Just before departure time the British Cabinet had learned that word of the expedition was leaking out. Exactly how much information had spilled no one could tell, but of one thing everyone in the Cabinet was certain; it could easily reach Vichy.

Some Free French officers had dined at a table in the back of the Coq d'Or, a fashionable London restaurant, and they had been overheard drinking loud toasts to the success of their landing in Africa. De Gaulle himself had openly gone to Simpson's to purchase some tropical uniforms. And when his train left London for the docks at Liverpool, a crowd of French-speaking well-wishers gathered on the platform beside the coaches and shouted out: "*A Dakar! A Dakar!*"

The British Cabinet, therefore, had been tempted to cancel "Operation Menace," but after some deliberation it decided to gamble on the success of the plan, and it allowed the ships to steam away for Dakar.

(4)

The fleet skirted far out into the Atlantic to avoid the torpedoes of the U-boats, and in a few days it reached the heat of the tropics. The sea was calm. Schools of porpoises frolicked in the swells between the ships. The troops on board the *Westernland,* said General Spears, whom Churchill had made representative to Free France and who accompanied de Gaulle on the mission, "were a strange assortment. There were some Legionnaires and many North Africans, and some of the entertainments they gave were excellent, but one gathered there were casualties most nights from knife fights, and I was very annoyed to fall flat outside my cabin over a corpse in the blackout one night.

"Part of one of the decks had been set aside for de Gaulle and myself. Two armchairs had been provided . . . [De Gaulle] sat there for many an hour, often in silence, but [he] did sometimes speak of his family, which he told me was the second oldest in Paris, having had a known residence there for over three hundred years. And on one occasion he said that when the war was over he would turn his back on public life in any form and withdraw to the country. 'That is an illusion,' I said. 'You will find you simply cannot do so. . . . No, *mon Général,* you have condemned yourself to a life sentence from which there is no reprieve . . .'"

Despite the stifling airless heat in the cabins and mess hall below, de Gaulle was in a good mood. Spears never saw him laugh so much, either before the trip or after: de Gaulle told few jokes of his own, but after the punch lines of others' stories, especially the vulgar tales, he would roar with glee and repeatedly smack the fist of his right hand against the palm of his left.

Other Frenchmen, too, were having a good time. "All this week," Robert Cremel wrote in his diary, on September 8, "I've been enjoying myself for the first time in a long while. I've learned to keep watch and to steer and I'm happy to be useful. To tack, to keep the ship's journal, to steer in zigzags—I've learned all the secrets. We are now coming to the end of the voyage. I don't know what to expect: battles, glory, trouble, disappointment, or perhaps death, eaten up by crabs and sharks. We'll see in a few days and I hope with all my heart that whatever it is, it will help to free France."

But a difficulty had arisen.

The fleet had maintained radio silence throughout the voyage and since its departure from England it had received only the broadcast bulletins of the B.B.C.—nothing of immediate interest to the expedition. But on September 13, a Friday, the flagship *Barham* brought in a most alarming communiqué.

Six Vichy ships, three destroyers and three cruisers, had left their berths at Toulon on the southern coast of France and had steamed out through the Straits of Gibraltar into the open sea. Whether Vichy or Berlin had learned for certain where de Gaulle was going, whether the

Vichy French Naval Command was ignorant of de Gaulle's expedition but wanted to reinforce Dakar just in case, or whether the Vichy ships were bent on retaking French Equatorial Africa, was unclear to either de Gaulle or Admiral Cunningham. One thing, however, was becoming clear: the Vichy squadron's course was taking it directly toward Dakar.

(5)

Admiral Cunningham stopped the fleet that night for a personal conference with de Gaulle. From the deck of the *Westernland* Spears was watching the approach of the Admiral's launch: as the *Westernland* wallowed, he wrote, "in the slowly heaving sea which gurgled as it gently slapped the sides of our ship far down below the deck we stood on, we watched the lovely silvery road laid by the moon across the ink-blue sea. Then like a vast shadow silhouette drawn across it, appeared the great bulk of the *Barham*. A moment later a dot could be perceived on the dazzling track. . . . It was the cutter carrying the Admiral."

Admiral Cunningham bore a telegram from Churchill. "His Majesty's Government have decided," the Prime Minister had said, "that the presence of French cruisers at Dakar [will make] the execution of the Dakar operation impractical. . . . Close blockade of Dakar from seaward is not possible with the naval forces available, and therefore, presence of de Gaulle's force . . . would not appreciably influence situation at Dakar. Best plan appears for General de Gaulle's force to land at Douala with the object of consolidating the Cameroons, Equatorial Africa and Chad. . . . The British portion of the force would remain for the present at Freetown [in British Sierra Leone, south of Dakar]. Unless General de Gaulle has any strong objections to the latter course, it should be put into operation forthwith."

General de Gaulle did, indeed, have strong objections. He met in his room aboard the *Westernland* with Spears and Cunningham, arguing vigorously against what Churchill had wired. "It was a strange council of war," Spears said, "held in the dark and hideously hot and airless cabin, where the participants with shiny, streaky yellow faces clutched long glasses containing warm whiskey."

De Gaulle was blunt: doing nothing at Dakar, he thought, was "the worst possible solution." The Vichy ships would have only to wait for the return of the British fleet to England—where it was desperately needed—and then, with an open sea before them, swoop down upon Douala and recapture all the colonies the Free French had taken in Equatorial Africa.

Fighting at Dakar, de Gaulle admitted, might easily produce a defeat, but doing nothing at Dakar, he insisted, would certainly lead to disaster.

Admiral Cunningham wired Churchill that he had agreed with de Gaulle, and after much coded argument up and down the Atlantic, the reluctant Churchill gave his permission for the expedition to go ahead. The fleet steamed down to Freetown in Sierra Leone to replenish its fuel supply and, on the night of September 21, it set sail again for Dakar.

Cunningham had been worried, however, and to protect the ships at his command he had sent the Free French Commander Thierry d'Argenlieu in a destroyer to warn the Vichy ships away from Dakar. Two of those cruisers had developed engine troubles and at d'Argenlieu's insistence they had sailed immediately back to Casablanca. But the rest of the Vichy ships had escaped in a rainstorm; by September 21, they had reached the arm of land that jutted out from Africa and formed the harbor at Dakar. They turned at the battery fortress and docked at the piers.

The Free Frenchmen aboard de Gaulle's ships were having premonitions that not all was right. "Visit on board the boat by General de Gaulle," Robert Cremel wrote just before he reached Dakar. "At last we know the role which has been assigned to us, a glorious and dangerous role [attempting to land at the port]. I am glad and proud. Perhaps eight hours from now I may no longer be alive. It's not important. Except for my parents no one will miss me, and it is for them only that I would like to live, to see them again. That's why, before setting out, I ask God's help and protection."

(6)

In Dakar itself Free French sympathizers were making their secret preparations for de Gaulle's arrival. A Senegalese schoolmaster named Kaouza had paddled by dugout canoe through a violent storm at sea to Bathurst in neighboring British Gambia. There he had loaded his canoe with Free French tracts and returned to Dakar. After landing on the coast just a few miles below the city he had given the leaflets to a messenger who met him on the beach. The messenger had cycled away in the nick of time: no sooner had he gone than Vichyist police had arrived on the scene and arrested Kaouza.

Then, on the night of September 22–23, Lieutenant Hettier de Boislambert, who had accompanied Leclerc to the Cameroon, joined a few companions in Dakar to sabotage the city's communication system. Again and again during the night they slipped out of the shadows to snip the telephone wires that ran out to nearby bases. They even planted a *plastique* in the telephone switchboard of the city's Marine Arsenal, but when the sun began to rise over the rooftops to the east, they had finished only part of their work and they had to break off for fear of being discovered.

De Boislambert dashed to the Palace Hotel, headquarters of the local Army garrison, to demand that Colonel Chaubet, the Commandant, rally his men to the Free French cause. Chaubet was still in bed when de Boislambert burst through his door. The Colonel was in no mood to listen to a rebellious young Lieutenant, and after de Boislambert had left the bedroom, Chaubet sent the youth's name and description off to the Dakar police.

As de Boislambert came down the front steps of the hotel, and looked out toward the broad expanse of quays and piers that formed Dakar's harbor, he noticed the billows of fog rolling in from the ocean. Something was different, however, about this fog: two dark forms, two dark forms with wings, two olive-drab airplanes were emerging from the mist. He watched as they drew closer. They were single-motor reconnaissance planes, roaring across the piers and dipping down toward the streets that led up the hillsides away from the harbor. One of them seemed to pause directly over de Boislambert's head. The pilot's arm dropped something from the cockpit. De Boislambert thought at first it was an explosive, but as the object touched the cobblestones he discovered what it really was.

The airplanes were dropping red, white and blue Gaullist leaflets over the streets and rooftops of the city. "Frenchmen of Dakar," the pamphlets proclaimed, "Join with us to deliver France!"

(7)

The Franco-British fleet had dropped in the bay outside the harbor, and de Boislambert could hear de Gaulle's voice booming through a loudspeaker on the deck of the *Westernland*, announcing his presence and assuring the citizens of Dakar of his friendly intentions.

De Boislambert hurried down the cobblestone street to the quay. A motorboat was bouncing through the fog and docking at the wide central pier directly in front of him. The boat was carrying a white flag of truce. Three men were climbing out, Captains Perrin and Bécourt-Foch, the latter the grandson of Marshal Ferdinand Foch, and Commander Thierry d'Argenlieu, the former monk who had joined Free France. And striding down the pier to meet the three Gaullists was the Commander of the Port, gleaming in his gold-braided kepi and his starched tropical whites.

De Boislambert could see through the rolling mist that d'Argenlieu was handing the Port Commander something in a white envelope. Inside, de Boislambert later learned, was a letter from General de Gaulle to Dakar's Governor Boisson: "In the vast movement for French recovery which is sweeping our Empire," de Gaulle had written, "you have a great part to play. Your hour has come. I ask you to join me in order to pursue the war for the purpose of liberating the Fatherland. I am quite near you with a considerable military naval and air force . . . I await your answer with confidence, *Monsieur le Gouverneur-Général ...*"

The man in the gleaming white uniform, the Port Commander, took the letter from d'Argenlieu's hand, and then did something that for a moment caused de Boislambert to stand still on the quay in puzzlement. Instead of shaking d'Argenlieu's hand, or gesturing to the other Free Frenchmen to come with him, the Port Commander walked quickly away, back up the pier. Then de Boislambert saw why.

Directly below him on the steps running down from the quay to the pier, a group of soldiers in French uniform had set up a machine gun and aimed its barrel parallel to the pier straight toward where Commander d'Argenlieu and his two aides were standing.

(8)

The two Free French scout planes de Boislambert had seen earlier had flown a few miles up the coast to the Wakam airport where they were supposed to seize the facilities and radio their aircraft carrier, the *Ark Royal*, to send larger Swordfish planes ahead for a landing.

Twenty minutes after the scouts had set out, the radio operator aboard the *Ark Royal* removed his earphones and passed a message to an officer hovering by his side: the planes were approaching the Wakam runway. The radio room was silent again for a moment, and officers stood about tensely waiting for further reports. Then the carrier's radio buzzed with welcome news. The scouts' pilots were safely inside the Wakam terminal. The *Ark Royal* could send on the Swordfishes.

One after another the Swordfishes roared along the deck of the carrier and swept up into the fog that was enveloping the sea. By the time the fourth Swordfish had cleared the end of the ship's runway, the first was radioing back a safe landing at Wakam.

Suddenly, however, the radio operator aboard the *Ark Royal* tore off his headphones again and rushed through the doorway to find his commanding officer. The first Swordfish had touched ground, the operator had learned, but had taken off again immediately, and its pilot had urgently warned the other planes also to turn back to the ship. The pilot had spotted flashes of gunfire coming from the Wakam terminal, and realized that, somehow, the two scout pilots had walked into a trap. Moments later the *Ark Royal* radioed the flagship *Barham:* "All aircraft recalled Further departures canceled."

In that same moment a French military truck from the airport was gunning along through the fog to the jail in Dakar. In the back end of the truck lay the two scout pilots, tied, handcuffed and being searched for names of Gaullist agents in Dakar.

(9)

Hettier de Boislambert was standing on his tiptoes on the quay beside the pier, squinting over the fezzes and kerchiefs of the Senegalese who had crowded along the waterfront. The Port Commander was calling out to the Free Frenchmen at the end of the pier to give themselves up, and the machine gun on the steps of the quay was aimed directly at their chests. For a moment nobody, neither the Africans along the quay nor the Vichyist soldiers on the steps nor the three Free Frenchmen at the end of the pier, moved. Then d'Argenlieu and his men leapt off the pier into their speedboat and, in that same moment, by instinct, de Boislambert did the right thing. He yelled.

The machine gunners wheeled around to face him, thus allowing d'Argenlieu to push his starter button and speed away from the pier toward the open sea. The machine gunners turned back to open fire upon the little boat but it was moving too fast—the bullets splattered harmlessly into the water.

Then the guns on the Vichy destroyers that had recently reached Dakar took aim on d'Argenlieu's boat. At first they kept missing, booming shells fore and aft and rocking it with their violent ripples. D'Argenlieu had almost reached the submarine net across the mouth of the harbor when the guns stopped blazing. A cloud of smoke arose where the boat had been.

"It has been the fate of all to wait and wait for news," wrote General Spears, who was in the bridge of the *Westernland* that morning, ". . . but those who have had to undergo this ordeal in a fog, uncertain towards which point the ear should strain, know that its damp opacity is far worse than darkness." For more than an hour the men of the *Westernland's* bridge had been hoping to hear news from d'Argenlieu. They had heard the rat-tat-tat of machine-gun fire somewhere off in the distance, and shortly thereafter they had almost felt the boom of the destroyers' shells, but they could not make out what was really happening in the warm, sticky, gray wetness of the Atlantic fog.

Then, at nine-fifteen that morning, Spears and de Gaulle heard the putt-putt of a motor penetrating the mist. It grew louder and louder. At last they saw the prow of a launch emerging from the fog. A little boat bumped against the side of the ship.

D'Argenlieu was still standing at the wheel of his boat but his white uniform was covered with red and both of his companions were lying, wounded, in their own puddles of blood. D'Argenlieu stayed conscious just long enough to tell what had happened on the pier.

(10)

Lieutenant de Boislambert had slipped away from the quay, trying to escape detection by mingling with the crowd of pro-Gaullist Senegalese demonstrating in the plaza in front of Government House. The Africans thought that if de Gaulle would free them from Vichy control he would later grant them independence from France, but Governor Boisson was reacting with vengeance. He appeared on the front porch of his residence, screaming down to his policemen and ordering them to disperse the milling throngs of Senegalese. The police did so without delay, flailing into the mob with iron clubs and fixed bayonets. Shortly after that Boisson issued another order, and by ten o'clock the guns in Dakar's battery fortress and aboard the destroyers in the harbor opened fire on the Franco-British fleet. Despite Admiral Cunningham's wiring that he "would be obliged to return blow for blow if the firing does not stop," Dakar's guns continued to blast away, starting a fire on the cruiser *Cumberland* and preventing de Gaulle's ships from moving any closer to the harbor. Boisson's men also found and arrested a number of Gaullists in the city's streets. One of these was Hettier de Boislambert.

De Gaulle's fleet fired back at last but the fog was too thick for accuracy and at eleven-thirty that morning, being noticeably outgunned by the fort and the ships in the harbor, it retreated. De Gaulle realized now that he could not take Dakar by sea.

Perhaps, though, he might be able to move in by land. He and General Spears transferred to the *Commandant Duboc,* a sloop that could cruise in shallow waters, and, leading the other sloop filled with Legionnaires and French Marines, they sailed twenty miles down the coast to a much smaller port below Dakar called Rufisque.

At three o'clock the *Commandant Duboc* drew close to the piers of the town and the landing craft began putting the troops ashore. But de Gaulle and Spears could still see nothing. "The minutes slopped their damp way around the clock," Spears said, "as we wallowed athwart the warm, glaucous, sticky rollers, engaged in a . . . game of blind man's bluff." For a good half an hour de Gaulle and Spears had no idea how many of their men had been able to establish a beachhead. No word had come back from shore.

Then, through the thickness of the fog, they heard the droning of a plane overhead, "an unmistakable Vichy plane," Spears said, that had to have come from Dakar. It was passing back and forth over the *Commandant Duboc,* trying to pinpoint the sloop's location, obviously under orders to bomb the ship.

The *Duboc's* radio crackled alive with a message from the *Barham.* The news was anything but encouraging: two fast cruisers, Vichyist, had broken out of Dakar and were speeding at full throttle toward Rufisque.

Someone in Rufisque must have sent word to Dakar of the Free French landing! This meant that the telephone lines that de Boislambert had so carefully snipped during the previous night had been repaired. Even that part of "Operation Menace" had failed.

For once in his life, possibly the only time, de Gaulle asked for someone's advice. Spears was standing beside him in the bridge of the sloop, and de Gaulle looked down at him, the arrogant look completely gone from his eyes. "What do you think we should do?" he asked. De Gaulle's face was pale as it had been when Spears found him hiding by the column that night in Bordeaux.

"There is absolutely no choice," Spears answered. "We must turn away to sea as fast as we can!"

For the next two days the Franco-British fleet hung around off the coast by Dakar, lobbing shells and dropping bombs into the fog, hoping thereby to force Dakar to surrender, but de Gaulle was too weak and Boisson was too strong. Ships in Dakar's harbor at one point opened fire on the city's Moslem quarter, where the Cross of Lorraine was decorating many of the huts of the Senegalese, and killed more than one hundred persons. Despite the fog the battery fortress managed to hit several of the Franco-British ships and it pierced the shell of the destroyer *Resolution* so often that the ship listed at forty-five degrees and took on more than a hundred tons of water.

At one-thirty on the afternoon of September 25, 1940, Winston Churchill sent another telegram to the fleet: "With all the information now before us," the Prime Minister said, "we have decided that the enterprise against Dakar should be abandoned. . . . You should forthwith break off."

There followed another conference between de Gaulle and Admiral Cunningham, this time on the bridge of the *Barham*. As the officers gathered around waited for de Gaulle's decision, he began to chain-smoke, throwing down a constant stream of burning cigarette butts. "Down they came," said Spears, "like incandescent meteorities with an appropriate escort of match ends." Cunningham shoved an empty pompon shell case toward de Gaulle for him to use as an ashtray. Hardly noticing it, de Gaulle vaguely tossed a cigarette in its direction, and missed. Cunningham pushed another shell case toward him, and another, and still another, until he was surrounded by them "as if he had been a pompon firing in a heavy engagement."

At last de Gaulle had made his decision. "We concur," he said, "in breaking off."

Moments later the Free French contingent in the Franco-British fleet set sail for its new home in Equatorial Africa.

(11)

Under the scorching tropical sun that afternoon the men of Free France gathered on the deck of the *Westernland* to mourn their dead. As the bodies draped in the tricolor slid into the warm sea, the sailors and Legionnaires wept without shame and without hesitation. One of the dead had been a young midshipman, a favorite of everyone aboard who had met him. After the 100-mm shell from the battery fortress had struck the bridge of the cruiser where Robert Cremel was standing, his comrades had found a diary in the breast pocket of his tunic.

The days that followed, de Gaulle wrote later, were cruel. "I went through what a man must feel when an earthquake shakes his house brutally and he receives on his head the rain of tiles falling from the roof . . . I, in my narrow cabin, crushed by the heat, was completing my education in what the reactions of fear could be, both among adversaries taking revenge for having felt it and among allies suddenly alarmed by a setback."

In Washington, President Roosevelt spoke of his poor opinion of de Gaulle's tactical judgment and said that Free France must be as "leaky as a sieve"; in London Prime Minister Churchill told Roosevelt's emissary, Averell Harriman, that "de Gaulle has perhaps done his best, but it amounts to very little." *Newsweek* exclaimed that Dakar was an "inglorious failure" and *Time* said that "the British have a weakness for lost causes," but that this was the worst of them all, "because the job looked so easy and the repercussions of failure were so drastic."

Concluded *Time:* Charles de Gaulle was a "mediocrity, who by accident had achieved world prominence, not to be taken very seriously."

THE
ATTACKERS

General Erwin Rommel, commander of the Seventh Panzer Division.

General Heinz Guderian, creator of the Panzerkorps, who led the Germans into France at Sedan in May, 1940.

German tanks and motorcycles crossing the "impenetrable" Ardennes Forest.

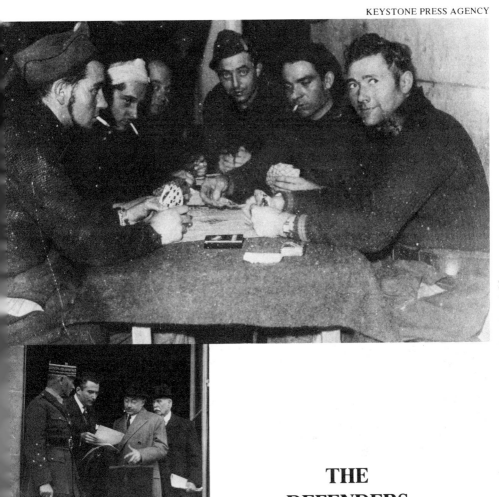

THE DEFENDERS

Top: German propaganda photo of French soldiers playing cards on the Maginot Line.

Bottom: (from left to right) Maxime Weygand, Paul Baudouin, Paul Reynaud and Philippe Pétain conferring after the German breakthrough at Sedan.

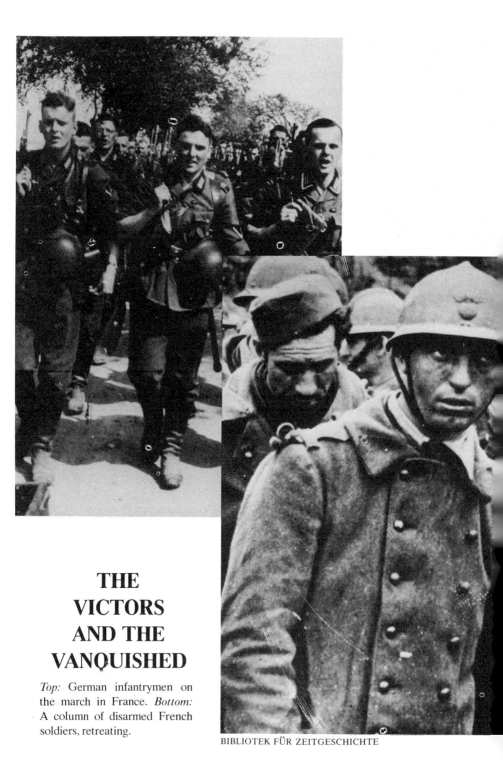

THE
VICTORS
AND THE
VANQUISHED

Top: German infantrymen on the march in France. *Bottom:* A column of disarmed French soldiers, retreating.

BIBLIOTEK FÜR ZEITGESCHICHTE

THE AFTERMATH

THE
FACES OF
DE GAULLE

Cadet at St. Cyr.   Lieutenant in the infantry, 1917.

Top: Tank commander near the Maginot Line, early in 1940.
Bottom: Reviewing the troops with King George VI.

De Gaulle in his London office during World War II.

"TO ARMS"

Two of the high-ranking military men among the few who responded immediately to Gaulle's call. *Top:* Vice-Admiral Emile-Henri Muselier with Gaulle at the BBC studio in London. *Bottom:* Lieutenant-Commander Thierry d'Argenlieu.

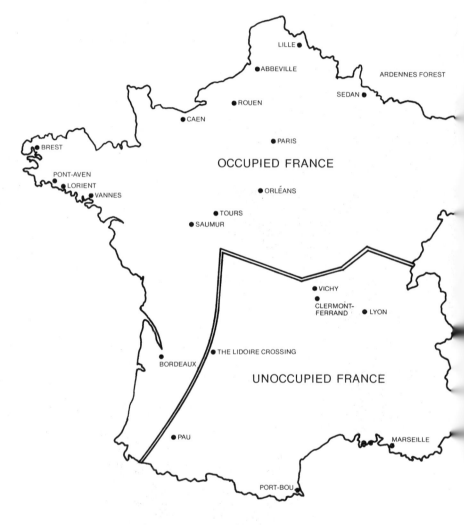

FRANCE 1940-1942

MERS-EL-KEBIR

CASABLANCA

TRIPOLI

BEIRUT
DAMASCUS

TOBRUK

JERUSALEM

BIR HAKEIM

CAIRO

LIBYA

EGYPT

MURZUQ

KUFRA

AR

CHAD

ERITREA

FORT-LAMY

ETHIOPIA

DOUALA

BRAZZAVILLE
LÉOPOLDVILLE

AFRICA 1940-1942

Breton fisherman slipping across the Channel to enlist in Free France.

CROSSING OVER

ACTION IN AFRICA

Left: Felix Eboué, the Gaullist governor of Chad. *Right:* Leclerc (Philippe de Haute-clocque), who led Free French columns from Chad against Italian bases in Libya. *Bottom:* A Free French patrol in Lybia, December, 1940.

IMPERIAL WAR MUSEUM, LONDON.

IMPERIAL WAR MUSEUM, LONDON.

De Gaulle with Churchill, March, 1941.

ATTACK
ON THE
LEVANT

ft: General Legentilhomme, wound-
on the road to Damascus. *Right:*
neral Catroux, de Gaulle's repre-
ttative at the talks in St. John of
re. *Bottom:* Spahis from Syria who
ght with Free France in the Middle
st and Africa.

Free French troops attacking a Vichyist position in Syria.

GERMAN SOLDIERS
IN NORTH AFRICA

FREE FRENCH SOLDIERS
AT BIR HAKEIM

(ALL) IMPERIAL WAR MUSEUM, LONDON

Top: Rommel in his command car in North Africa. *Bottom:* General Koenig, Free French commander of the outpost at Bir Hakeim.

PART THREE
Free France in the Field

Chapter 13

THE TALL STORKLIKE GENERAL DE GAULLE, WEARING A YELLOW SLICKER, WAS CLUTCHING THE RAIL OF THE COMMANDANT DUBOC, WATCHING THE FLAT RECEDING COASTLINE OF NIGERIA BOB UP AND DOWN IN THE storm. The downpour was incessant. Gusts of wind were curving the trunks of the waterfront trees, and steep yellow waves that crashed into the breakwater were shooting fountains of spray up against the blackened sky. At last the shore disappeared from sight, obscured partly by the rain clouds in front of the coast and partly by the swells of the ocean that sometimes rose high above the horizon. De Gaulle turned from the railing to go to his cabin below. It was the morning of October 6, 1940, and the General was en route to the Free French–controlled territories in Equatorial Africa, hoping to make a new beginning after his humiliating defeat at Dakar.

As he crossed the slippery boards of the deck, several of the *Duboc's* crew members noticed how pinched and haggard his face had become: the lips were pressed tight, the lines beside his mouth had grown deep, the bags beneath his eyes seemed blacker than ever, and the eyes themselves were feverish and blazing. In the three weeks since Dakar, three weeks of steaming heat and condescending welcomes from British officials along the coast of the African hump, de Gaulle seemed to have aged. His face was grayer, his paunch was broader, his pace along the wet deck slower. He seemed to the watching crewmen, for the first time, old.

He ducked his head to vanish beyond his cabin door, going off, alone as usual, to find ways of combatting the many enemies he saw closing in about him.

One such enemy, of course, was the Axis: although by now, in early October, the Germans had given up plans for an early invasion of Britain, their U-boats were torpedoing more and more of the ships carrying food to Britain; and the motorized armies of their allies, the Italians, had pushed effortlessly sixty miles into Egypt, the British Middle Eastern headquarters, threatening both the Suez Canal and the British-held oil wells in Iraq. The stakes were high, for de Gaulle as well as for the British. Since neither America nor Russia had entered the war, if Britain fell Free France would lose its sole source of support. If Britain collapsed, so would Free France.

Many Frenchmen, too, seemed hostile to de Gaulle. His own Admiral

Muselier, the flamboyant pirate who had escaped from Marseille, had called him a fool for having lost at Dakar; other Frenchmen in London, some of whom had recently bolted from Free France and who resented his cold abruptness, had dubbed him *"Général de Gauleiter"*; and Vichy France had dispatched General Maxine Weygand to North Africa to seal Morocco and Algeria off against Free French penetration.

But the most insidious threat—de Gaulle feared—would come from his closest ally, Winston Churchill. Churchill's problems were staggering, demanding all his energy and concentration, and now, after Dakar, his dealings with de Gaulle would stem from nothing but expediency. Churchill would try to dangle de Gaulle from a string like a puppet, make him play role the British had written, extract from him whatever military assistance Free France could offer, and then drop him, letting him fall limp out of sight of the audience. The Prime Minister would have no other choice.

De Gaulle, of course, being de Gaulle, had no intention of letting himself be used. In rebelling against his War College professors in the 1920's, in denouncing the idea of the Maginot Line in the 1930's and in fleeing from Bordeaux in June, 1940, he had risked his career in the hope of rendering France "some signal service," in the hope of restoring to France both her freedom and her honor. He was not about to end up as one of the expendables of history. But now, as he rode the creaking, groaning, pitching *Duboc* toward his obscure territories in tropical Africa, difficult questions began to confront him: How to remain his own man? How to turn weakness into strength and ignominy into fame? How to render that "signal service" to France before the British could cast him aside.

As he looked out his porthole at the brackish tossing sea, he realized that he had long ago seen the course he must follow—and what he had realized made him feel even older and more exhausted than before. For the course he must follow, he foresaw, would condemn him to a lifetime of loneliness.

He knew he had to go to war against the Axis armies, wherever he could reach them—necessity and honor demanded that. He knew he must convince the world that Free France, not Vichy, was the rightful government of France—his feel for propaganda demanded that. He knew he must "adopt without compromise the cause of national recovery," to act "as the inflexible champion of the nation and of the State," and to be intransigent about the fights of Free France—his sense of what would "win from foreigners respect and consideration" demanded that. But to accomplish these things he would have to lead, and to lead he would have, as he had once written, to "stage-manage" his effects, combining "theatricality of manner" with "sobriety of speech," "economy of words and gestures," and—"silence." For nothing, he had written, "enhances authority more than silence." There should be in his designs and demeanor a "'something' which others cannot altogether fathom, which puzzles them, stirs them, and rivets their attention," and his orders should be "swathed in the robes of nobility." This would prove that he had "vision," and he could "act on the grand scale," and "so establish his authority over the generality of men who splash in shallow water." If, despite his weakness, he could act *as if* he were strong, he could lead the French "by dreams."

As he glanced up at the rain dashing against the glass in his porthole, he wondered if he was really cut out to bear the burden of leadership. The price one must "pay for leadership," he had once said, "is unceasing self-discipline, the constant taking of risks, and a perpetual inner struggle. . . . Contentment and tranquility . . . are denied to those who [would lead]. The choice must be made, and it is a hard one. . . . One day somebody said to Napoleon, as they were looking at an old and noble monument: 'How sad it is!' Came the reply, 'as sad as greatness.'"

Could he do it? Could he suppress the longing for friendship, forsake the few quiet moments he had known with his men in London, forbid to himself the sharing of jokes he had so enjoyed on the voyage to Dakar? Could he cease being *Charles* de Gaulle and henceforth be *General* de Gaulle? The dehumanized symbol of the grandeur of France? Could he "climb to the heights and never then to come down"?

But as he studied the storm on the sea outside, he knew what he had to do: He *must* endure. There was no other way.

That evening in the ship's mess hall, at supper, it seemed to the crew that he had willed his doubts away. As he sat down at the head of the table he nodded politely but coldly to his men. Bodily he was present but spiritually he was detached. He seemed to have become almost a deity, serene and impertubable, who worked in mysterious ways that awed but resentful subjects on earth could never hope to comprehend.

After the meal, however, he sat down beside the Captain under a rain-filled awning on the quarter deck. They were facing the ship's stern. De Gaulle lit a cigarette in silence, looking out at the wake, still luminous as it spread back into the darkness. A wave rolled up against the ship's side; the *Duboc* skidded and groaned. He crushed out his cigarette and lit up another. A gust of wind made its tip glow red-orange in the night.

Then he leaned over to the Captain and, for the last time during the war, he confided in someone outside his family.

"You know," de Gaulle said, "what's the hardest for me is the feeling of being alone. Always alone."

He went to bed shortly, ready to start the war again from the remotest regions of Africa.

Chapter 14

(1)

ANOTHER FREE FRENCHMAN, TOO, GILBERT RENAULT, THE ONE-TIME FILM PRODUCER AND NOW SECRET AGENT FOR THE DEUXIEME BUREAU, HAD BEEN STARING OUT AT THE OCEAN THINKING ABOUT THE FUTURE. As he swished his cognac around the sides of his snifter, and lifted the glass to his lips, he looked out the dining-room window of a British hotel at the harbor of Plymouth beyond. What a splendid setting, he mused, this would make for one of his movies! British ships had been sailing in and out of this bay since the days of King John and the Magna Carta: it was from here that Drake had sailed for the New World and Cook had set out for New Zealand; it was from here, just inside the breakwater, that in 1815 H.M.S. *Bellerophon* had dropped anchor and held prisoner a man named Napoleon. What a shot it would make! Napoleon Bonaparte, pacing endlessly about his cramped quarters, scowling now and then out at that same breakwater, that same lighthouse, those same green Devon hills! Then Renault remembered, barely, that he was no longer really in films, and he put his snifter back down on the white linen tablecloth.

It had happened so fast; his hasty training in British intelligence codes, his drawing a supply of pounds and francs, his purchase of a light tan raincoat and a tweed jacket in Piccadilly, his preparing a cover—he would go to Spain and Portugal on the pretense of financing a movie on Christopher Columbus—and now, at the end of August, he could scarcely believe that in the morning a seaplane would fly him to Lisbon, the first stop on his circuitous route back into France. It seemed unreal. All he could grasp was that he was off to perform a small but necessary service for his leader, de Gaulle, and that, soon, after long months of absence, he could be with his family once more. Renault sighed, and looked longingly at the dancers on the restaurant floor.

A small band in the corner of the room was playing, "There'll Always Be an England," and a couple from the table next to Renault's brushed by his shoulder as they walked onto the floor. The girl's hair was styled in a pompadour and her beau, Renault could see from the pip on the lad's shoulder, was a Second Lieutenant in the British Army. Other couples began to swirl about the floor. Renault could make out a few more insignia: a Captain's three pips, a Major's crown, rings of gold on blue sleeves that denoted commissioned officers in the Royal Navy. The band shifted to "Blue Moon" and still more couples crowded, clinging, on to the floor until Renault was the only person in the room still seated at a table.

Despite his longing to be with Edith again—the sight of the couples made him remember his wedding in 1929—Renault felt comfortably drowsy and peaceful. "We might have been thousands of miles away from the war," he wrote; it was almost as if the Germans no longer existed. After the dance was over, he finished his cognac and went upstairs to his room, sure of getting a good night's sleep.

(2)

The Germans, however, were very much in existence, and they were tightening their grip on the French. The *Wehrmacht* was systematizing the looting of food and objets d'art, an S.S. group was starting to track down Jews who had fled from Germany into France, the *Abwehr*, the German Army's intelligence division, was cracking down on the few French who dared sell anti-German newspapers, and the Gestapo were setting up offices in Paris.

Gestapo headquarters were in the rue de Saussaies. German sentries in gray uniforms and steel helmets guarded the building around the clock, and a swastika fluttered from a flagpole atop the roof. Inside, up one flight of stairs and down a narrow corridor, was the Cabinet Room, with an ornate long table and an expensive deep red Oriental carpet. In the corner of that room, behind desks that overlooked the canopies and sidewalk tables on the street below, worked two officials who formed the Gestapo's chief interrogation team in Paris. The Gestapo were not well known yet in

France but they were beginning to learn, and practice and perfect, the art of tracking down enemy agents.

Nor had the French begun significantly to rebel against the forces of the Occupation. Many of Renault's old friends, all of them once patriots, he would soon discover, had aged and grown tired, and the Vichyist newspapers he was about to start reading reminded him of revivalist sermons. "The expiation theme," he said later, "set in motion by Pétain, had been exploited from every angle, and very insidiously. France, they shouted in chorus, deserved her defeat. It was a blessing from heaven in disguise. France must redeem herself, do penance, and the Germans were there to see that she practiced the fasting and the abstinence. . . . And the Lord before whom the sinner must bow down was no longer the Son of God, but the Nazi colossus. In her humiliation she would find redemption, under the guidance of the Marshal, a modern Moses, aided by his warden, Pierre Laval."

But what would disturb Renault even more than the newspapers themselves were their readers. In railway stations, hotel lobbies and sidewalk cafés throughout Occupied France he would witness the same scene for months: "Frenchmen with their noses buried in these very papers. . . . [And] on the faces of none was the slightest sign of protest, the smallest proof of disgust."

(3)

To Renault, however, as to many Frenchmen at this time, the Gestapo were just people, just like any other chance acquaintances among the enemy with whom one would converse. For unlike his austere and awkward leader, General de Gaulle, Renault loved people. People had always felt free with him and he with them: that, plus hard work and a talent for organization, had carried him from a boyhood in provincial Brittany to the fast-moving, fast-talking world of the Paris cinema. But now it was 1940, the Germans were occupying France, and Renault's old habit of talking with strangers was not exactly the best way of screening himself from the Gestapo's attention.

He still had to learn this when, two weeks after his arrival from England, he stood in line to board a plane at the Lisbon airport, and heard a gutteral voice speak out behind him.

"Here's the Frenchman," the voice was saying in a Teutonic-accented French. "The one who tells such good stories."

After his landing in Lisbon two weeks before, Renault had flown to

Madrid to establish his cover as a movie financier and to persuade Jacques Pigeonneau, a French consul, to carry coded messages from France over to Portugal in his diplomatic pouch. Pigeonneau had agreed, and had told Renault about another French official in Lisbon who might smuggle those messages out to Great Britain. On the plane back to Portugal, Renault had met and swapped stories with a tweedy-looking German. After making the suggested contact in Lisbon, Renault had decided to fly back to Spain again before going off to France. And now, as he was waiting in line to board the plane for Madrid, he heard behind him the voice of that same tweedy German, pointing him out to a friend.

"You remember," Renault heard the tweedy German say, "the story about Churchill and the cup of tea."

"Ach, ja, ja!" Renault heard a deep, rumbling reply.

Renault turned to look at the source of that powerful voice: the man was tall, bullnecked, and dressed in a brown suit that was too tight around the shoulders and the back. Renault and the big man were introduced. The German's thick hand surrounded Renault's in a handshake. Renault failed to understand the man's name, but he did catch one thing: the German worked for the Gestapo, and was on his way back from Argentina to Berlin.

"You'll have to tell me your stories on the airplane," he said to Renault, booming out the words.

As Renault settled down in his seat in the four-engined Lufthansa aircraft, his mind drifted ahead to his final destination in France. Before he tried to enter France and recruit on-the-spot spies for Free France, he reflected, he would have to find a way of getting his wife, Edith, and their children, living then in her mother's place in Brittany, safely down to Spain. Perhaps an old friend, the porter at the Palace Hotel in Madrid, where Renault had a room reserved, could help him find a way—and then an elbow in the ribs broke into his thoughts.

It belonged to the beefy Gestapo man. "I'm all ears," he boomed.

"You know," Renault said, hesitantly, "these stories are extremely well known."

"Nein, nein," came the resonating voice. "Tell me about Vinston Churchill and the cup of tea."

Renault repeated the story he had already told the tweedy German: Churchill, Hitler and Mussolini were having tea beside the carp pool at Fontainebleau, near Paris, arguing about who would finally win the war. Churchill proposed a wager, and whoever lost the bet would have to admit that he had lost the war. "What's the wager?" Hitler asked suspiciously. Churchill proposed that whoever could catch one of the carp in the pool without ordinary fishing tackle would be declared winner of the war. Hitler agreed, aimed his revolver, fired and failed to hit any fish. Mussolini tried next: he stripped off his uniform, beneath which he always wore a bathing suit, splashed into the pond and began trying to catch the fish with his hands. Naturally, they all slipped away. Then it was Churchill's turn. Dipping his teaspoon into the lake, he threw a teaspoonful of water over his shoulder. He did it again, and again and again. Hitler and Mussolini watched with their mouths agape. "What the hell are you doing?" the Führer finally demanded. Churchill looked up from the water's edge. "It will take a long, long time," he said, "but I do believe that in the end we shall win the war."

Renault sat still when he had finished, watching. Perhaps, he thought, he had gone too far, for the German was frowning heavily and mumbling. Suddenly, however, the Gestapo man roared with laughter.

"*Wunderbar,*" he exclaimed. "Mussolini in the water with the fish!"

At the Barajas airport outside Madrid, the Gestapo man's hand engulfed Renault's in another handshake. "Thank you very much for the story," the German said. "I shall be a great success in Berlin with it."

He grinned at Renault.

"I surely hope we meet again," roared the German.

The man had seemed so oafish, Renault thought, as he walked toward the customs shed. Perhaps the Gestapo in France were not so terrible, after all.

(4)

As autumn came, however, the Gestapo was starting to spread its net beyond Paris, with regional headquarters at Dijon, Bordeaux and Rouen, cities from which they could watch Alsace-Lorraine, the provinces along the English Channel, and the French Atlantic coast. The Germans were sensitive about each of these parts of France—Alsace-Lorraine was close to the Reich, Brittany and Normandy on the Channel looked onto England, and Atlantic coast harbors were vital to U-boat warfare against Allied convoys. And in each of these regions, the Gestapo was posting occasional black-rimmed notices, the left side in German and the right side in French, notices that listed the names of Frenchmen executed for having committed acts of violence and sabotage against the forces of the German occupation.

Implicit in these posters was a message for men like Gilbert Renault: stay out of Occupied France.

Renault, however, in Spain, had not seen the warnings. In mid-November, 1940, he set out to enter Occupied France.

(5)

As the three bicycles started down through the woods on a rainy November night, their headlamps illuminated the gnarled tree trunks and the barren branches bent low enough to scrape against the faces of the riders. On the lead bicycle pedaled a man named La Bardonnie, fortyish, wearing shabby britches, and bending his bald head low enough to avoid the branches over the road. His young farmhand, Le Rat, rode in the rear. And, in the middle, was Gilbert Renault, a bicycle clamp holding his trousers above his ankles and his upper-middle-class thighs still trembling from having climbed up this steep hill only an hour before. He wa: wearing the light tan raincoat he had bought in London over his Piccadilly tweed coat.

After his encounter with the Gestapo agent, Renault had sent a letter through his hotel porter to his wife in Brittany, asking her and the children to join him in Madrid. In late October, then, he had set out for Unoccupied France, renewing old friendships and following a chain of contacts that had led him to the Château la Roque, forty miles east of Bordeaux. The master of the estate, La Bardonnie, had told him that by cycling to the cottage of a Gaullist named Beausoleil, Renault could slip across the nearby Demarcation Line into Occupied France. La Bardonnie himself would use his identity card to cross the Line legitimately, meet Renault and guide him to a safe place on the other side. They would rendezvous on the bank of the Lidoire, a little stream that was part of the boundary of the two zones of France.

As the three bicycles swung on to the National Highway 136, the main road from Ste-Foy to Castillon and on to Bordeaux, the rain began to fall harder. The black tarmac glistened beneath the beams of the lights. The lamps illuminated a house or two, set back from the road, and then the three men reached a cluster of thatched-roofed cottages, huddled around an ancient stone church. It was the village of La Mothe-Montravel. La Bardonnie squeezed the brake lever on the handle of his bicycle.

"This is Beausoleil's place," he said.

The three men swung their legs to the ground and walked along a gravel path to a small cottage. The door was half open, and through the doorframe Renault could see the dancing flames of a fireplace.

A lamp with a yellow shade hung from a beam, shining on the face of an old peasant who was pulled up to a table, slurping from a bowl of soup. "His wife," Renault said, "a small, wizened old woman with gray hair, their son Pierrot, a young winegrower of about thirty with a cheerful open face, and his wife Simone, a strong-looking woman, blonde and pretty, shook our hands in turn." Pierrot offered Renault a glass of his tangy red wine.

La Bardonnie explained that Renault wanted to cross the Line.

"Off we go, then," Pierrot said after Renault had finished the wine.

As La Bardonnie and Le Rat pedaled away into the darkness, Pierrot Beausoleil explained his plan to Renault. They would go first to Pierrot's mother-in-law's cottage—she knew better than he where the Germans had strung barbed wire—and she would lead them as far as a German sentry post beside the Lidoire. Pierrot would show Renault the way from there.

Pierrot's mother-in-law was at home, and after bundling herself up in a heavy sweater, she took them across the no-man's land, a field some five hundred yards wide, separating the Vichy French and the German frontier posts. The sky was murky black and the soil beneath Renault's feet felt spongy. He shivered. The rain was sharp against his face. Then he bumped against Pierrot's back.

Renault could barely make out the young man's arm, pointing across to a farmhouse. One of its windows was yellow with light.

"They can't see us," Pierrot whispered, "but don't speak out. Voices carry here. Sometimes the German patrols stop for a drink there."

They slogged along in the dark again. Renault nearly slipped down the side of a ditch. Pierrot stopped once more. Renault could see a red glow on top of a bridge.

"Quiet now," Pierrot whispered, "We're right next to their post. Next time, don't wear that light raincoat. They might spot it in the dark."

"It's all right now, Mother," Pierrot whispered again. "You don't have to come any farther. I can make it from here."

He began then to lead Renault across a meadow. Soon, they stopped again.

"This is the Lidoire," Pierrot said. "Take off your shoes."

Renault did so. He could hear the stream bubbling along in the night.

"Ready?" Pierrot asked.

"Ready."

"Off you go then," Pierrot said. "And good luck."

Renault felt for the stream with his bare feet: the bank was soft and steep, and the mud squished up between his toes. He inched ahead carefully, his right hand clutching his shoes and socks, and his left hand extended sideways for balance. He slipped, and splashed into the water loudly. He stood still, listening, but all he could hear was the murmur of the stream. The pebbles were smooth beneath his feet as he pushed through the racing current; the water around his knees was chilly. He stopped at what felt like midstream: from the opposite side and off to the right he saw a tiny spot of glowing red—the tip of a cigarette. He waded on for another few yards, then his toes dug into the mud on the other bank. His knuckles scraped against a root, a hand met his, grasped it and hoisted him up to the top of the bank.

The hand was La Bardonnie's. Renault rose to his feet. He was standing now on the soggy ground of Occupied France.

La Bardonnie guided him across another field to the cottage of a friend, an old man named Rambaud. As soaked and cold as he was, Renault was elated. In the morning, of course, he would leave to spy under the very noses of the Gestapo, but so far at least, the Germans had seemed so easygoing and unthreatening.

Chapter 15

(1)

DUST BILLOWED UP AS A CAR SKIDDED TO A HALT IN FRONT OF THE ONE-STORY STUCCO FREE FRENCH HEADQUARTERS BUILDING AT FORT-LAMY, IN CHAD. PHILIPPE DE HAUTECLOCQUE, "LECLERC," WHO IN THE SUMMER had played a key part in the liberation of the French Cameroon, stepped from the car. He was slender, and dressed in khaki. His blue eyes, normally turned down at the outer corners, squinted even more in the brilliant sunlight; on his epaulets were the five stripes of a colonel in the Free French Army. It was early December, 1940, and on the orders of General de Gaulle, Leclerc had arrived to take command of the base at Fort-Lamy. Briskly and erectly, he strode through the door of the stucco building, plunging immediately into the assignment on which he had come.

His instructions had come from the General personally, after de Gaulle's landing in Equatorial Africa: from Fort-Lamy Leclerc was to launch three small Free French attacks upon the Italians, who had declared war on France only days before Pétain's asking for the Armistice.

The first was to be aimed northward at the Italian outpost of Murzuq in southwestern Libya, in the hope of shaking the Italians' morale and causing them to transfer troops down from the Mediterranean coast where they were fighting the British. The second was to sneak up upon Koufra, close to the Egyptian border in eastern Libya, for Koufra was an important base on the air route from Tripoli to Italian-controlled Ethiopia. And the third was to strike at Eritrea, an Italian-governed portion of

Ethiopia that lay along the Red Sea and from which the Italians were threatening Allied convoys steaming up toward Suez.

Each battle would be only a minor skirmish, fought in obscure African outposts, and since Free French resources were limited, each would be undertaken jointly with the British. But, in de Gaulle's judgment, each expedition was vital to the future of Free France. Each was a gamble, pitting tiny numbers of Free Frenchmen against the sun, the desert and numerically superior forces. If they succeeded, they would help relieve the pressure upon Britain's oil reserves in the Middle East, and give Free France the reputation of being a winner. But if they failed—as far as de Gaulle was concerned, Free France must not fail.

Failure, however, was precisely what most officers in Fort-Lamy were predicting for the three expeditions. No sooner had Colonel Leclerc laid his kepi upon the desk of his new office than he began to hear the objections.

Fort-Lamy, he heard, had no trucks or tanks or planes that would work. And even if he could put together a force, said the officers, launching expeditions from the place would prove impossible. Fort-Lamy was considered desolate, dry and scorching for half the year and sunk deep in swamps for the other, virtually cut off from the outside world. Beyond the fort, furthermore, lay barren stretches of steppe where nothing grew but tufts of weeds and stunted thorny bushes, and past all that was the desert, sometimes hard and flat as a floor but at other times rough and uneven, with limestone outcroppings and ever-shifting dunes of sand. One could navigate only by use of the compass and sextant, and with the heat and thirst that came upon any traveler in the region, the slightest mechanical breakdown would spell inevitable death. Fort-Lamy did have an airport, and from there one could get to Brazzaville or Khartoum or Cairo, but the place was good for nothing else but sitting, sweating and drinking.

But Leclerc had seen defeatism before—in France during the spring of 1940—and he was ready to try anything General de Gaulle had asked of him.

For a month he scarcely slept. He climbed over heaps of junk outside the fort, looking for rusty gun parts that might be scraped clean, and broken carburetors and mufflers that might be pieced back together. He watched his pilots, Sainte Pereuse, Lagar, Noël, Ezanno, Romain Gary, take off for training missions in the Blenheims the British Air Ministry had assigned for his use. He drilled his French officers and their men, Legionnaires, Saras, Tuaregs, Senegalese, teaching them the few scraps of information he had heard about how to survive in the desert. At last, at the beginning of January, 1941, he felt he was ready. He had patched together some trucks and tanks, he had supplied his men with canteens of water and wine and, by radio, he had coordinated his plans with the British in faraway Cairo. Then, once again, he heard the counsels of defeat.

"Don't tell me," Leclerc said, "what I can and cannot do."

His first expedition, under Jean Colonna d'Ornano, who had earlier come to Chad with René Pleven, left Fort-Lamy on January 8, 1941. Its objective was Murzuq, far up the desert in Libya.

(2)

From the big mahogany desk in Carlton Gardens, in London, where, after his return from Africa, de Gaulle spread out *The Times* every morning to follow the news from Libya, there seemed good reason to hope for d'Ornano's success.

The Italians were now on the run. On December 6, 1940, the British General Sir Richard O'Connor had struck back at the Italian positions at Sidi Barrâni, on the Mediterranean, and had captured forty thousand prisoners. On December 16, he had hit again, seizing Sollum, another port town, and the long string of forts the Italians had built on the lip of the escarpment that paralleled the coastal plain. On January 5, then, he had forced the surrender of Bardia, taking forty-five thousand more Italians, and, on January 20, he had conquered Tobruk—bagging thousands more prisoners of war. And, said *The Times,* a Free French contingent serving under General O'Connor "made a brillant contribution to the capture of Tobruk."

The good news, however, had failed to soften de Gaulle. Good news or bad news, he believed, the British wished to use Free France for their ends alone. So he protected himself in the only way he knew: he acted as if he were, in the words of a Free Frenchman, "a statue in a public square, outwardly cold, impassive, unapproachable."

Not even the good news from Africa could make him unbend.

(3)

The procession left Fort-Lamy on the night of January 8, 1941. In the lead, jouncing along atop a camel, was the hawk-nosed Colonna d'Ornano, his long skinny limbs enveloped in the flowing robes of the desert; next came a short column of camels, then half a dozen small tanks and armored cars, then a few trucks filled with black African soldiers, following the narrow road that was turning into nothing but two deep ruts in the plain.

The column pushed ahead in the night, moving through a "nightmarish, weird, surrealist terrain—along an enormous dry riverbed, past sudden oval valleys, with black soil floors, across an eroded tableland . . ." Occasionally a truck would jerk to a stop. The engine would begin to labor and the wheels to spin against loose sand, filling the air with the sweet smell of burning rubber. Black enlisted men would get out of the truck's rear, stretch strips of canvas and tin in front of the trapped wheels and shovel sand away from the tires until they could push the vehicle up onto its new road. The column would then move forward again until the tires of another truck bogged down in a trap of sand.

The column traveled only at night. No motorized vehicles had ever taken this route before, and the men in the rear truck kept sweeping the sand with their cloaks to hide their tracks from Italian aircraft that might fly over their path by day.

Two nights later the ground began to rise: before him in the moonlight d'Ornano could see the jagged peaks of the Tibesti Mountains in northwestern Chad. He waved his men ahead. In the morning, after reaching a plateau beyond the mountains, he rendezvoused with a small British–New Zealand detachment from Cairo under the command of a Major Pat Clayton, waiting to drop in the morning onto the desert sand below. Murzuq, their destination, was only one day away.

At dawn, a day later, four officers, Jean Colonna d'Ornano, Pat Clayton and two of Clayton's subordinates, William Shaw and Chrichton-Stuart, were lying stomach-down on a ridge four miles from Murzuq. Through their binoculars they could see a road leading across the desert and disappearing into a thick palm-tree grove, about a mile outside the town. The dome of a mosque rose above the trees, and to the left of that emerged an Italian flag, flapping atop what seemed to be either the fort or the nearby hangar. The four officers wished they could get in for a closer look, but there was no cover between them and the palm trees, so they decided to attack immediately.

As the column approached the fort, Italian sentinels, standing outside the gate, seemed to think that the column was a detachment of their own reinforcements arriving, for they presented arms and snapped off sharp salutes. But the salutes turned quickly into panic. When the sentries saw who had really come, they rushed inside and slammed the gate shut.

Crichton-Stuart's patrol of Coldstream Guards drove its armored cars behind the protection of some huge boulders, dismounted and brought its guns into action against the fort, while d'Ornano and Clayton raced in another car toward the airfield. Camels tethered around the hangar moaned in fear. Clayton swung the car across the airstrip and d'Ornano fired rounds into the gas tanks of three unattended Italian airplanes. Clayton then wheeled back toward the hangar itself. He had almost reached it when a burst of machine-gun fire from the neighboring fort forced him to race back behind the huge boulders. When he had braked the car to a stop he turned to speak to d'Ornano. Colonna d'Ornano did not answer. He was lying dead across the gas tank of the car, his rifle clutched in his long bony fingers.

Clayton decided to withdraw across the desert: his forces were too weak to take the fort.

But the Anglo-Free French column could be proud of its effort: it had destroyed three aircraft, blown up a large gasoline tank, captured four machine guns and inflicted several casualties upon the defending Italians. And as the detachment picked its way back across the desert, a radio message reached it from British headquarters in Cairo: "Report at once how many fit to join French in operation against Koufra."

For, on January 19, a second Free French column, under Colonel Leclerc himself, had set out for Libya.

(4)

Other reports reaching de Gaulle's desk were just as good. The Italians were in headlong flight along the Mediterranean coast toward Tripoli and the British were right behind them in rapid pursuit. One problem had emerged—British supply lines from Egypt were stretching thin—but this seemed of small importance because the Italians were beaten and the Germans had failed to come to their support. The British were confident of keeping control of the Western Desert.

De Gaulle, however, was as watchful and cold as ever. "There was an intellectual arrogance in his speech and manner," wrote a journalist, "a disdain for the rest of humanity such as I had never encountered in a human being. Here was a man so wrapped up in his own consciousness it was as if no one else in the world existed. I agreed completely with every word he spoke. But they were uttered with a bitterness, a fanaticism that might lead anywhere."

(5)

That fanaticism for the moment was directing his men to a faraway Italian outpost in the Libyan desert. The small column from Murzuq had joined with Leclerc on January 25, 1941: The objective was Koufra, whose fort and airbase linking Tripoli and Addis Ababa seemed lost in the vast whiteness of the desert. Along with his new detachments, Leclere left the oasis at Faya the next morning. Five days later his men ran into trouble.

A British patrol under Clayton and Crichton-Stuart had reached a well at Bishara, seventy miles south of Koufra. Around the well, Clayton discovered, fresh tread marks were still indented in the sand. The Italians must be nearby. He had his men move out quickly and into a range of low hills overlooking the oasis. He was too late. As his trucks were dispersing through the rocky valley, Italian armored cars appeared around the crests of the hills, and a squadron of two-engined Savoia airplanes dipped down to strafe his patrol. Three of Clayton's trucks caught fire and he himself received a piece of shrapnel in the shoulder. He saw that he had to surrender.

Four of his men, one wounded in the throat and another in the intestines, did manage to escape—on foot. Ten days later, after walking semidelirious across the burning sand, they found Leclerc's column, moving up toward the oasis at Sarra. The four men were safe for the moment, but by this time the Italians realized that a column was approaching Koufra.

For on February 3, a formation of Blenheims from Fort-Lamy—the Lorraine Squadron—had conducted its first raid on El Tag, the Italian fortress at Koufra. Twice more in four days the Free French airplanes bombed the fort, and then, on February 7, Colonel Leclerc himself appeared in an armored car outside Koufra.

An Italian motorized detachment came out of the base to stop him. He divided his force into two columns: one attacked the Italians from the front, but the other, supposed to sweep around from the flank, became mired in a stretch of loose sand. Only the accuracy of the first column's guns prevented the Italians from destroying his units. The enemy raced back to the fort to avoid being encircled in the open desert.

Then Leclerc besieged the airbase and the fort themselves. Each night for three weeks his artillery bombarded the fort, each night for three weeks his infantry attacked the airstrip's defenses, and each night the Italians counterattacked, dropping bomb after bomb on the Anglo-Free French dugouts. And by the end of the three weeks the Allied force had nearly exhausted its supply of water. Even Leclerc was ready to quit. He gave his men one more night to succeed.

On the night of February 28, the Allied infantry climbed over the barbed wire around the air base and ran immediately into a hail of Italian machine-gun fire. Leclerc's men tried again and again, and when they were almost ready to give up the effort, they realized that the machine guns in the fort had stopped firing. The Free French artillery had finally done the job.

When morning came Leclerc looked toward the top of the fort and grinned. Hanging from the tip of the flagpole was a white flag of surrender. Soon the tricolor rose in its place.

"We shall stop," Leclerc proclaimed to his men that night, "only when the flag of France also flies above Strasbourg and Metz."

(6)

General de Gaulle, however, was far less sanguine. A disturbing intelligence report had reached his mahogany desk in London: long convoys of German ships, well protected by the *Luftwaffe*, were docking at the piers of Tripoli and unloading wooden boxes, motorcycles, patrol cars, anti-aircraft guns and huge twenty-two-ton tanks. The intelligence report, sent by an Allied spy in Tripoli, ended on a disturbing note. The commander of this German expeditionary force was an "obscure general" named Rommel. Characteristically, de Gaulle responded by insulting the British. A Member of Parliament, Harold Nicolson, who was also working in the Ministry of Information, was shocked when de Gaulle accused him and his ministry of being pro-Pétain (the British were being correct—and no more—toward the Vichy government), and Churchill's personal physician, Lord Moran, likened the General to a "human giraffe, sniffing down his nostrils at mortals beneath his gaze. . . . He is so stuffed with principles that there is no room left for a little Christian tolerance; in his rigidity, there is no give."

In this way, de Gaulle was convinced, he could prove to the people of France that he was his own man, not Churchill's. But there was another reason, too, in the early spring of 1941. The third expedition from Fort-Lamy was running into real trouble.

(7)

The scene these Free Frenchmen faced at dawn on March 15, 1941, seemed truly formidable. The Eritrean plain on which they were camped was about two miles across, already hot in the early morning sun and offering no shade except that of a few dried thorn bushes. But more awesome than the ravine was the sheer cliff of razor-backed ridges towering just ahead of them and extending as far as they could see both to the left and to the right. There was only one gap in the cliff, the Dongolass Gorge, and that was what the Free French and the other Allied Forces had been ordered to cross.

Late in January these men had left Fort-Lamy, Spahis from North Africa, Senegalese of the Third *Bataillon de Marche*, men of the *Bataillon Etranger* who had already seen fighting against the Germans at Narvik, in Norway. In command of the Free French expedition had been Colonel Magrin-Verneret of the Foreign Legion (his code name was "Monclar"), whom General Spears described as "fair, fresh-skinned, very closely shaved, bespectacled and soft-voiced," looking "for all the world like a youngish priest"—except for the hole a bullet had once carved in his skull. On February 18, the detachment had reached Mersa Taclai, on the Red Sea coast of the Anglo-Egyptian Sudan, and there had joined a larger Allied force under the command of Lieutenant General Sir William Platt. Their objective was the port of Massawa on the coast of the Italian-controlled Ethiopian province of Eritrea, but to get there they had to reach the main road through Keren, and Keren lay over the mountains, on the other side of this impossibly steep cliff that could be easily defended by a few well-placed Italians.

"Don't let anybody think that this is going to be a walk-over," General Platt had said to his officers on the evening of March 14. "It is not. It is going to be a bloody battle and it is going to be won by the side which lasts longest."

The air was breathless and hot the next morning, and a thunderstorm, threatening to break, hung over the valley. Just after sunrise the Allied infantry, Scots, New Zealanders, Indians and Free French, moved out, each man already soaked and dripping under his pack as he crossed the valley floor. In the heat and humidity their thirst grew unbearable. Then, as the men began scrambling over the boulder at the base of the Dongolass Gorge, they ran into enemy gunfire. The Italians had watched them coming, and were so protected by a tunnel overlooking the gorge that Allied artillery had no success in dislodging them. By nightfall it was evident that the first Allied attack had failed.

The fighting continued unabated for a week. Each day the Allied forces assaulted the gorge and each day the guns of the Italians drove them back. The Allied supply problems were mounting: every vehicle in Platt's command was working around the clock, more and more engines were breaking down, and no trucks were left in reserve. To the troops in the valley the savage fighting seemed to be producing little but mounting casualty rates. At the end of the week General Platt settled down in his tent to figure out a new approach to the problem.

The break in the action, however, brought little relief to his men. The nights were cold, the days were hot, and each morning at sunrise clouds of millions of flies would buzz to life, settling on corpses and human excrement, spreading dysentery and desert sores, and so helping further to weaken the thirsty, hungry troops. The Free French especially suffered from thirst. One of the Battalion Garby's water parties, said a British report, set out to find water for its unit but, on the return journey, drank empty every container they had filled.

The lull soon come to an end: on the evening of March 24, word went out to the troops that they would attack once more in the morning. General Platt had decided to try a new approach: in addition to rushing the Dongolass Gorge itself, he would have commandos sneak up behind the Italian positions in a tunnel that covered it, trying to do by surprise what he had failed to do by assault.

While the mass of his force scrambled into the valley again at dawn for a diversionary frontal attack on the gorge, a few men under a Brigadier Rees wormed their way across the ravine, between the boulders at the base of the cliff and up the rock wall until they had reached the tunnel's mouth opposite the one over the Dongolass Gorge. There they stopped to rest, while Rees tiptoed ahead through the tunnel to see if the Italians were aware of his presence. They were not. He rejoined his men and spent the rest of the morning in the cool of the tunnel. In mid-afternoon he was ready to move. After a final mug of tea strengthened with rum, Rees and his men set out through the darkness of the shaft. They moved ahead stealthily for some five minutes, and stopped, listening. They heard gunshots from the other end of the tunnel, evidently aimed at the gorge below. They moved again, creeping along in the blackness for still another few minutes. The firing was louder, and they heard shouts in Italian. Then, again, they tiptoed ahead, and now they could see the square of light that formed the tunnel's mouth. They kept moving forward, closer and closer to the light, and then, bent over before them, they saw the back of an Italian machine gunner, feeding a new belt of ammunition into his weapon. The man had just started to fire upon the gorge again when a shot from the tunnel cut him down.

The surprise was complete, and although the fighting raged bitterly throughout the rest of the afternoon, the Allies had now captured the advantageous position. That evening Colonel Monclar wired a communiqué to de Gaulle: "In a series of hard engagements," it said, "over extremely difficult terrain and in burning heat, the troops vied with each other in courage and maneuvering ability and broke the resistance of the Italians, who fought bravely wherever they met them. They captured 915 prisoners, including 28 officers."

The route to Massawa was now clear, and early in the afternoon of April 10, Colonel Monclar led his Legionnaires and two Indian brigades into the streets of the fallen Eritrean port.

(8)

But in March, General Rommel had stood on a platform in downtown Tripoli to watch a parade. Hundreds of tanks had passed him, rattling and clattering on the macadamized street, then disappearing around a corner after receiving his salute. After the parade, he had gone immediately off to the desert, where he shocked the British commanders with the boldness of his tactics.

The Axis was once again moving toward the oil of the Middle East, and as it did the stony-faced General de Gaulle began to fear more than ever both for the future of the Allied cause and for Free France's ability to control its own destiny.

Chapter 16

(1)

TO THE OUTGOING GILBERT RENAULT, HOWEVER, THE TASK AHEAD HAD SEEMED REMARKABLY EASY. HE HAD TO BE CAREFUL, HE KNEW, BUT HE HAD FAITH IN HIMSELF, FAITH THAT HIS WARMTH COULD RECRUIT AGENTS for Free France, faith that his skills could organize ways of relaying intelligence to England, faith that his talkativeness could keep him out of trouble with the Germans. So, blithely, he had set out in November, 1940, from the River Lidoire, off to see what he could do to spy upon the occupation forces of the Third Reich.

Later that month an Atlantic fog was rolling up against the kitchen window of a second-story apartment in the rue Carnot, in the Breton port of Vannes. The sun had arisen, theoretically, along the south coast of Brittany, but to the women silently and groggily munching croissants around the kitchen table inside, it still seemed like night outside, so thick and dark was the mist. This was Renault's family: his mother, his sisters Maisie, Hélène, Madeleine, Isabelle. Old deaf Uncle Sauvage was still in bed. Suddenly Hélène looked up from the table—she was in her late teens and pretty like her sister-in-law, Edith Renault. She thought she had heard a knock downstairs. Then she bit into her croissant again, deciding it was too early in the morning for anyone to be calling.

But she heard the noise again and crossed to the window over the stove. A man was standing on the sidewalk below. All she could make out in the gloom was a receding hairline and a tweed jacket, then he looked up and she recognized his square jaw. Squealing with delight she raced down the stairs to let him in.

Gilbert Renault had come home.

"How is Edith?" the women asked as they hugged and kissed him at the foot of the stairs. "Is her pregnancy going well?" "How are the children?" "How's baby Manuel?" Maisie giggled. "We heard you on the B.B.C.," she said [like many Free Frenchmen Renault had spoken anonymously to his family over the air, telling them he was fine], "and all Uncle Sauvage could say was, 'Bah! Bah!'"

"And you, Gilbert," asked his mother, "what brings you here?"

"I'll tell you when we get upstairs," he answered.

He followed the girls up the staircase that led to the second-floor flat. At the top of the stairs he looked down the long corridor to his left. It had all started behind the last door down there: that was where, in June, he had told Edith of his plans to go to England.

"And now, Gilbert," his mother was saying as he sat at the kitchen table, "you were going to tell us why you are here."

Renault tried to look mysterious, and then grinned.

He was on a secret mission for General de Gaulle, he explained—his mother smiled knowingly—and when he had written to Edith, asking her to join him in Madrid while he produced the Columbus film, well, that was only a cover. Now that he was in France, he was using a slightly different disguise. His identification card, forged in London, said that he was on the sales, rather than the financial, side of the insurance business. But, in reality, he had become a spy, and had come to Brittany to see what kinds of naval facilities the Germans were constructing along the coasts.

Then it was Renault's turn to pose some questions.

"Have the Germans bothered you about my brother Claude's absence or mine?" he asked his mother.

"No, not at all, Gilbert," she answered.

"What's become of my brother Philippe?"

Philippe, a fisherman, had been out to sea on the day Renault had sailed for England, and had been ordered by the Germans to leave his boat down the coast at La Rochelle. He had gone home after that, the girls told Renault, to his home on the Ile-aux-Moines, near Vannes, where he and his wife lived with her father, a Major Legros, now the owner of a trawler.

"Are they home now?" Renault asked.

Philippe would be out to sea again, his mother thought, but Major Legros should be home by the next morning.

A gusty November wind had blown the fog away the next morning, and as Renault stood in the tiny cabin of Major Legros' trawler, he could see the gulls being tossed squawking and whirling about the winter-gray Atlantic sky. A rope was slapping against the mast that rose from the top of the cabin. Renault's finger pointed to a gap in the Breton coastline.

"Can we get any closer?" he asked Major Legros.

"I think so," came the answer, "but they might be watching, you know."

Earlier that morning, after he found Major Legros breakfasting in his cottage, Renault had explained what he was doing for Free France, and had asked if the Germans were servicing ships or submarines in the region. Yes, the Major had said, grinning with pleasure at being asked to help, they were supplying U-boats in Lorient: would Renault like to take a look?

The gap in the shore was widening fast, and Renault could make out individual clumps of leafless trees, scattered behind the beach. Then, through the gap, he saw a tiny red and black flag.

The boat moved still closer: it was bobbing up and down in the current outside Lorient. Then Renault whistled loudly. Below the red and black flag stretched a huge building, an enormous warehouse. Three or four cranes stood beside it, for its roof was not yet completed, but beside the pier that extended from the front of the building, rested the wet, gray, cylindrical hull of a German U-boat.

The message the scene conveyed was clear: it was from Brittany that the Germans would be striking out against the Allied Atlantic convoys; it was in Brittany, therefore, that Renault should establish his first network for the gathering of intelligence.

It seemed so simple. All he had to do was recruit men who had access to Brittany's ports, visit them regularly on the pretext of adjusting their insurance complaints and find a way of relaying their reports to England. All he had to do was find the right men; the rest would be easy.

(2)

Renault was right about one thing. The Germans were using the ports of Brittany to their very greatest advantage. "The only thing that ever really frightened me during the war," Churchill has written, "was the U-boat peril. Invasion, I thought, even before the air battle, would fail. After the air victory it was a good battle for us. . . . But now our lifeline, even across the broad oceans and especially in the entrances to the island, was endangered. . . . How much would the U-boat warfare reduce our imports and shipping? Would it ever reach the point where our lifeline would be destroyed? Here was no field for gestures or sensations; only the slow,

cold drawing of lines on charts, which showed potential strangulation."
And Brittany was the key to the Germans' success.

But Renault was wrong about something else. Nothing was going to
be easy, for the Gestapo had stepped up its surveillance of Brittany.

(3)

The drawbridge where Renault stood in February, 1941, gave him a
splendid view of the harbor at Brest. Directly below, tied with thick long
ropes to the side of a pier, two German submarines rocked gently back and
forth with the current. Farther along toward the harbor's entrance and
towering over the German destroyers anchored there were the battlements
of the fortress that had guarded the harbor since the thirteenth century.
And beyond the harbor's mouth, he could see the sail of a Breton fishing
boat, riding the waves to sea as its predecessors had done for hundreds
of years.

Renault continued along the drawbridge, walking toward the arsenal
at its end.

After leaving his family in Vannes, he had learned, early in January,
that his little son, Manuel, had died in Madrid of diphtheria. He had immediately rejoined Edith, but not even the birth of a new son, Michel,
had erased the pain of the loss. And, for a time, Renault had almost decided to stay in Spain, giving up his work for Free France. In February,
however, after learning that London would soon parachute him a radio
transmitter, he had found his spirits lifting again and he had set off to
Brittany to recruit a chief for his network there. A contact along the coast
had told him about a naval officer named Philippon, whom the Germans
had relegated to tending garden in the arsenal at Brest, but who, by merely
walking along this same drawbridge, would keep track of ship movements
in the harbor below.

As Renault reached the end of the drawbridge, a German policeman
with a shiny badge hanging from a chain about his neck, came out of the
arsenal gate and stopped him.

"*Papirzz,* please," the German said.

Renault produced his identity card from inside his tweed jacket, and
gave the man an anxious smile.

The German squinted at the card, then grunted, "*Gut.* You can go
on."

"Excuse me," said Renault, deferentially, "can you tell me if a Commandant Philippon is inside? I believe he works here."

"Commandant Philippon?" the guard said. "I expect he's in the garden."

"In the garden?" asked Renault.

"Yes, up there. You can't miss it."

Renault was able to wander at will through the naval arsenal. He found the garden and asked a German sailor if Philippon was there.

"You're out of luck," the sailor said. "He's just gone home."

Renault went off immediately in search of Philippon's apartment.

The naval officer who opened the door was startlingly handsome: the gold braid and buttons, the five stripes against the dark blue of his sleeve, his keen eyes, his neat dark hair, his perfectly chiseled face brought Gary Cooper to mind. Perhaps, Renault thought whimsically, instead of asking this man to spy, he should hire him to play the part of Christopher Columbus. But Philippon had invited him in to the living room, and was asking: "What can I do for you?"

"I'm trying to get information about the German base here in Brest," Renault said, "and I've been told you might help."

The keen eyes looked sharply at Renault. "Sit down, will you?" said Philippon.

They sat in armchairs at each side of a little window. Renault explained who he was and what he was doing. Philippon sat in silence for a moment.

"Yes," he said to Renault at last, "I've heard about you. But I haven't committed myself to working with you."

"Yes, I know," Renault responded, "and that is why I've come to ask you if you will."

Philippon stared out the window again. Then he spoke up.

"I can't give you an answer at once," he said, "I shall have to think about it. Come back and see me in a few days. Shall we say at the end of the week?"

As Renault stood up to leave, he noticed a plaque on the wall bearing the name *Ouessant*. Philippon had been second-in-command aboard the submarine *Ouessant*, Renault knew, a ship laid up for repairs in Brest when the Germans had arrived. It had not had time to escape. Its commander had ordered it scuttled.

"May I ask you a question?" asked Renault as he reached the door. "Yes?"

"If your submarine had been able to leave port in June last year, would you have gone to England?"

"I was not in command," Philippon answered.

"What about the commander?"

"I think that he would have gone," said Philippon, "at that time at any rate."

"At that time?"

Philippon's eyes looked sharp again: "Much has happened since," he snapped. He must be referring, Renault thought, to the British attack upon Mers-el-Kébir.

That Saturday afternoon, Renault knocked again at the door of the flat. Philippon led him into the living room.

"I must explain why I had to ask you to come back again," said Philippon.

Renault sat down, waiting for the officer to continue.

"You see," Philippon said, "there's some question of our having to take an oath of loyalty to Marshal Pétain, and I did not want to run the risk of having to break this oath in advance."

Renault nodded understandingly.

"I have been to see my commanding officer, Captain Courson," Philippon went on. "I asked him whether, if I were ever in a position to pass on information to the English, such an action would be against the oath to the Marshal. He answered that, if he were ever in such a position, he would not hesitate to do so. Consequently . . ."

Philippon's voice trailed off for a moment. He looked out at a distant gull, making a "V" with its wings. Then his handsome face turned back to Renault.

"Consequently," Philippon said, "I am ready to help you."

Renault shook his hand warmly, and after a few minutes of relaxed conversation over a glass of cider, set off for the inland town of Angers, where Philippon had recommended a young radio operator to him. The boy had been an operator aboard the *Ouessant*. His name was Bernard Anquetil.

(4)

By the early spring of 1941, the Gestapo was tightening its surveillance of Occupied France, especially in the areas where pockets of resistance had sprung up. In Brittany a tax collector who was also a poacher was visiting fellow Britons in his official capacity, and then leading them along secret paths through the woods to shoot at remote German outposts. In Normandy, aircraft factory workers would slice through vital rivets with acid, causing the planes to disintegrate in the air. And in Paris, a band

of students had marched in silence up the Champs-Elysées, each carrying
two fishing poles—in French, *"deux gaules"* —as symbols of their support
for General de Gaulle.

The results were inevitable: arrests, executions and an increase in the
number of Gestapo trench coats and gray fedoras quietly infiltrating the
regions around Brest, Rennes, Nantes, Caen, Rouen—and Angers.

Bernard Anquetil lived in Angers.

(5)

"Bernard Anquetil?"

"Oui, monsieur?"

A pair of Harold Lloyd glasses was staring at Renault. Behind them
was a timid-looking boy in his early twenties, with hollow cheeks and
blond hair plastered straight back from his forehead. This was Bernard
Anquetil, standing behind the counter of a radio repair shop in Angers
where Renault had found him on a rainy morning in the middle of March.

"I've come to see you on the introduction of the second-in-command
of the submarine *Ouessant*," Renault said. "Would you have lunch with
me?"

The boy's thin lips parted slightly: *"Oui, monsieur."*

He followed Renault through the shop door into the drizzle outside.

As they were finishing their carafe of wine in the restaurant, Renault
turned sharply to look at the street outside. He had been explaining his
mission to Bernard, showing the lad a letter of recommendation from
Philippon in Brest, and saying that he would soon need a radio operator
to relay his networks' data to England, but a sound from outside had interrupted his monologue. It was a rhythmic metallic clacking sound from
the pavement outside. A detachment of Germans was goose-stepping by.
The clacking grew louder and became intermixed with the hoarse gutteral
commands of the sergeants. The procession lasted for several minutes,
then it had marched out of sight, and Renault turned back to talk with
Bernard Anquetil.

The boy's thin face was gray with fright.

Renault gave him a reassuring smile, waiting until Bernard's cheeks
had returned to their normal pasty white.

Then Renault leaned forward and grasped Bernard's forearm. "Will
you be my radio operator?" Renault asked.

Bernard seemed to have lost control of his jaw. Finally, after a struggle, he stammed out, *"Oui, monsieur."*

"Are you sure?"

"*Oui, monsieur.*"

"All right, then," Renault said, "I can't use you right away. I've got people fixing up a transmitter on the other side of the Line, and I haven't decided yet where to install it here. When I need you, I'll let you know. Don't worry, Bernard. There shouldn't be much trouble. The Germans have no idea who you are."

As they skirted the puddles on the sidewalk going back to Bernard's shop, Renault felt elated. He prided himself on being a judge of men. Bernard would overcome his fear, Renault was certain, and perform important services for Free France.

(6)

But even though they did not yet know his exact identity, the Gestapo were waiting for the likes of Bernard Anquetil. They had covered northern France with converted ambulances and paneled trucks equipped inside with radio receivers and earphones and outside with revolving netlike antennae, designed to track the direction from which a clandestine radio signal was coming. A pair of such trucks would first pick up a forbidden radio signal, somewhere in or around a city, separate widely to learn its approximate location, and then, creeping slowly along the city's curbs, follow the signal until they could pinpoint the exact building from which it was coming.

These vans, of course, were at a disadvantage if the radio operator broadcast at irregular times and got off the air soon after he had started. But the Resistance networks in France learned such tactics only through experience, and in the spring of 1941 neither Bernard Anquetil nor Gilbert Renault had the necessary experience.

Chapter 17

(1)

GENERAL DE GAULLE, HOWEVER, DID HAVE EXPERIENCE—AT LEAST AS HE SAW IT—EXPERIENCE IN DUPLICITY, EXPERIENCE IN CONSPIRACY, EXPERIENCE IN BRITAIN'S TRYING TO "PUSH HER INTEREST AT THE expense" of Free France.

His list of complaints was long. Early in the summer of 1940, British officials had insisted on the right to censor Free France broadcasts over the B.B.C. Later that summer His Majesty's government had sought to enlist French refugees in England into the British military. And in January, 1941, without consulting de Gaulle, Scotland Yard had arrested Free France's Admiral Muselier on the grounds that he passed military secrets to the Vichy government. In every instance, as de Gaulle saw it, the British acted as if they were the lords and the Free French were the serfs, useful for doing dirty work but possessing no inherent rights of their own.

Each time, of course, de Gaulle had fought back: he had won the right to speak freely on the radio, he had thundered until the British allowed him first shot at recruiting the Frenchmen, and he had shown that the documents incriminating Admiral Muselier had been forged at Vichy's London consulate.

On each of these occasions, de Gaulle wrote, the matter was settled quickly, at "least in appearance. The rounding-off would be done at a friendly party, not without our partners attempting, at a venture, in the midst of the optimism arising from restored understanding, to obtain some advantage by surprise. Then relations would become as close as before;

the basis of things remaining, however, undetermined. Because, for Great Britain, there was no such thing as a case tried and done with."

Many around him, including Free Frenchmen themselves, thought de Gaulle was being paranoid, that the British were simply bunglers, inconsiderate, taking no time to think of others in their own quest for survival.

De Gaulle, however, saw darker motives in the corridors of Whitehall. In an interview with Félix Gouin, a journalist, he insisted that "the fight to the death [the British] are at present waging against the Reich aggravates that ruthless love of power which is the dominant characteristic of their race. That is, no doubt, what causes them to encroach on others' interests."

The General, wrote Gouin, "stopped for a few moments; his hands were shaking slightly, his expression brightened and from his lips fell those astonishing words which still ring in my ears . . . : 'You see,' he said, 'my duty is straightforward. Until the victory I am accountable for what makes France a great people and a great country. I will surrender none of those elements which go to make this greatness. And the weaker I become,'—he hammered the point home in a voice suddenly harsh—'the more intransigent will I be to defend our rights and make them respected. . . . What would have become of the fatherland,' he added, 'if Joan of Arc, Danton, Clemenceau had wanted to compromise?'"

The question to de Gaulle was critical. The British, he was convinced, would soon encroach once again upon his rights. He was sure that he knew which rights, and he was sure he knew just when.

(2)

There was good reason for de Gaulle's feeling of urgency: the grip of the enemy was closing fast around the oil of the Middle East.

In Libya, on February 20, 1941, for the first time, British and German armored cars had engaged in a brief skirmish; a few days later planes of the *Luftwaffe*, flying over the hump of Cyrenaica, had crippled the port of Benghazi; and on March 31, General Rommel had "sat high on the roof of his [armored car], dangling his legs through the open doorway," and watching his tanks advance into Marsa Brega, even farther along the coast toward Egypt.

In the Balkans, in March, the Germans had wooed and won a useful new ally, Bulgaria. Soon the *Panzers* began rumbling across a bridge on the Danube, and by the end of the month, the *Wehrmacht* and the *Luftwaffe* were poised in southern Bulgaria, ready to launch an attack against next-door Yugoslavia and Greece.

And in the French mandates of Syria and Lebanon, closer still to the oil wells in Iraq, German agents disguised as tourists and hunters were entering the region with Vichy's approval—Marshal Pétain had openly declared himself a collaborationist—and were preparing the ground for an outright German takeover.

The Allied forces around the Mediterranean were reeling. There seemed only one way to keep the pincers from snapping shut on the vital oil deposits, and that solution, de Gaulle felt, boded ill for the sovereign rights of Free France.

(3)

He began glaring out his defiance as never before.

"I remember very well the first time I met General de Gaulle," General Spears' wife, the novelist Mary Borden, wrote of these months, "and the curious discomfort I felt when he stalked into the room. It was almost like fear. It was certainly mingled with a painfully strong feeling of revulsion. He had brought Madame de Gaulle to dine with us. . . . A gentle, charming, slight, timid figure, I turned to her with relief, watching de Gaulle out of the corner of my eye, not wanting to look straight at him. I watched him through the evening. His face never showed the slightest change of expression as he talked. No flicker of interest lifted his hooded eyelids. I was fascinated, the novelist came into play. I began to study him.

"I believe pride is the basis of his character," she went on. "I think he felt the dishonor of France as few men can feel anything, and that he had literally taken on himself the national dishonor, as Christ according to the Christian faith took on himself the sins of the world. I think he was like a man during those days who had been skinned alive, and that the slightest contact with friendly, well-meaning people got him on the raw to such an extent that he wanted to bite, as a dog that has been run over will bite in its agony a would-be friend that comes to its rescue. The discomfort I felt in his presence was due, I am certain, to the boiling misery and hatred inside him.

"His one relief, in fact his one pleasure, was to hate. And he hated all the world, but most especially those who tried to be his friends. . . . To come to the British as a suppliant, with the disgrace of his nation burned on his forehead and in his heart, was intolerable. . . . The weaker his position became the more arrogant he became. The Prime Minister . . .

[was] using him, he would use them. He would wring out of them the arms and equipment he needed, but he wouldn't pretend to be grateful. He hated them for giving him what he had to have. One day he would pay them back. . . ."

Mary Borden had no love for General de Gaulle: but his sympathizers among the British were equally aghast. During his weekdays in England he lived at London's Connaught Hotel [he weekended with his family in a series of cottages far from the center of London] and one night invited General Spears and a few other Britishers to dine with him in his private sitting room. "As we sat round the gas fire after dinner," Spears said, "de Gaulle said suddenly, following a thought unperceived by the others, 'You know, I really am Joan of Arc.'"

And Harold Macmillan, later to be Prime Minister, said, simply, of de Gaulle in this period: "He was never rude by mistake."

(4)

The pincers were gripping still tighter on the oil in Iraq. One morning in mid-April, General Rommel was off by himself in Libya, lying on the ground as shells were exploding all around him. "I watched [him]," wrote his adjutant, "intently studying the ground ahead through his glasses. His firm mouth is tight lipped now; his prominent cheekbones stand out white. His cap is perched on the back of his head. 'Fort Pilastrino,' he mutters."

Rommel was looking, for the first time, at the British defenses by Tobruk, the great fortress on the Mediterranean coast the Allies had seized from the Italians. The hunter's urge, his adjutant thought, was taking possession of the General. "*Leutnant,*" Rommel commanded. "Orders to the *Panzers!* Attack those stone ruins ahead. . . !"

The Germans were sweeping down from the north as well. Early in April, after the Germans had already attacked Yugoslavia, the *Luftwaffe* launched a devastating bombing attack against the Greek port of Piraeus, outside Athens. And on April 24, the British Army, having fought unsuccessfully on Greece's behalf, began the second of its great wartime evacuations, this time not from Dunkirk in France but rather from the beaches of the Peloponnese in Greece.

And in Syria, General Henri Dentz, the Vichyist Commander-in-Chief, was approving the landing of a *Luftwaffe* squadron on an airfield near Damascus.

The more the pincers tightened, the more quickly the British wanted to act to save the oil; and the more quickly they wanted to act, the more vigilantly, and bitterly, did de Gaulle defend what he believed the rights of Free France.

(5)

He had long since developed his mode of attack. "Acting on a precedent perfected by practice," General Spears said, "General de Gaulle, when he had a really difficult controversial problem to settle with, say, a minister, would sail in looking like thunder. The less sure he was of his ground the more stormy he appeared. He would slam down his kepi as aggressively as a bull preparing to charge strikes the ground with his hooves, sit down looking furious and sway his head like a cobra. He would then unleash a stream of accusations that were extremely rude to the person or the department concerned and make remarks that were quite intolerable. The Englishman facing him would be intensely embarrassed, then grow angry, but the angrier he grew the more tongue-tied did he become. Whereupon, suddenly, de Gaulle would spring up, seize his cap and say, 'I will come to hear your answer at ten tomorrow morning,' and stalk out.

"At such time," Spears continued, "I have on occasion spent the evening with the British target of de Gaulle's wrath. Generally he did not enjoy his dinner, and was obviously thinking of all the things he would have liked to have said but had not, and I guessed that he probably woke in the night rehearsing the phrases with which he would blast the irascible Frenchman next morning.

"The next day came and so did ten o'clock, bringing de Gaulle to the same office where, to the bewilderment of the Englishman, he would be all smiles and politeness, positively exuding *bonhomie*. The Englishman was so relieved at not having to produce his carefully rehearsed remarks that there flowed from his lips a cataract of amiability, and he would immediately concede 50 percent of the General's demands of the previous evening, which was more than the General had reckoned on obtaining."

In this manner, de Gaulle had been able to bludgeon one concession after another from the British.

(6)

But Erwin Rommel was on the move. He had captured two crucial passes on the Libyan escarpment, just next to the Egyptian frontier, and had driven off a British counterattack in which the Allies had lost more than one hundred tanks. To his men he had become a hero, and whenever they saw him step from his dusty Volkswagen on a tour of inspection, they cheered. A legend was spreading across the desert and up to London, the legend of the brutally swift, ruthless, cunning and omnipresent "Desert Fox."

The reports from the eastern Mediterranean were equally grim. On May 20, 1941, the Germans attacked the island of Crete, to which the British had fled from Greece, and six days later had driven the Allies across the sea to Egypt.

The British promptly set in motion their last-ditch plan for the defense of the oil. The Free French took part in the campaign, too, but even as they did, de Gaulle warned that the British were simply using them, that when the campaign was over, the British would withhold the prize that was rightfully theirs.

(7)

The idea was to launch an invasion against Vichy-held Syria and Lebanon, lands that bordered on the oil-producing regions of Iraq and the Persian Gulf. General Sir Henry Maitland Wilson was to organize a three-pronged operation in Palestine, designed to capture Damascus and Beirut and, in so doing, block further German progress in the eastern Mediterranean.

De Gaulle had no quarrel with these objectives as such, but he suspected they masked a hidden and insidious British plot. After their liberation from Vichy, he had demanded, Syria and Lebanon should remain French—Free French. Gaullist control of these lands would symbolize Free France's emergence as the legitimate government of France. But if the British refused his demand, if London controlled the region after Free Frenchmen had given blood for victory, de Gaulle would look like a stooge, a hireling, a mercenary, a chump.

And what had caused de Gaulle in the weeks before the campaign to glare, thunder, pound on desks and twist his lips with more invective, was the fact that the British had given no clear promise to turn Syria and Lebanon over to Free France after the victory.

He had, of course, pounded and shouted and slammed down his kepi, but the one person de Gaulle could never intimidate was Winston Churchill, and the most concrete assurance the General received from the Prime Minister was a wire, on June 6, 1941, saying that "we have sought no special advantage in the French Empire and have no intention of exploiting the tragic position of France for our own gain."

And on the morning of June 8, as the Allied columns began to march across the reddish-brown sands of the Syrian desert, de Gaulle was still skeptical. Why had Churchill, he insisted on knowing, not given a point-blank promise of Free French control of the Levant?

Chapter 18

(1)

"YOU KNOW, OF COURSE, THAT WE HAVE VISITORS?"
THE HANDSOME COMMANDANT PHILIPPON WAS TALKING TO RENAULT
AGAIN IN BREST. RENAULT HAD BEEN BUSY SINCE THEIR LAST MEETING
three months before: he had moved his family back to Brittany (after
Manuel's death Edith had found Madrid unbearable), carried several packets of messages across the Line of Demarcation, and smuggled a radio
transmitter up to Bernard Anquetil. Never once had a German questioned
him, never once had anyone seemed to notice anything unusual about his
travels up and down the Atlantic coast of France. Everything had seemed
so easy. Even the work Philippon had been doing.

"By visitors," Renault asked, "do you mean the *Scharnhorst* and the
Gneisenau?" Renault had heard rumors that these battleships had returned
to Brest after a successful raid in the Atlantic where they had managed
to sink twenty-two British ships.

"Yes," Philippon responded in his precise way. "Would you like to
see them? I really think you must."

"I should indeed," said Renault.

"Then come with me."

The warehouses inside the harbor gate were bustling with Germans
who seemed to pay no attention to the two Frenchmen. Philippon led the
way along a quay from which sea gulls were diving and dipping for fish,
and took Renault into the great stone fortress that towered over the piers

of the harbor. When they had climbed to the battlements, Philippon stopped, and pointed.

"Do you see the ships?" he asked Renault.

"Where?"

"There, immediately below you."

Renault looked down from the fort. A series of broad wharves below him, each with a large warehouse in its middle and railroad tracks along either side, jutted out into the harbor. He saw several destroyers, cruisers and submarines. But nowhere did he see anything large enough to be the *Scharnhorst* or the *Gneisenau.*

"We're right above the docks of La Ninon," Philippon explained. "Do you see them now?"

Renault kept looking but he could still see no sign of the battleships.

"Look more closely," Philippon said, and he aligned Renault's shoulders with the spot toward which he had pointed.

Renault, suddenly, leaned forward.

"Yes, that's it!" exclaimed Philippon.

Renault was astounded. "The two warships," he wrote, "each at its dock were entirely covered with nets over which boughs were spread. We were barely a hundred yards away, and yet, from where we stood, one could have said that we were looking down on a great expanse of sand on which, here and there, grew sparse marine vegetation. The shape of the docks was camouflaged too. The whole thing resembled a natural continuation of the cliff."

"What do you think of *that?*" asked Philippon, almost proudly.

Renault shook his head in grudging admiration.

"These are splendid ships," Philippon went on. "They've both had to take refuge here on account of the same mechanical trouble. It's fortunate for our English friends, for they have a chance now to bottle them up here, whereas, on the open sea, they have practically no rivals."

"But," Philippon continued, "I understand they'll soon be fixed and out to sea. And I won't give much for the Atlantic convoys when they do."

A few mornings later, as Renault crossed a bridge over the Loire at Saumur, near Tours, he gave the side pocket of his tweed jacket a satisfied pat. The pocket was bulging with paper, a long folded strip of paper on which he had diagramed the harbor at Brest and the location of the *Scharnhorst* and *Gneisenau.* In a few more days he would cross the Demarcation Line to pass the map to England through Jacques Pigeonneau in Madrid. At the moment, however, he began fingering another bundle of papers, this one tucked away in his inside pocket—a coded dispatch for Bernard Anquetil, who now lived and broadcast for Free France in his uncle's attic here in Saumur.

Renault's walk was bouncy. He had had no trouble getting the map out of Brest or gathering reports from his agents along the coast. Now, if he could only calm Bernard's fears, if he could only persuade the boy that, to keep up with the ever-growing number of dispatches, he should broadcast a little longer each day.

As Renault turned off the bridge toward Bernard's attic, Renault glanced briefly at the château that dominated the city, failing to realize the building's significance.

(2)

The blue-gray pointed turrets, the huge towers, the gray walls with narrow slits for windows, and the thick solid stone perimeter of the château shot up steeply into the sky. Some of the nearby châteaux were lovelier—water lilies in the River Indre gave an air of tranquil luxury to Azay-le-Rideau; some of the châteaux were more stirring to the imagination—Chinon had inspired the retelling of the legend of Sleeping Beauty; some of the châteaux were more graceful—Chenonceaux was built atop a series of arches over the River Cher. But none of the Loire châteaux was grimmer, more menacing, more dominating of its countryside than the cloud-scraping Château de Saumur.

In this château, unknown to Renault, the Gestapo had recently established its Saumur headquarters.

And in an attic in one of the insignificant-looking houses below the château, a gray stone house with a sloping dark slate roof, Bernard Anquetil lived, broadcast and looked more frightened than ever behind the black rims of his glasses. For he had seen Gestapo in the restaurant around the corner where he took lunch, and he had seen their trucks a few times on the bridge, drawing steadily closer as if they had picked up his beam.

But the greater the number of dispatches that came in from Renault, the tighter Bernard's thin lips pressed together as he forced himself to stay on the air.

(3)

A battered old Peugeot was sputtering along Route 136, early in June, 1941. Its driver, a Dr. Pailloux, a wizened old Gaullist dying from cancer of the throat but with still enough fight left to defy the Germans, was taking Renault, as he had done several times before, to the Lidoire, where Renault would cross the Demarcation Line. It was late in the afternoon and Renault was drowsily watching a farmer in his field when Dr. Pailloux's veiny hands jerked sharply on the steering wheel. Renault looked ahead toward the road. A man was pedaling his bicycle just in front of them — a man in the uniform of a German customs guard.

Almost imperceptibly Dr. Pailloux pushed his accelerator down, speeded up, crossed into the left lane to pass the bicycle and then, when the car was far ahead of the German and well out of his sight, stomped on the brakes beside a stone monument and told Renault to get out.

On Renault's previous trips across the Line, Dr. Pailloux's routine had been, Renault explained, "to turn down a lane beside the monument, pass the railway, put me down, and turn around. I would then walk back, looking as if I belonged to the place, see that all was clear on the main road, which was much frequented by the German customs men on their way from Castillon to the frontier post, and, if I saw no one who aroused my suspicions, cross over and get to Rambaud's [the farm in Occupied France that was Renault's last stop before crossing the Lidoire] as quickly as possible." This time, however, Dr. Pailloux had changed the pattern.

"Aren't you going to go down the lane, as you usually do?" Renault asked, puzzled.

"There's no need," Pailloux rasped. "You can see there's no one on the road."

"But we've just passed a German customs man on a bicycle," Renault persisted.

"He's too far away to see us," the old man snapped. "Please get out."

Renault could see that the old doctor was frightened, so he got out, waved good-bye and sauntered off for the Rambaud farm. As he walked along, he gave the map in his tweed jacket pocket another satisfied pat, thinking the doctor had been overly cautious.

The late afternoon sun was pleasantly warm and as Renault crossed a vineyard to the Rambaud farmhouse, he took no trouble to check back along the dirt road he had followed from the main highway. A thickset, middle-aged peasant, Rambaud, welcomed him into the house. As Renault walked into the kitchen, he could see that Rambaud's wife and old mother were just sitting down to supper. "You must eat with us," Rambaud said. "The sun's still up and you won't be able to cross the stream for another hour or so." The two women also, the solid and smiling wife and the parchment-skinned mother, gestured Renault into a chair. He sat down at the table, opposite the door, open because of the heat. He sipped from a glass of Bordeaux, leaned back in his chair and began to feel sleepy again.

He had forgotten all about the man on the bicycle, the German customs guard.

Then he heard the screech of bicycle brakes. Renault looked out the door. The German guard was walking down the path, directly toward Renault.

(4)

Far to the north that same evening, in Saumur, Gestapo radio vans had several times picked up a radio signal. They had known it to be a clandestine broadcast, because it was in code, but it had always gone off the air before they could pin down its location. This evening, however, it had been on the air longer than usual, and the vans had narrowed down a sector of a few blocks from which it was coming. Then the radio had gone silent again.

And in an attic in Saumur, the skinny, gray-faced Bernard Anquetil leaned back from his transmitter in relief. If only these piles of dispatches from Renault would stop growing! If only he could get off the air sooner these days! It was so nerve-wracking to have to stay on the air this long. Could he keep it up? Would he be able to do it if the stack of coded messages grew any higher? Would he have the courage to do his duty?

Bernard Anquetil was beginning to have his doubts.

(5)

The eyes of the German customs guard traveled up and down Renault's tweed jacket. Something about it must have aroused the German's suspicions.

"Your *papirzz!*" he demanded of Renault.

"But why?" asked Renault.

The German gave no answer, merely repeating, peremptorily, "Your *papirzz!*"

Renault extracted his forged identification card from inside his tweed jacket and handed it over to the guard. The German squinted at it, then commanded, pompously, "Follow me!"

As they reached the highway the German barked at Renault to walk in the middle of the road. The German was on Renault's left, pushing the bicycle with one hand and holding the identification card in the other. They came to a crossroad.

"Turn to the left," the guard ordered.

"But where are you taking me?"

"No questions! Keep moving!"

After the German had led the way under a railway bridge, Renault realized where they were heading. Outside the nearby village of Capitourlan was a border post where, he had heard it rumored, German officials searched suspects. Almost without his realizing it his hand felt for the map in his pocket. Then, in a flash, he saw how he might escape.

On the right side of the road was a railroad embankment, five or six yards high, and just beyond that, he calculated, lay the neutral strip between the two zones of France. Renault thought fast. If he could lag behind by a step or two he could jump the German from behind, throw him down and scramble up and over the embankment to disappear into the dusk.

Renault grinned broadly: it would be just like in the movies. He hadn't gone into the film business for nothing!

He slowed his pace; the German with the bicycle began to move ahead. Renault lingered behind still further; the customs man moved two steps in front. Renault edged over to his left. He bent his knees, very slightly. He crouched to begin his jump. Now! he thought—and then he stopped. By chance, another German had pedaled up behind them on his bicycle.

(6)

Bernard Anquetil had harbored no such illusions. He knew that if he continued broadcasting he would be caught.

A tug-of-war raged behind those Harold Lloyd glasses and those pale blue eyes, a moral battle, a struggle between fear and conscience. Should he stop transmitting, and save his skin, or should he keep on transmitting and save his honor? His dilemma grew sharper every day. As the packets of data from Renault's networks got thicker, the time required to relay them to England grew longer and the danger of detection became graver. After several weeks of this, Bernard could stand the turmoil no longer.

For several nights late in the month of June, before the curfew, the citizens of Saumur could see his ghostly figure, now on the bridge, now near the château, now in the restaurant around the corner from his uncle's house, always alone, always intense, always seeming at war with himself. Then, on the night of June 30, he seemed to have vanished.

Bernard Anquetil had gone back to his radio.

(7)

His mentor, Renault, had never experienced this kind of anguish. His confidence remained high even as he was shoved through the door of the guard house outside Capitourlan: he still believed he could outwit these oafish Germans.

A German officer was seated behind a wooden table inside. The guard who had come to the Rambaud cottage talked vehemently to the officer, pointing several times toward Renault's tweed jacket. Renault pressed his hand against the pocket of his jacket to keep the map of Brest from sticking out.

The officer looked at Renault's identification card, and then asked, in halting French, "What were you doing at the farm?"

"I was there on my business," Renault said.

"Your business?"

"Yes. I am in insurance."

"Insurance?"

The German was frowning in puzzlement and Renault saw his chance to direct the man's attention away from the map in his pocket. He leaned forward, opened a pocket dictionary lying on the table and flipped the pages until he had come to "insurance."

"Ah, here we are," Renault said helpfully, "'insurance,' see it?"

"*Ach, ja.*"

Renault pointed to "insurance inspector" on his identification card. The officer compared those words with the one in his dictionary.

"I work for the Eagle Star Insurance Company," Renault said, with hardly a pause. "It is in Zurich. Do you know it? Zurich?"

"*Ach, ja.*"

The officer was beginning to study him, however, and Renault immediately tried another diversion. If he could just keep talking, he was sure, he could escape from this mess.

He took the German officer by the arm and led him to a large map of France, pinned to the wall behind the table.

"You see," Renault said, "I'm from Vannes."

He put his finger on the map; the German bent forward and squinted.

"*Ach, ja,*" he said, "Van-nes."

"Yes," Renault put in fast, "Van-nes, Vannes. You see on my identification card that it was issued at Vannes. Good. I am an insurance inspector for the whole Atlantic coast from Brest to Bayonne. I am always on the go visiting my clients—Brest, Quimper, Lorient, Vannes, Nantes, La Roche-sur-Yon, Bordeaux, Bayonne. All this side of the Line, you see. I call on the agencies and their clients. I verify their policies. I listen to their complaints. This evening I was with one of our clients, Monsieur Rambaud. I had to see him about his fire insurance. I went to see him in the car of another of my clients. I had just finished my business and was sitting down at the table with the family because, as you know, there's not much in the restaurants these days, when your man came and took me away. I can't imagine why. I have to leave for Bordeaux this evening."

The German looked dumbfounded at this flood of words. Bewildered, he gave back Renault's identification card and said, "*Gut*, you may go."

With that Renault was off to Madrid with his map for the British, relieved but amused that in the confusion he had created the German had even forgotten to search his clothing.

And in early July, after he had returned to Occupied France, he learned the good news: in a bombing raid over Brest, the R.A.F. had severely damaged both the *Scharnhorst* and the *Gneisenau*.

In early July, however, he also learned the bad news: Bernard Anquetil was under arrest.

(8)

When the Gestapo entered Bernard's attic, Renault heard, the boy had apparently fought back as hard as his undernourished body would allow and had actually broken loose on the sidewalk below. A bullet in the leg, however, had cut him down. The Gestapo had fallen on him where he lay, beating him into senselessness, and as they carried him back to their car, one of his pale blue eyes dangled forth from his face.

An icy feeling took hold of Renault as he heard the story. "I could see [Bernard] walking beside me, in the rain at Angers," he wrote, "as I gave him instructions on what he had to do. I knew that he was frightened then, but I knew, too, that he would carry on to the end. Why on earth did I send him those last messages?"

But Renault's icy feeling arose from more than guilt and surprise. Bernard, he heard, was still alive in a cell of the Château de Saumur — and from him the Gestapo torturers were trying to learn the identities of Renault, his family, and all his networks.

Renault at last had learned the true nature of the Gestapo.

Chapter 19

(1)

L ATER THAT SAME MONTH, IN JULY, 1941, AT THE OPPOSITE END OF THE MEDITERRANEAN, GENERAL DE GAULLE WAS ENCOUNTERING AT FIRSTHAND WHAT HE CALLED THE "PERFIDIES" OF INTERNATIONAL DIPLOMACY.

On June 8, the three Allied columns under the overall command of General Maitland Wilson had left their bases in Palestine and invaded Syria and Lebanon. An Australian column, having swung up through Iraq to strike at the citadel at Aleppo, had, for some reason, expected a friendly reception at the border and marched up to the Syrian frontier post wearing slouch hats instead of helmets. Blasts of machine-gun fire cut into their ranks and a hard-fought battle began to rage below the slopes of Mount Hermon, still capped with snow. A second column, Free French, under General Legentilhomme, headed for Damascus—and straight into a sandstorm that "was blowing like a wind out of a furnace. Clouds of yellow dust were rolling down the [road] to envelop . . . the few starved trees and the straggling troops in billows of yellow fog." Then, as soon as the storm subsided, a Vichy fighter plane dived from across the mountains to strafe the column. The Free Frenchmen scrambled into the roadside ditches and in the process General Legentilhomme broke his left arm. Later, as a nurse was splinting his arm, he gave a sour cackling laugh and said, "One must be a little mad to be Free French." And, after a week of steady advances, the third column, mainly Australian and Scottish, had moved up the mountainous coastal road of Lebanon to the Litani River beyond Tyre. A Scottish commando unit set out to sea to land behind the

Vichyist position along the shore, but when it waded up onto the beach it discovered that the enemy was waiting for it behind a row of seventy-five cannons. A murderous burst of fire swept along the seashore and soon the beach was littered with the crumpled corpses of young Scots soldiers.

By the end of that first week the Allies had incurred hundreds of casualties and their attack, for the moment, seemed to have stalled.

(2)

General de Gaulle, however, was concerned not only with *whether* the Allies would win but also with *how* they would win. The day after the opening of the Syrian invasion, on June 9, he had boarded a plane in Jerusalem (he had flown there from London through Brazzaville to be with his men at the battle's beginning) and took off for British headquarters in Cairo. As his plane rose from Jerusalem, tiny white villages appeared on the ridges below, and the dark-green orange groves, contrasting with the drabness of the Palestinian desert, stretched down to the blue of the Mediterranean.

De Gaulle, however, an aide noted, paid no attention to the beauties of nature below the plane's wing: his mind was on the future, pondering the fate of Syria and Lebanon, wondering if, after their liberation, the British would seize these lands from Free France and place them under London's control.

(3)

That liberation itself, however, was scarcely complete. The three Allied columns had, to be sure, regrouped and started their drive again. The northernmost unit, the Australians, broke through the Aleppo; the middle detachment, the Free Frenchmen under Legentilhomme, seized Kinetra, a town well down the road to Damascus; and the southern units, Australian and Scots, moved up the coast to Sidon, where the only enemy soldiers they encountered were two dead Senegalese lying jumbled in the gateway of the town.

But Vichy was not yet ready to quit. General Dentz, the Commander-in-Chief for Syria and Lebanon, announced from Beirut that if his troops failed to fight back against the Allied invader, the Nazis would take reprisals against their kinsmen in German prisoner-of-war camps. And Dentz was getting help. Guns and food were coming into Syria from Crete, planes bearing the black crosses of the *Luftwaffe* were strafing the conquerers at Aleppo, and on June 16, a force of *Junkers* bombed the small British fleet that was shelling the Vichy coastal batteries.

Behind the Allied lines near Damascus, dust-covered ambulances were crowding wounded Free Frenchmen into a schoolhouse that was doing duty as a clinic. "When I call to mind," a British nurse wrote later, "those suffocating, fly-infested schoolrooms smelling of blood and gangrene and sweat and disinfectant, the beds crowded so close together that stretcher bearers could pass in and out only with the greatest difficulty, I feel again, not the physical suffering of the men's mangled bodies—that I was used to, it was an old story—but the festering pain of their minds. And as they tossed and writhed in their beds, as they raved in delirium, I knew that one thought tormented many, namely, that this had been done to them by their own people."

By the end of the second week of the Allied invasion, the outcome was still uncertain. From Jerusalem, General Wilson had his troops pause to await supplies and reinforcements: they needed more of everything—guns, men, airplanes, ammunition. Then, at the end of June, 1941, he ordered the final push through Syria and Lebanon.

(4)

But General de Gaulle was elsewhere, fuming and thundering into the offices of British officials in Cairo. One such Britisher, Oliver Lyttleton, a member of Churchill's War Cabinet, has described one of these sessions with de Gaulle. The General "was white with suppressed passion," Lyttleton remembered. "He strode into my room with his staff, greeted me frigidly, and launched the most violent complaint about the British attitude [toward] 'the French territory of Syria and the Lebanon.'"

These days in Cairo were infuriating to de Gaulle—and to the British as well. The more he tried to pin them down to concrete promises about Syria and Lebanon, the more evasive they seemed to become; the more evasive they appeared, the angrier he grew; and the angrier he became, the more exasperated and standoffish the British appeared.

Then, late in June, the question became critical for de Gaulle. According to all reports from the front the Syrian-Lebanese campaign was reaching its climax.

(5)

The Australian column had pushed past Aleppo, new fighter planes were protecting the British offshore fleet, and the Free French column was approaching Damascus.

The British journalist Alan Moorehead rode up to observe the capture of Damascus. From Rosh Pinna, in Palestine, he wrote, "You turned down upon the lower road past the Sea of Galilee and Tiberias and Nazareth . . . and a succession of villages too Biblical to be real. Military traffic was on the road everywhere. . . . We drove hard . . . up out of Palestine and across that arid black lava country where the Arabs were threshing a brilliant yellow harvest . . . and on up the road where Legentilhomme had been wounded. . . ." Then he reached palm groves and orchards around Damascus. "[This] garden town on the edge of the desert was so beautiful that Mohammed had refused to enter it lest he anticipate heaven. This was the burial place of Saladin and John the Baptist . . . the oldest inhabited city in the world, and probably the most ancient hotbed of intrigue in the Middle East."

The Allied force hit Damascus in a three-way thrust. The Free French cavalry pounded onto its dusty streets from the east; Legentilhomme, despite his broken arm, marched up the main road from the south; and a detachment of Indians and Australians, attached to Legentilhomme, fought their way into Mezze, a suburb lying on the heights to the west of the city.

This time the Allies met with success: Damascus fell quickly beneath their blows. Beirut, too, soon collapsed, and as the Allied column on the coast reached its outskirts, Lebanese girls ran along the streets beside the tanks, waving hastily made flags that bore the Cross of Lorraine.

The fight for the Levant was over. Free France had at last won a victory in the field. But de Gaulle feared that it was about to lose one at the conference table.

(6)

He had, to be sure, extracted certain promises from the British. The Armistice, he had demanded, must provide for "honorable treatment for all the [Vichyist] military and all the officials" in the Levant, allow all "military and officials [in Syria and Lebanon] who are willing to serve with the Allies" to join Free France, and guarantee "the rights and interests of France in the Levant." De Gaulle had also insisted that a Free French representative, General Catroux, be allowed fully "to participate in the negotiations." And the British had agreed to each of these points.

But would they live up to their word? As the day of the talks approached, de Gaulle tells us, he began to suffer the gravest of doubts.

(7)

The conference began on July 12 around a table in the British officers' mess at St. John of Acre, a coastal Palestinian town once conquered by Richard the Lion-Hearted. General Wilson sat alone on one side of the table; General Catroux of Free France and General de Verdilhac, the Vichy delegate, sat by the opposite side. Wilson started by declaring that he had an announcement to make.

General Catroux, leathery and sad eyed, studied the olive trees outside that ran down to the shore, and could hear the lapping of the waves against the beach. He was gentler, less suspicious than de Gaulle. But even Catroux was worried: what did this Wilson have in mind?

As Wilson began, his pistol strap jiggled up and down with his magnificent paunch. He was all soldier—later in the war, on Capri, he would sponsor a club "for colonels and generals only"—and he had no use for time-wasting frills like diplomacy and lengthy negotiations. He wanted to get on with the war. He looked over at the mournful-eyed Catroux, and his great voice boomed out decisively.

He wished to thank the Free French for their contribution to the victory in Syria and Lebanon, and of course he would be delighted to have Catroux sit in as an observer. But the British were in charge here, they had paid for the war, and it was they alone who would deal with Vichy. Catroux could have no direct part in the talks.

Two nights later, on Bastille Day, 1941, the rest of the news reached de Gaulle in Cairo. Of the three substantive promises the British had made, not one had appeared in the terms of the Armistice.

And, in the weeks that followed, de Gaulle received an even more grievous insult. Only a fifth of the twenty-five thousand Vichy troops in the Levant joined Free France. The others, some of whom steamed from Beirut to the accompaniment of a British military band, wanted nothing to do with General de Gaulle.

(8)

At Dakar Free France had fought, made mistakes and lost, but in Syria and Lebanon, it had fought, and won and *then* lost. De Gaulle felt betrayed. The British had used him, he was convinced, allowed hundreds

of Free French to die on the Syrian desert, then cast him aside, contemptuously, giving him no role in running the Levant. Once again de Gaulle
heard the chortles of Radio Vichy: he was a fool, a hireling of the enemy,
a charlatan who claimed to represent France but who had done nothing
more than go to war against his own Army.

What could he do? General de Gaulle saw only one way to resurrect
the cause: From now on he and Free France would have to go it alone,
risk martyring themselves for the grandeur of France, and prove their
steadfastness against the most fearsome enemy of all, Erwin Rommel, in
what the "companions" to this day remember as the "hell of Bir Hakeim."

PART FOUR
Confrontation with the Reich

Chapter 20

(1)

A YOUNG MESSENGER FROM THE RADIO ROOM OF CARLTON GARDENS WALKED PAST THE DOOR OF DE GAULLE'S OFFICE ON THE MORNING OF MAY 27, 1942, CROSSED THE ORIENTAL CARPET THAT COVERED MOST of the spacious floor, reached the front edge of the broad mahogany desk, saluted and handed across a message typed out on a flimsy sheet of nearly transparent white paper. The boy stood at attention, awaiting the General's reaction to the message, nervous in the presence of his awesome leader.

De Gaulle had changed since the previous year's campaign in Syria. He had aged considerably. His face was waxy, his waistline had spread, and deep furrows ran down from the corners of his mouth. But that, given his eighteen-hour days and the pressures of the war, seemed natural. What surprised the people around him was the change in his manner.

He had always been remote and brooding, but each of the crises he had faced, the fall of France, the failure at Dakar, the bad relations with the British over Syria and Lebanon, had sharpened and intensified these traits. No longer did he share jokes with his men, no longer did he inquire about their families, no longer did he storm as he once had at tongue-tied British officials. He seemed to have shrunk—and grown—into a symbol. He made few public appearances now and when he did, dressed in

his crisp uniform and white gloves, and wearing on his left breast no decorations except a small Cross of Lorraine, it was only behind a podium
and only in the presence of the tricolor of France. His eyes revealed nothing of the thoughts within, and whenever, in conversation, he digressed
from the business at hand, it was solely to discuss the greatness of France,
past and future. His listeners frequently left his office feeling that he was
both composing and acting out the next chapter of that Gallic saga. Whatever he said seemed memorized, as if he were acting out a part. The private de Gaulle, Charles, had vanished, and the public de Gaulle, the General, invariably spoke in the third person, lacked flesh and blood and even
bodily functions. General de Gaulle was an abstraction, France was an
abstraction, and General de Gaulle *was* France. He struck many as having
lost touch with reality.

Reality, however, was closing around him fast, and as the messenger
watched the General's eyes move heavily down the typed lines on the
flimsy paper, he wondered how de Gaulle would respond. The information on the paper was of the greatest significance for the future of Free
France. Everything for which de Gaulle had worked and struggled during
the last two years, the creation of an alternative-in-exile to the Vichy government, the prestige of Free France and his men in the field, and his own
reputation as the symbol of the honor of France, everything now was at
stake. This time, surely, the messenger thought, General de Gaulle had
to show some flicker of human interest.

The young man was surprised. De Gaulle handed the paper back,
courteously, and thanked the messenger in a correct, precise voice, but
nothing had changed the heaviness of his gaze and his face still looked
clammy, waxen and lacking in all earthly compassion.

Word spread quickly through the offices and corridors of Carlton
Gardens. Heads shook in bewilderment, and a few brave souls wondered
aloud if the General were mad — or was it, simply, that, head in the clouds,
he no longer cared?

For, the message had said, thirty-six hundred Free Frenchmen, alone,
were at that moment looking out from the Libyan outpost at Bir Hakeim,
watching and waiting as the tower of dust that was Rommel's *Afrika
Korps* rumbled directly toward their positions. If they stood fast, they
would become heroes and recapture the honor France had lost in 1940;
if they fled or surrendered, they would be sneered at as cowards, no better
than the men of Vichy France. The fate of Free France — and the lives
of the men — stood in the balance.

Yet General de Gaulle had failed to display the slightest sign of emotion.

(2)

The Free French had nearly missed this chance to prove themselves, for Bir Hakeim was part of the British-controlled Gazala Line in Libya, and by the spring of 1942, London was refusing to have any more to do with the arrogant and troublemaking leader of Free France. De Gaulle, indeed, had invited such treatment. Regardless of why Britain had kept control of Syria and Lebanon—whether, as de Gaulle claimed, she had designs on the French Empire, or whether, as London insisted, British troops were simply better equipped than the Free French to defend the region against Axis invasion—the results of the British action had been devastating to de Gaulle, a blow to his pride and, in his words, "an intolerable attack upon the rights of Free France." And so de Gaulle had fought back, as only de Gaulle could.

His kepi had crashed down upon British desks from Cairo to London, his narrow head with its plastered-down black hair had swayed rapidly back and forth, and his pouting mouth had puffed into a circle of scorn to denounce both the character and the motives and the morals of the officials facing him from behind their desks. One such Britisher, Oliver Lyttleton, had been convinced that when de Gaulle arose in the morning "he said to himself, 'France is dishonoured. Where and when am I going to be insulted today?'" And at one point Winston Churchill had removed the wet chewed cigar from his mouth to bellow at the General: "My God, you sound as if you think you are France herself!"

"If I am not France," de Gaulle had retorted, "why are you talking to me?"

In the short run such tactics had worked because by the late summer of 1941, the British government, throwing up its hands in exasperation, had recognized Free France's control over Syria and Lebanon. In the long run, however, these tactics had been self-defeating. The British disliked being bullied, they resented being called inept and disloyal, and they had resolved to freeze the General out of their future military operations.

De Gaulle had battled back: he was determined that Free France prove its worth against Germans. Early in the autumn of 1941, he had started again to make the rounds of British offices, demanding this time that the Free French forces be given a part to play in the coming contests with Rommel on the Libyan desert. General Ismay, Churchill's Chief-of-Staff, had refused, explaining that the Free French Army was too dispersed, too poorly trained, too cheaply equipped to be of any use. De Gaulle had tried again in November. The British had offered this time to use the Free French but only if their tank, artillery and infantry bat-

talions were absorbed into the larger British units. De Gaulle had refused
to accept this condition: he had feared that if the Free French were under
British command they would lose their distinct identity. He had tried
once more in December, but now he had played politics, leaking hints
that if the British refused his help he would send his troops to fight against
the Germans on the Russian front. The British had given in immediately,
authorizing the Free French General Pierre-Marie Koenig to command
an all-French detachment of thirty-six hundred men at Bir Hakeim, an
isolated outpost at the exposed end of the Gazala Line. Koenig's job there
would be to await the expected onslaught from General Rommel and to
tie him down long enough for the Allied forces farther up the Gazala Line
to regroup and prepare their counterattack.

No sooner had Free France won the right to fight in Libya, however,
than another problem arose: The Free French were no longer in a mood
to fight.

(3)

The rot of discouragement had afflicted Free France. Intrigues and
conspiracies were buzzing behind closed doors in Carlton Gardens, Admiral Muselier and a number of other French in London were rebelling
openly against what they called de Gaulle's authoritarian character, the
troops in Africa were spending more time drinking than drilling, and
the men in Syria and Lebanon, seeing new equipment from America distributed first to the British units and only at the end—if there was any
left to distribute—to their own detachments, so that they lacked enough
equipment even for training, were resorting to grumbling and looting
and frequenting brothels. The Syrian campaign had wrecked their morale. Partly because they had had to fight fellow Frenchmen and partly
because humiliation and discrimination had followed their victory there,
the Free French in the Levant were losing their stomach for warfare. Free
France was becoming apathetic.

De Gaulle took harsh steps to chop away this rot. He summarily fired
Muselier, he ordered Colonel Leclerc to get the men out of Chad to harass
outposts in Libya, and he bludgeoned and thundered and bullied until
the British allowed the French in the Levant to have their share of arms
and equipment.

But he needed more than intransigence to raise the morale of Free
France. He had to be bold: "The confidence and enthusiasm of others,"
he wrote, ". . . are due only to leaders who show their worth in action,

face difficulties and overcome them, stake their all upon the throw." He had to be unflinching: only thus could he, he believed, draw "to himself the hopes and wills of everyone as the magnet draws iron." He had to be aloof: "there can be no authority," he stated, "without prestige, nor prestige unless he keeps his distance." So it was that he had asked his men to risk their lives at Bir Hakeim, that he refused to exhibit the slightest trace of worry, that he grew as stony and forbidding as a fortress on a distant hill.

So it was that he tried to remake Free France in his own image.

One Free Frenchman, the novelist Romain Gary, has told how this worked. The troops in Africa, during one of the General's tours of inspection there, had prepared for his amusement a naughty revue in the best manner of the Paris burlesque, but as de Gaulle sat stiffly in his front-row chair, his arms crossed and his kepi resting across his knee, he failed, from the opening notes to the climactic chorus, to laugh, budge, twitch, squirm or even frown. "I do seem to remember," wrote Gary, "one fleeting moment when I was doing a lot of high kicking, dancing the can-can, while a fellow actor screamed, as the part demanded, *'Je suis cocu'*—I do seem to remember that I just caught, out of the corner of my eye, a very slight quiver of the moustache on the face of the leader of Free France. But perhaps I only imagined it. There he sat, very erect, with his arms crossed and looked at us with a sort of merciless concentration." And although the two hundred men in the audience behind the General had roared raucously at the dress rehearsal the night before, they now sat, like their leader, rigid and silent, neither laughing nor daring to smile. "Let those who maintain," Gary concluded, "that General de Gaulle is incapable of making contact with crowds or of communicating his feelings think this over."

This went on for several months and then, early in March, 1942, General de Gaulle felt his men were once more ready to fight. He ordered them to ship out immediately for the camp at Bir Hakeim.

(4)

They embarked from every point of Free France's far-flung domains: from the carpeted offices in Carlton Gardens and the drizzling fields of Aldershot, outside London; from the steamy bases in tropical Africa (at this same time, Leclerc was launching another expedition from Chad against the Libyan outposts) and the repair shops and recreation centers in the Levant. They were an odd mixture of detachments and men: the

2nd and 3rd Battalions of the Foreign Legion under the command of Lieutenant-Colonel Amilakvari, a Georgian; the 2nd *Bataillon de Marche de
l'Oubanghi Chari*, from Africa, under a Lieutenant Colonel de Roux; the
Bataillon du Pacifique—South Sea Islanders who had rallied to de Gaulle—
under Lieutenant Colonel de Broche; colonial infantrymen from the *In-
fanterie de la Marine*, under Major Savey; artillerymen of the *Fusilier-
Marins* under Lieutenant Commander Amyot d'Inville; Captain Lequesne's
22nd North African Company and Captain Jacquin's 2nd Anti-Tank Company. A medical team from Britain went along; so did sappers and signals
specialists, a fashion photographer from Paris, a Major Savet from Damascus who once had been a monk, and Claude Renault, who, two years
before, had escaped to England with his brother, Gilbert. De Gaulle stayed
behind in London to keep an eye on the British, and General Pierre-Marie
Koenig, tall, effervescent, hook nosed, and one of de Gaulle's earliest recruits, was in overall charge of the defenders at Bir Hakeim, the elite of
the Free French forces.

They gathered first in Cairo, in mid-March, 1942, and, after ogling
the belly dancers in cabarets near the Pont des Anglais, started out by
truck, train and boat for the sparkling harbor and gleaming white walls
of Tobruk. From there they traveled up the five-hundred foot coastal
escarpment and onto the gravel-strewn plateau where a minefield stretched
thirty-five miles southward across the Libyan desert to form the Gazala
Line. Inside the minefield lay a series of isolated forts, each surrounded
with mines and barbed wire, equipped with guns that faced outwards
in every direction, and supplied with enough water, food and ammunition
to withstand a fortnight's seige. The idea was that while the German
tanks, roaring out of Rommel's camps to the west, could surround or
bypass these forts at will, they would not be able to proceed far toward
Egypt or even Tobruk lest British tanks sally forth from the forts and
strike at the Germans' flanks. As the Free French units rode from Tobruk
along narrow lanes cut through the minefield, they passed through the
box called Knightsbridge, manned by English Guardsmen, through El
Adem, held by an Indian brigade, through the Cauldron, defended by
South Africans and Englishmen, and finally, they reached the bottom—
and most exposed—end of the Gazala Line where the fort called Bir Hakeim
was built around a white rectangular fort and two dried-up cisterns that
the French immediately nicknamed "the Mammaries." As they looked
around their new home their mouths fell agape with surprise and dismay.

Bir Hakeim sat atop an undulation in the desert, and a low, scarcely
visible ridge ran along the southern edge of the base. The bleached gravel
and the flat rocks along the ground offered no defensive cover for the

scrubby bushes, and camel thorns never rose more than two feet in the air. The desert cooked for fourteen hours a day—one Frenchman broke and fried an egg on the roof of his armored car—then turned frigid after the sudden blackness of night. Almost every afternoon, just before the evening meal, the sandstorms came, progressing slowly, tall and tawny, solid as a wall, and then making all movement impossible save huddling under blankets and spitting out sand from between one's teeth.

This was the middle of March, and for the next two months, General Koenig's men worked feverishly, partly to protect themselves against Rommel's expected assault and partly to relieve the dreadful monotony of Bir Hakeim. They crisscrossed the base with slit trenches, dug holes for their tents, carved out wider holes, ten feet square, for the hospital tents, and hollowed out still more holes so the ambulances could park with their noses down, out of reach of the sandstorms. They cleaned, checked, recleaned, rechecked, their handguns and their ammunition, then spent innumerable days going over the anti-tank weapons, the anti-aircraft and Bofors guns, the machine guns, tanks and trucks, the armored half-tracks, the ambulances and the jeeps. Occasionally they picked up the German radio station in Belgrade that broadcast *"Lili Marlene,"* and they went on weekends for rest and recreation in Tobruk. And, of course, they ate: instead of the standard British rations of cold bully beef and tinned peaches, Hajali, their Lebanese cook, was somehow able to dish up hot stews, pease puddings, *pommes frites, crème au chocolat,* beer, coffee and, naturally, good red wine.

But nothing relieved the boredom of the ever-blistering sun, the almost daily sandstorms, the fleas, the flies, the ticks, the whitish gravel waste stretching blindingly down in every direction toward the horizons, and the lack of anything to do but dig more trenches, clean more guns, scratch more fleas and eat more food. Two months had gone by, nothing had happened, and all the men in the garrison could think about was having one moment of real live action.

Then, at the end of May, they got exactly that.

(5)

General Koenig had received the first warnings on May 15. Rommel's camps, said a message from Tobruk, were unusually active. Koenig got ready: He hurried in more food and supplies, had his men perform gas-mask drills, for he had heard that the Germans were using gas in Russia, and forbade further leaves to Tobruk. Looking out from the rectangular fort in the middle of Bir Hakeim, he began to study the dazzling white desert for signs of Rommel's arrival.

More warnings reached Koenig on May 24—Rommel's *Panzers* were aligning themselves in battle formation. Koenig radioed out to his men in the trenches inside the barbed-wire perimeter to be ready to fight, and he kept his own field glasses trained on the western horizon, watching for the telltale black dots that would inevitably show up against the sky.

Then, during the night of May 26, the men in Bir Hakeim heard the sputter of engines and the rattle of treads somewhere out in the darkness, and high in the black sky, above the Gazala Line, saw the red streaks of parachute flares. But the noise stopped and the lights went out, and the desert again was silent and dark. Perhaps, the French thought, the Germans were feinting. The men in the trenches relaxed. A few even began to doze.

They soon woke up.

(6)

Just after dawn that morning, a British tank commander, a Brigadier Filose, looked through his binoculars and saw a pillar of dust against the sky to the south of Bir Hakeim. The dust spread higher and deeper, and along its bottom was a row of moving black dots. "Looks like a brigade of Jerry tanks coming this way," he said into his telephone to Tobruk. Then he looked again and this time cried out in alarm, "Good Christ! It's more than a brigade! It's the whole bloody *Afrika Korps!*"

Chapter 21

(1)

ARLIER THAT SAME MONTH, JUST BEFORE DAWN ON MAY 7, 1942, A
BATTERED GRAY PICKUP TRUCK CLATTERED TO A HALT IN FRONT OF THE
BULLETIN BOARD OUTSIDE THE TOWN HALL OF CAEN, IN NORMANDY.
The plump middle-aged little driver, René Duchez, a house painter–
paperhanger and a member of Gilbert Renault's cell group in Caen, clambered down from the running board to read the latest notices. One piece
of paper, neatly typed and thumbtacked to the board, caught his eye. It
was a request for cost estimates for a wallpapering job in the Caen headquarters of the Nazi *Todt* organization, named for a Dr. Todt and respon-
sible for German engineering and construction activities along the coast
of France. Anyone interested and qualified was invited to submit his estimate in an office of the town hall that lay just across the brick courtyard.
The deadline for submissions, however, had been five o'clock the previous
day. Duchez placed his hands upon his plump behind, cocked his head
to one side, pursed up his lips and calculated his chances.

The immediate chief of his network, the huge, bearlike André Girard,
who owned a construction business in Caen, had recently asked his men
to seek information about the defensive wall the Germans were building
on the coast all the way from Dunkirk in the north to Biarritz in the south.
He wanted to know about everything, the texture of the sand around the
wall, the height and quality of the barbed wire, the thickness of the blockhouses, the location of the gates that led into the wall. Someday, Girard
said, when the liberation began, the invading Allied armies would need

all these facts, and more. One place to find such information, he suggested, might be in the *Todt* headquarters of Caen.

And now René Duchez saw an opportunity to get into the *Todt* building. The notice, of course, said it was too late, but then, Duchez thought as he grinned to himself, he had dealt with these bureaucrats before and, well, it might be worth a try.

He sauntered into the tiled lobby of the town hall where a French official with a gray face and rimless glasses in the *Bureau Civil* said coldly that the deadline had passed. Duchez widened his eyes, however, in a pleading, spaniel look, and the official informed him that he could apply directly to the *Todt* headquarters on the avenue Bagatelle.

The *Todt* organization had taken over three adjoining buildings on the Avenue Bagatelle, one for storage, another for administration and a third, a four-story stone mansion that faced the street, for the *Abteilung Technik* (the Technical Division) that handled *Todt* contracts and blueprints. A white picket fence covered with coils of barbed wire blocked this building off from the road. At the end of the fence, on the left, was a black and white striped sentry box.

Duchez's ancient truck shuddered and lurched to a stop in front of the sentry box. He had just climbed down from the driver's seat, when a sentry, rifle pointed toward Duchez, stepped out.

"*Halten!*" the sentry barked.

Duchez looked straight ahead, vacantly, and ambled past the sentry toward the buildings beyond. The rifle barrel jabbed into his ribs.

"*Halten!*" the sentry commanded again.

Duchez's palms lifted toward the heavens in a gesture of innocence. He had come to submit an estimate for papering, he tried to explain, but the sentry, not grasping his rapid French, kept poking him in the ribs and shoving him back toward the truck. Another sentry came down from the stone mansion to investigate. Duchez tried again to explain why he had come. Standing beside the sentry box, he flapped his hand up and down its side, miming the gestures of a man papering a wall. This, he hoped, would make the sentries react.

It did. A fist cracked into his ear and, while a torrent of punches and kicks rained upon him from seemingly every direction, he felt himself being dragged across the street, through a stone doorway and on to the hard concrete floor of a ground level office. There, a monocled German Captain asked him, in fluent French, if he knew the penalty for making fun of the Führer.

Despite his predicament and the soreness of his ribs, Duchez began to giggle. He had not dreamed of mocking the Austrian paperhanger, he said, his belly quivering with suppressed laughter, he had come looking for work, and he had simply been trying to show the sentries that he wished to do the papering job for the *Todt* organization.

The Captain dismissed the sentries and sent Duchez up two flights of stairs to the Lieutenant who was in charge of the wallpapering estimates. Yes, said the Lieutenant after listening to Duchez's request, bids had come in but the *Todt* organization had not yet awarded the contract. The job would be simple, the German went on, entailing the papering of only two rooms in the *Abteilung Technik* across the street. Would Duchez care to submit a bid?

Duchez thought fast, he was willing to do this job at a loss. "Twelve thousand francs," he said.

"That's it, then," the Lieutenant said. "Present yourself tomorrow morning to Major Schnedderer, second floor, *Abteilung Technik.*"

How strange, Duchez thought the next morning as he stood in front of Schnedderer's desk, how very queer, in fact, that such a ferocious-looking officer, Teutonic, bald, bullnecked, with a thick, red, dueling scar on his right cheek, should be so fascinated with the roses and pansies and silver-colored cannon in Duchez's book of samples of wallpaper. Perhaps the good Major had a secret side, perhaps at heart, he was an interior decorator—then a knock on the door interrupted Duchez's reverie.

"Come in," Schnedderer called out.

A young officer entered, clicked his heels, snapped, *"Heil Hitler,"* and handed Schnedderer a thick folded paper that looked like a blueprint.

"Thank you," said Schnedderer, "I was waiting for these."

As Duchez watched the retreating back of the young officer, he noticed, on the wall beside the door, directly opposite Schnedderer's desk, a large gilt-framed mirror. Then he turned back to the desk.

Schnedderer had shoved the pattern book aside with a sigh and had unfolded the paper lengthwise across the desk. It was a blueprint, Duchez could see, but more than a blueprint; it was also a map, an enormous and detailed map of something that looked like a coastline.

Duchez stood motionless, trying to look idiotic, watching.

Schnedderer had forgotten Duchez's existence. He leaned back from the desk and held a corner of the map up to the light from the window.

Duchez could see its details in reverse, letters that spelled out Le Havre, next the mouth of a river and finally a coastline smooth at first then plunging sharply downward. He edged away from the desk, staring at the cypress trees out another window and hoping that his face looked stupid. But his mind was fast at work—he tried to hide his sense of exhilaration, the lightheadedness of hysteria. For he knew what he had seen: a *Todt* map of the portion of the coastal wall along the Normandy coast.

Through the corner of his eye Duchez saw Schnedderer refold the map, push it to the front edge of the desk and begin again to study the book of wallpaper patterns.

Someone else knocked at the door, this time a German sergeant who muttered something in a harsh and gutteral German. Schnedderer rose from his chair, walked away from Duchez, and opened the door to an inner office directly behind the desk. Schnedderer stood in the doorway, resting his beefy shoulder against the doorjamb, his back to Duchez. He was dictating something to a clerk inside. The Sergeant left the main office, passing on his way out the gilt-framed mirror that hung on the wall.

Duchez was alone with the map.

He leaned sideways toward the desk, and peeked under the top corner of the map. He dropped it quickly, as if it were hot. This was both a map and blueprint as he had realized before, but it was also a minutely detailed blueprint, showing not only the overall outline of the wall, but also the placement of its guns, the location of its exits and the size of its rooms for the storage for ammunition. It was a complete picture of the Atlantic wall.

He looked up quickly toward the inner doorway. He could still see the back of Schnedderer's square bald head.

Duchez acted by instinct. His right arm stretched out. The map was in his hand. Three strides carried him across the room to the gilt-framed mirror. His right hand, still holding the map, rose to the glass. He looked back at Schnedderer again. The major was still talking to someone in the inner office. Duchez's right hand slid the map lengthwise behind the mirror, and then he tiptoed hurriedly back to the desk and once more stretched his mouth into an idiot grin. In that moment Schnedderer came back to the desk.

"Come back on Monday, then," he said to Duchez. "I want you to use the paper with the silver cannon on the dark-blue background."

Duchez left, having no idea whether or not Schnedderer had noticed that the map was missing.

(2)

But time was running out for Duchez and his Commander-in-Chief, Gilbert Renault.

For several months after Bernard Anquetil's arrest, Renault's operations in occupied France had continued smoothly. Bernard had died without talking, and Renault himself, based in an office above the Ermitage

Cinema on the Champs-Elysées, had expanded his network—being a devout Catholic, he called it the Confrérie de Notre Dame—into the bustling ports and smoky cities along the Atlantic and Channel coasts of France.

He was no longer direct and open and affable. His eyes now glanced furtively up and down sidewalks, and he changed his appearance and cover names with increasing frequency. Sometimes he was Monsieur Morel, a movie producer, who wore a fashionable gray tweed suit; sometimes he was Monsieur Raymond, representative of a Swiss insurance firm, attired in an old Basque beret and a shabby raincoat with a frayed and soot-darkened collar; sometimes he was Morin or Jean-Luc or Rémy; sometimes, before leaving his office, he placed a piece of cardboard inside the heel of his left shoe to alter his walk.

But whether he was bringing reports from Biarritz or Brest to Paris, whether he was recruiting agents beneath the skirts of the Eiffel Tower or in smoky basements in Montmartre or in crowded cafés in the Left Bank, his technique was always the same. Had the man slept well the night before? If he had, that revealed an inner repose. Did he ask Renault hard questions? If he did, that showed a sense of caution. Or did his hands drum nervously on the café table, and when his fingers lifted from the tabletop, did they leave behind little spots of perspiration? If they did, that indicated a nervousness that could easily produce poor judgment and hasty decisions. And if Renault found the man acceptable as an agent of the Confrérie de Notre Dame, his instructions were always the same: Never write down more than you must—if the Germans stop you and find a revealing name or address on a matchbook in your pocket, they will arrest you and probably sentence you to death before a firing squad. Never use your real name or address—even your toughest colleague can break and reveal your whereabouts when the Gestapo lower a knife to his testicles. Never be late for a rendezvous and never loiter once you are there — if you stare too long at a shop window or sit too long on a park bench, someone might notice and wonder, and lift a receiver to call the Gestapo. Never broadcast at regular times, if you are a radio operator, and never stay on the air for more than five minutes at a time—that was how Bernard Anquetil was arrested.

The work was slow and risky and Renault proceeded with painstaking caution. Then, by the winter of 1942, he had recruited the agents and radio operators he wanted, organized them in cell groups and courier chains, and set out for London from a secret field in Normandy to report on his progress to Passy. Colonel Passy was delighted with the results, and outlined a project upon which the Confrérie de Notre Dame could start work immediately. British reconnaissance planes had spotted peculiar new construction work along the French channel coast, blockhouses and excavations that looked like the beginnings of a gigantic defensive wall. Could Renault get more information about it?

Renault agreed and, on an afternoon late in March, went shopping in Selfridge's department store for cigarettes, chocolates and a box of expensive cigars, for his flight back to France.

Just as Renault returned to the *Deuxième Bureau's* (now called, officially, the *Bureau de Contre Espionnage, Renseignements et d'Action*) headquarters in Duke Street, however, to say good-bye to his friends there, an alarming radiogram reached Passy's desk.

The Gestapo, it said, had arrested seven of Renault's radio operators in and around Paris.

(3)

The German orderly in the hall outside where Duchez was working could stand it no longer. It was a Monday morning, May 11, and for the last two hours the orderly had heard nothing but the squish of the wallpaper against glue, the steady slapping of the brush—and Duchez's singing. It was loud singing, it was nasal singing, and Duchez seemed never to run out of mushy sentimental songs. Finally, in a burst of temper, the orderly called through the door: "Will you please *shut up!*"

Duchez came out to the hall, brush in hand, apologizing profusely. Then, before returning to his work, he said, humbly, "When it is convenient, please, I would like to see Major Schnedderer."

"Well, if you do," the orderly snapped, "you'd better take the train to St. Malo [west of Caen, on the north coast of Brittany]."

"Any time will do," Duchez said, thinking that Schnedderer's office might now be empty. "When will he be back?"

"Back?" the German exclaimed. "Never to here. He's been transferred to another unit. Major Keller has taken his place."

Duchez spent the rest of the day working in silence, his brain too busy even for singing. The next morning, after having finished the two rooms he was supposed to paper, he put his plan into operation.

He cornered a young Lieutenant in the hallway of the *Abteilung Technik* and asked him when Major Keller would like for him to start. "Start what?" the Lieutenant asked. "Why, naturally," Duchez explained, "papering Major Schnedderer's office. Major Keller will know what I mean." The Lieutenant went off to confer with Major Keller. Half an hour later he returned and informed Duchez that the requisition sheet said nothing about Schnedderer's office itself. So, what was Duchez talking about?

Duchez went upstairs to Schnedderer's old office to clear up the confusion that he himself had created.

"I had offered to paper this room free," he explained to Major Keller, "you know, as a gesture of good will."

Major Keller saw no objection and told Duchez to come back the next morning to paper the room. He even patted Duchez's round shoulder and called him, contemptuously, a "good Frenchman."

As he walked out the door, Duchez glanced to his left: the gilt-edged mirror was still hanging against the wall.

Duchez re-entered the office the next morning, Wednesday, May 13, carrying a load of buckets and wallpaper, and settled down to do his work. First he pushed the desk, the chairs and the file cabinets to the center of the floor. Next, he covered them carefully with his dustcloth. Then he straightened up, letting his eyes shift about the room to see if anyone was watching, and deciding that no one was, walked across the office floor until he had come to the gilt-edged mirror hanging at an angle against the wall.

Finally, as imperceptibly as he could, he peeked around the frame of the mirror to see if the Germans had discovered their map.

(4)

"January, February, March, April, May, June, July, August, September, October, November, December, one, two, three, four, five, six, seven, eight, nine, zero. J for John, J for John, John, do you hear me? Over."

An Englishwoman's voice had been speaking through Gilbert Renault's earphones, as he sat in the darkened cockpit of the Lysander that was to fly him back to France. He glanced down at the luminous dials on his watch: it was ten-thirty on the night of March 28, 1942. He was at the Tangmere airport, outside London, awaiting the lift in his stomach that would signify the moment of takeoff. He heard a click in his earphones, then his pilot's voice saying: "J for John speaking. J for John speaking. I hear you loud and clear. Over."

Out in the darkness the propellor was turning, vibrating the plane's cockpit, then the aircraft edged forward, wheeled around and stopped. Renault missed the signal from the ground but he did feel the shaking and the rattling as the throttle opened wide and the plane rose in a lurch from the runway. Then the airport was beneath him, its shadows sharp in the pale light of the moon. Soon the Lysander reached the coast, and was over the English Channel.

"J for John, J for John," the woman's voice said again, "Good luck to you, good luck."

Renault let out an ironic laugh. That afternoon, in Passy's office, he had learned about the arrest of his seven radio operators. "You're not going back to France, are you?" Passy had asked him, incredulously, but Renault had answered, "Yes. I must." No one else, he said, knew enough to coordinate the activities of the Confrérie de Notre Dame—and, he thought to himself, the news meant that he would have to get his family out of France before it was too late. But now, in the cockpit of the Lysander, he was experiencing the dry cotton mouth and the dripping armpits of fearful anticipation.

Far below, now, on the ground, Renault could see the faint blinking of lights. He knew he must be over France, for those lights, red and green, seemed to be strung out along a railroad track. The sky was clear—much too clear for his liking. A ribbon of silver came into view. That was the Loire, at Saumur. The shadow of a huge château fell across the houses, and Renault shivered. That was where Bernard Anquetil had been imprisioned. And Renault's landing site was only a few miles away.

The pilot banked over the town: Renault could see the silhouette of the Lysander shadowed against the sloping slate roofs. The plane descended and Renault picked out three lights set in a triangle below and then a fourth, winking up at the plane. This would be the landing zone.

The pilot circled back and lowered the nose of the plane toward the base of the triangle. The wheels hit down on the grass, bumped along for a distance, then turned so abruptly that Renault's ear smacked against the window beside him. The pilot raced the engine, trying to move the Lysander closer to the middle of the triangle of lights, but the tires simply spun around in one place. He tried again—still no success. He shouted over to Renault: "Stuck! We're stuck! The tail wheel is stuck in the ground!"

Then Renault looked out across the fields: shadowy figures were racing headlong toward the airplane; familiar faces loomed out of the darkness. They were Renault's men, and as soon as he had climbed from the airplane, they scrambled around to the Lysander's tail and lifted. The plane jerked forward. A bag of dispatches tumbled aboard, and as the men waved farewell, the motor roared to life and the plane lifted from the grassy runway to disappear into the night.

Gilbert Renault was back in France.

(5)

Beneath the Eglise St-Pierre in Caen on the evening of May 13, across the cobblestones of the Avenue des Touristes and through a café window on which a sign said, "Paul. Vins. Tabacs," the roly-poly René Duchez, still wearing his paint-splotched white work coat, was standing at the zinc-bar and sipping from a glass of applejack. He was in no hurry to join his friends, the members of André Girard's cell group, who were playing dominoes at a nearby marble-topped table. Instead, he was studying an old German soldier, whom he had nicknamed "Old Albert," and who was sipping a cognac at another table across the room. At last Duchez finished his glass. He hung up his work coat on a rack beside Albert's *Wehrmacht* raincoat, and pulled up a chair alongside his friends. But he was acting strange, uncharacteristically quiet.

"Double six," said one of the men. "How goes it, René?"

"Fine," Duchez answered, and grinned mysteriously.

He rose again at once and sauntered toward the door. He glanced out at the street, down to his right.

The men at the table exchanged glances. Duchez had told them several days before about the map, and they had been certain that he was spoofing, but as they watched him lean out the door now, they sensed that he was concocting something—but what?

Some bicycles pedaled past the window, a girl clumped by on her stiff wooden shoes, and on the steps of the Eglise St-Pierre, a few older women in starched white caps were hawking baskets of anemones. That was all the men could see outside—it was a perfectly normal scene for a late afternoon in Caen. Then the men at the table looked out again, and this time they saw what Duchez was watching.

The bicycles had disappeared and the women with the flowers had retreated up the steps of the church into its doorway, for a low black Citroën, nosing its way toward the square, was slipping past the church and parking at the curb directly opposite the café. Two men in raincoats sat in the back seat: under their gray felt hats, their skulls were shaved clean. The men in the café knew instantly what that meant: agents of the Gestapo.

Duchez was wandering back to the table.

"Be with you in a moment, old friends," he said with a wave, "I forgot my cigarettes."

He meandered over to the coatrack, where his paint-smeared rag hung beside Old Albert's Army raincoat, and returned with a mangled pack of Gauloises.

"What have you been up to, old goat?" one of the men asked him in a whisper. "We've been sitting here all afternoon, trying to figure how to get your Atlantic wall map out of the *Todt* building."

"Assuming, of course," muttered another, "that there really is such a map."

Duchez leaned back in his chair with a grin. He blew out a ring of blue smoke. A domino clicked upon the table, and a voice said, "Pass." More dominoes clicked; Duchez took another puff. Then he spoke up, whispering through the side of his mouth:

"I have the map," he said, "right here."

Fingers were motionless, glued to the dominoes; eyes lifted to Old Albert's table, across the room. He was still sipping his cognac, having, apparently, heard nothing.

"Not here, for Christ's sake, René," a voice muttered. "If you're not joking, get it the hell out of here."

Duchez glanced up toward the door. "No time," he said, "they're coming inside now."

The men bent over the domino board; no one had the courage to look up. They heard the café door swing shut and the heavy silence that fell upon the room, but no one dared raise his eyes to look at the men with the raincoats and the gray hats and the closely shaved skulls. Time seemed to crawl. Finally, Duchez got up. He walked to the bar and ordered another drink. At last he returned to the table and, with a grin, said that the Gestapo had left. Sighs of relief exploded around the table.

"Now then," said one of the men, "will you please tell us . . ."

But Duchez was on his feet again. Old Albert had finished his cognac and risen to leave. Somehow Duchez collided with him just in front of the coatrack. Duchez bowed in an elaborate apology and helped the old German into his raincoat. Then he came back to his chair again.

Once more his friends began to quiz him; once more Duchez was on his feet, this time to wave and yell loudly to André Girard, head of the Caen cell group, who was weaving his way through the tables to join the men.

"How's it going, old fellow?" Duchez called out. "What've you been up to?"

Girard pulled a chair up to the table. He was out of breath, anxious to catch the train that left before nightfall for Paris.

"Have you gentlemen got any dispatches for me?" he asked.

All eyes focused upon Duchez. He was grinning his most vacuous grin.

"Well," he said, "we do have some routine dispatches . . ."

Then he paused for effect, the men saw him pass a thick wide white envelope under the table to Girard.

"What's this?" Girard growled.

"Oh, not much," Duchez answered. "It's just a *Todt* map of the Atlantic wall."

Girard sat silent, without moving, on the edge of his chair, trying to piece together the words he had just heard. Finally, he spoke, in a weak voice, nothing like his usual bearlike rumble.

"Where did you find it?"

Duchez explained about his encounter with Major Schnedderer and how he had conned his way back into Schnedderer's office after Major Keller had taken charge. The Germans had apparently not missed the map, Duchez supposed, for, that very afternoon, he had found it right where he had put it—resting in the space behind the mirror on the wall. He had extracted the map and put it inside a roll of wallpaper that lay on the floor beside his brush bucket, and then, when he had finished papering the room, he had simply gathered up his equipment and left. And now, here it was.

Girard had recovered his poise. "You brought it *here?*" he exclaimed in as harsh a whisper as he could manage. "You've had it with you where the Gestapo could find it? You *fool*, what if they'd come to the table and searched you?"

"The Gestapo," said Duchez, with his most idiotic grin, "would have searched in vain."

"But how . . ." Girard felt at a loss again. Everyone else at the table was staring dumbfounded at Duchez.

"Well," Duchez smirked, "when I went to get my cigarettes, you remember?"—and he looked around the table in triumph—"I put the map in Old Albert's coat pocket. So when he rose to go, I simply took it back again. After all, we don't want Old Albert to get the firing squad, do we?"

Moments later Girard left the café to take the map to Gilbert Renault, with whom he had already scheduled a rendezvous in Paris. But last thing the men at the marble-topped table saw Girard do that day, before he crossed in front of the Eglise St-Pierre and passed out of sight, was to feel the bulge in his coat pocket, raise his thick-boned, hairy right hand to the back of his head, scratch and look back in absolute stupefaction, past the lettering on the window that said "Paul. Vins. Tabacs."

Chapter 22

(1)

A HUSH FELL OVER CARLTON GARDENS ON THE MORNING OF JUNE 8, 1942: THE TOWERING, AWKWARD FIGURE OF GENERAL DE GAULLE HAD STALKED INTO THE BUILDING, HIS ABDOMEN THRUST FORWARD, HIS ARMS straight at his sides, his slender wrists nearly reaching the edge of his tunic, his eyes glancing neither to the left nor the right and his lips pressed together into a thin white line. And he showed no reaction whatever to the news.

Until now, it seemed, General Rommel had merely toyed with Bir Hakeim, annoyed by the Free French raids upon his flank, but concentrating the bulk of his forces upon his immediate objective, the seizure of Tobruk. Suddenly enraged, however, as if a burr in his side had grown infected and painful, he had turned back from the coast, throwing all the *Panzers* he could spare against the minefields and barbed wire that surrounded Bir Hakeim. The British Command in Tobruk had asked the Free French to hold out until the night of June 10, but Bir Hakeim's supplies and energies were nearly exhausted, and throughout Carlton Gardens there across the inevitable question whether the men of Bir Hakeim had the stamina to hang on.

But General de Gaulle had shown no concern at all: one Free Frenchman in London likened him to a lump of wet potter's clay, and another was moved to quote a line from the Lamartine—"Nothing human throbbed beneath his thick armor." He seemed oblivious to what was happening to the defenders at Bir Hakeim.

(2)

Just after sunrise on May 26, the men of the garrison had looked out at the rosy ribbon of sunlight that was spreading across the eastern sky and saw a series of black dots spaced out along the horizon. The French watched closely over the sights of their machine guns and between the slits of their pillboxes. The blacks dots were drawing nearer, taking on the forms of heavy tanks, and in their wake came columns of trucks, filled, certainly, with well-trained infantry. The *Afrika Korps*, apparently, was preparing to strike. One French sentry, however, noticed something surprising: the markings on the tanks revealed that these were not part of the *Panzer Korps* itself—Rommel seemed to have disappeared to the east—but of two Italian divisions, the *Ariete* and the *Trieste.*

The Frenchmen in the trenches cheered and hooted: the Italians had a reputation for cowardice. In that same moment a wave of Stukas bombed the camp.

Bombs and shells exploded around the barbed wire, Italian infantry-men began picking their way through the minefields around the garrison, and the Free French slammed shut the three gates of Bir Hakeim, opening fire with every gun they had into the clouds of dust that were swirling around the desert. Six Italian tanks managed to break through the barbed-wire perimeter and roared off toward the white fortress in the middle of the camp. Captain Otte of the Foreign Legion, watching through the slit in his pillbox, was the first to see them come: he was sitting directly in their path. He telephoned out a warning. The tanks came closer—Otte fired back, ineffectually, with his machine gun. The lead tank drew within fifteen yards: Otte was looking straight up at the barrel of its gun. Then the French seventy-fives opened up at close range and a unit of Legionnaires scrambled over the Italian tanks, firing their revolvers into the observation slits. The tanks quickly withdrew.

A second wave of Italian tanks lumbered into the minefields during the heat of the late morning, but several exploded when they struck mines —one tank collapsed onto its side, the tread dangling from the sprocket—and by midday the gravel desert outside Bir Hakeim was littered with the hulls of burning Italian vehicles. The French settled back to await the next attack.

It came late that afternoon, in the midst of a sandstorm that left the French spitting out mouthfuls of sand every few moments. The dim shapes of the Italian tanks and crawling infantrymen loomed out of the fog. "Where are they now?" Frenchmen in the trenches asked each other, and fingers pointed left or right, out into the invisible distance. The tanks came within fifty feet of the barbed wire, and then the French seventy-fives blasted again: from down in their trenches the French soldiers could see streaks of flame flashing into the storm. And Italian crewmen, clothes aflame, leapt from their blazing tanks, most of them dead by the time they hit the ground, although their clothes kept burning for minutes thereafter.

By the end of the day the Italians had lost forty-five tanks, sixty prisoners, and had managed to wound only one Free Frenchman. The French, however, did not celebrate, yet. Rommel was still out there, somewhere, assuredly within striking distance.

(3)

At the moment he was far to the north of Bir Hakeim, racing along behind the Gazala Line toward Tobruk. His columns had spread out, a journalist noted, like "the fingers of a man's hand. The hand reached forward clutching at Tobruk from the south." One *Panzer* detachment had passed back *through* the Gazala Line, reaching Derna on the coast, eighty miles west of Tobruk. Another unit, swinging off to the right, had reached El Gobi, almost at the Egyptian border, and still other *Panzers* had reached the escarpment above Tobruk, "swarming everywhere," driving "through the night shooting out very lights, banging their guns off to make as much uproar as possible and giving the impression of great strength." Tobruk had locked itself in: "The fingers of the hand were beginning to tighten their grip."

At dusk, however, on May 29, Rommel saw that he had moved too fast. His supply lines, bent at a right angle around Bir Hakeim, were being harassed hourly by the Free French, and he himself had driven into a trap east of the Gazala Line, hemmed in on one side by the extensive minefield and on the other by the British 150th Brigade of tanks.

Five days passed: Rommel's blitz had exhausted itself and his forces were unable to get the supplies from around the corner at Bir Hakeim. Rommel did, however, see a solution. He decided to catch the British off guard by feinting toward the great semicircle of their tanks, then trying to squeeze out through the Gazala Line itself. He had also decided to deal with the problem of Bir Hakeim.

As Rommel's sappers cut passages through the British minefields, the bulk of his force began its retreat. His losses were heavy but he kept on going. Finally, after nineteen hours, he broke out of range of the pursuing British tanks and pushed southward to do what he knew he should have done in the beginning. He threw all his remaining units at the garrison called Bir Hakeim.

(4)

Bir Hakeim had had it easy, for a while. By day its guns had lobbed shell after shell at Rommel's passing convoys, and by night its patrols had scooted down from the ridge and across the desert to set German tanks and trucks afire. And the Germans had failed, so far, to retaliate with any effectiveness. British supply trucks, furthermore, coming from the north through gaps in the minefields were reaching the Free French with regularity. General Koenig was buoyant and smiling beneath his blue kepi, and his troops cheered and applauded like boys at a circus at the spectacle they would see to their north.

"We could stand on our hill," said a member of the medical corps, "and watch the battle [between Rommel and the surrounding Allied tanks]. It was hard to believe. We saw South Africans fight and maneuver the Germans, and watched the ponderous heavy tanks advance and deploy. Pillars of black smoke rose up in the still air all over the desert, marking for several hours an accurate aim and good hit. The French seventy-fives . . . took effect on anything that foolishly came within range . . .

"Then [at night] the big ack-ack shakes the ground and bursts high with a brilliant yellow flash. But the Bofors guns provide the show. Long streamers and strings of balls of red or green flames, spaced about five feet—or perhaps more—apart, but regularly and in perfect alignment, they twist and bend slowly and gracefully in the night air; and then one after another the balls of fire explode in sequence. [We] saw that display from Bir Hakeim . . . from there it looks like a bouquet of flowers, more or less. It is very beautiful, but deadly; it rains iron fragments."

The diversion, however, soon was over. On the afternoon of June 1, Lieutenant Colonel Broche, whom Koenig had sent out with an armoured unit to harass a German convoy, and who had bivouacked about a mile northeast of Bir Hakeim, began radioing frantic messages to Koenig's headquarters. At first Koenig could make no sense of them, for Broche's radio had been functioning badly. But at last Koenig did make out what Broche was trying to say: numerous tanks were rumbling across the desert, just north of his tent.

Koenig asked if the vehicles were hostile.

The radio was silent for a moment. Then it crackled again. This time Broche's voice came through clearly. His scouts had counted one hundred and fifty tanks, and yes, they were hostile, they were *Panzers* and they were beginning to fire upon his encampment.

Moments later Broche's armored cars came scuttling back into Bir Hakeim, followed by shells that kicked fountains of sand high into the air. Two Italian emissaries, carrying a white flag, soon appeared at a gate of

Bir Hakeim. General Rommel advised the camp to surrender, they advised Koenig, to avoid the useless spilling of blood.

"Gentlemen," Koenig told them, "thank your generals for their pleasant conduct but tell them that with us there is no question of surrendering."

(5)

Rommel responded without hesitation. As he studied Bir Hakeim through his field glasses the next morning, his feet spread wide on the gravel floor of the desert, he barked out orders for his forces to "pinch the life out" of the garrison at Bir Hakeim.

Huge field guns began immediately to shell the base, wave after wave of *Stukas* came dipping down and screaming toward the French fortifications, and German sappers started cutting gaps in the minefields to allow the *Panzers* to approach the barbed wire in safety.

That, however, was only a prelude—Rommel gave his troops a rest that night. On the next morning, June 3, he launched his attack in earnest.

(6)

"When a bomb falls on the desert," said one of the men at Bir Hakeim, "you see it leave the rack and straighten out as it falls shining in the sunlight. It whistles and then you see the smoke and dust burst and rise up like a giant gray-white cedar tree or a fat cypress, and then you hear the noise. It is more than a huge plume of smoke and dust and there are enough for a small grove. Always more than one of them fall."

The Stukas came in threesomes at dawn, wave upon wave, hurtling across the horizon, strafing the tents in the base and trying to aim their bombs into the honeycomb network of slit trenches. The French were well dug in—it took a direct hit to destroy a slit trench—but the bombs began quickly to take their toll. Mushrooms of dust and smoke billowed up around the camp. One bomb destroyed the rectangular stucco fortress that had been Koenig's headquarters, another fell upon one of the two large hospital tents.

General Koenig radioed for help from the Royal Air Force, and as the British fighters arrived from Tobruk, Frenchmen all across the camp lifted their faces up from the trenches, grinned, and counted the two dozen planes marked with the black German cross go spinning into the sand and explode.

"*Merci pour la R.A.F.,*" radioed, Koenig.

"*Merci à vous pour le sport,*" came the response.

(7)

But the German infantry had crept closer toward Bir Hakeim, and Nazi machine gunners had dug into the sand only a few hundred miles away. And from behind them the German eighty-eights were getting the range.

At midday on June 3, two English soldiers, whom Rommel had captured, appeared outside the camp gates. One of them, a Captain Tomkins, bore a message that Rommel himself had scribbled on a lined page from a German signal pad: "To the troops of Bir Hakeim," Rommel had written. "Any further resistance will only shed useless blood! You will suffer the same fate as the two British brigades which we exterminated at Got Saleb two days ago. We shall cease fire when you raise the white flag and come towards us without arms."

Koenig's only response was to send a message of his own to his unit commanders: "Soon we must expect a large-scale attack. The enemy will employ airplanes, tanks, artillery and infantry. It is my order and wish that every man will do his duty unflinchingly, either at his post or isolated from his comrades. Our task is to hold the ground, whatever the cost, until our job is finished. This order must be clearly conveyed to all the ranks. Good luck to you all."

(8)

Rommel struck the next morning with fury. "Three bombs," said an ambulance driver, "fell directly upon a Bofors gun and its crew of French Marines. That killed all but one of the men [there]. They had been standing up, manning the gun, aiming and firing it, and the bombs blew them to pieces. It set fire to the munitions truck, drawn up a few moments before, and so we went into the bright burst of the shells. The one man alive died in my car on the stretcher. His eyes were open, and he was not bleeding much though his right leg was gone at the hip. He lay in the wreckage, the other leg across the leg of the gun. In the midst of those bodies the spoiled gun stood still, pointing directly overhead. Even the dust was burned. It was black-gray, and the bodies of the young men had suddenly aged in that instant in which they were dismembered. The faces looked old and worn, like faces that too much bitter knowledge has aged. When the munitions truck had burned out, they were picked up and buried not very far from their gun, which stood up straight like a marker on that high place in the desert."

As the bombs exploded and the sand whirled and the powder reeked and the wounded screamed on stretchers on the one remaining hospital tent, Koenig kept an anxious watch on the sky, studying the heavy, clumsy Bombay troop carriers that lumbered through the German flank and parachuted down drugs, bandages, food, spare parts, bullets and hand grenades. Most of the crates smashed or became lost in the desert, and now, Koenig realized, fewer and fewer of the Bombays were managing to get through. British supply trucks had already stopped appearing at the gates of the fort and the men in the far outposts of Bir Hakeim were having to go for entire days without fresh water or nourishment.

By the evening of June 7, Koenig was deeply worried. For two days his men had enjoyed no sleep—Rommel filled the nights with red flares and machine-gun fire in the hope of keeping the French awake—and Koenig radioed Tobruk, asking how much longer the British Command wished him to hold out.

The answer came: Could he hang on for three more days?

That same evening, Rommel ordered his *Panzers* and assault troops to cross the barbed wire around Bir Hakeim.

Chapter 23

(1)

ANDRE GIRARD, THE BURLY HEAD OF THE CAEN CELL GROUP, CHECKED HIS WATCH AND LOOKED OUT FROM THE BALCONY OF THE FLAT AT 71 RUE CARDINAL LEMOINE, ON THE LEFT BANK IN PARIS. FAR ACROSS THE roofs of the city he could see the onion-shaped dome of Sacré-Coeur, gleaming and white in the morning sunshine. Just beneath the balcony, in a courtyard surrounded by moss-covered walls, a flock of pigeons murmured on the pavement and water trickled softly into the basin of an old stone fountain. Girard glanced at his watch again: it was eight o'clock in the morning of May 14, time to start the map of the Atlantic wall on its circuitous route to Gilbert Renault. Girard turned from the railing and walked back into his flat.

Girard felt queasy. He had brought the map into Paris the night before without trouble, but he had a premonition that something would go wrong: the map was hot property, and by now the Germans must surely have learned of its theft. He had to get rid of it, fast.

Girard's huge right hand poked down behind the cushion of the window seat where he had stuffed the map for safekeeping, took it out, folded it under his shirt, buttoned his jacket and peeked out through the keyhole that revealed the hallway and the head of the stairs outside. No one was there. Then he passed through an inner door that opened into a second, vacant apartment. This second flat was his escape route, for, in an emergency, he could hoist himself through its skylight and out onto the roof and, he hoped, safety. Girard locked the door of this second flat behind him, and walked down the six flights of stairs that led to an alley and the cobbled street beyond.

The map was on its way to Renault: Girard wondered if Renault would be at the designated spot to pick it up.

(2)

Renault was wondering the same thing. One of his arrested radio operators, he had learned, had revealed his name to the Gestapo, and during the week that Duchez was confiscating the map, Renault had gone to Brittany to engineer his escape from France. His plan, which he radioed in code to London, was to sail a fishing boat out past the tip of Brittany, transfer himself and his family to a British trawler and take the trawler to Dartmouth on the south coast of England. He had asked a fisherman named Alex Tanguy, an agent in Brittany, to lease a suitable fishing vessel.

"Well, I've found what you wanted," Tanguy said to him one morning as they stood on a quay in Lorient. "I've got the boat, but don't be surprised when you see it."

They walked along a pier together. Then Tanguy pointed past the ends of the planks into the water.

"Well," he said, "that's her."

Renault gulped in disbelief.

The boat was named the *Deux Anges*, and was about thirty-five feet long, unpainted, and encrusted with dirty white clumps of hardened salt. The men climbed aboard: Renault gagged from the smell of something rotten.

"What on earth did they use her for?" he gasped.

"I don't know," Tanguy mumbled. "Lobster, I think, or conger-eel. Something like that."

The *Deux Anges*, Tanguy explained, could make thirteen knots, but Renault remained apprehensive. The stench was nauseating, the boat seemed unseaworthy, and aside from the cramped lockers along the fore-deck and the tiny engine room below, there was no space at all for his family to hide.

"Was this the best you could find?" he asked Tanguy.

"As I told you," Tanguy answered defensively, "she's all there was."

Utterly dismayed, Renault returned to Paris where, a week later, he was scheduled to receive the latest reports from the Confrérie de Notre Dame. He planned immediately thereafter, to leave France—he only hoped he could survive the intervening week.

(3)

The map of the Atlantic wall was on its way to Renault. From his apartment in the Left Bank, André Girard had bicycled to the Boulevard Flandrin to visit Marcel Berthelot, a retired diplomat whom Renault had recruited into the Confrérie de Notre Dame a few months before. Girard took the map from underneath his shirt and spread it across the table in the kitchen of Berthelot's flat. The paper flopped over the edges of the table like a table cloth. Berthelot peered down through his gold-rimmed glasses—and whistled in amazement.

Berthelot saw instantly that this was a top-secret Nazi document, showing the location of every machine gun and piece of artillery on the Channel coast between Brittany and the mouth of the Seine. The map had to reach London, he knew, as soon as possible, but he also saw a serious obstacle.

Until recently, when documents and dispatches reached Paris from Renault's agents in Biarritz or Brest or Caen, a courier took the papers to the studio of a photographer, a Jean Pelletier, who microfilmed them in his darkroom, buried the copies in his backyard, and destroyed those copies only after learning that the original had reached England. But Pelletier was gone. He had also been a radio operator, one of the seven now in the Gestapo jail on the rue des Saussaies in Paris. And there was no one left who could inconspicuously photocopy the map of the Atlantic wall.

Berthelot did know two men, René Bourdan, an architect, and Paul Mollet, an industrial draftsman, who could copy the map by hand, but he was not sure how soon he could locate them, and besides, copying it thus would certainly take most of the day. And Girard's rendezvous with Renault was scheduled for four o'clock that afternoon.

"Look," Berthelot said to Girard. "Leave the map with me. Bourdan and Mollet know me. I'll try to get them to do the job, then I'll take it to Renault."

Girard agreed, and left. There was one thing, however, that both men thought and that neither said: they wondered if Renault would at that very moment be under arrest.

(4)

Renault was wondering the same thing, too, that afternoon as he waited for four o'clock, the time for the rendezvous. Only a few days before, someone, probably from the Gestapo, had visited his aunt, Lizette

Decker, at her house in Paris. Early in the evening she had heard her door-bell ring and, looking out from an upper-story window, saw a bare-headed young man standing on the pavement.

"Madame Decker?" he called up.

"Yes?"

"I've come from Raymond [Renault's alias at the time]."

Renault's aunt was not thinking. She assumed the young man was one of Renault's couriers, and said, "I'll come down at once."

But when she got downstairs and opened the front door, she nearly fainted with fright: a German policeman, who must have been hiding around the corner, was standing beside the young man in the raincoat.

"We would like to speak with your husband," the young man said.

"He's not here," Madame Decker responded.

"What do you mean, he's not here," the policeman demanded.

"Just that, he's under arrest."

"They let him go, didn't they," the man in the raincoat asked.

"Yes, but they took him away again, just a few days ago."

"Who did?" inquired the young man.

"The police. I have no idea where he is now."

Confused, the two men talked to each other in rapid German: the policeman seemed angry. At last they walked away, forgetting to ask Madame Decker why she had opened her door to someone who said he had come from Raymond.

The Germans, however, soon corrected this oversight.

(5)

A thin figure, in a shabby blue suit and gold-rimmed spectacles, was sitting on a wooden bench that paralleled the wall of the Metro car, and noticing his harried reflection in the window across the aisle. It was three o'clock in the afternoon of May 14, and Marcel Berthelot was late for his meeting with Renault. His two friends, René Bourdan and Paul Mollet, had worked through their lunch breaks to copy the map, and now Berthelot had the original on the slatted train bench beside him, wrapped and sealed in a brown manilla envelope. But although he still had another hour before he met Renault, he was worried about the time, for the Confrérie de Notre Dame's security regulations forbade his taking the train directly to the rendezvous point. He had, instead, to crisscross Paris several times, according to an elaborate scheme, in order to elude anyone who might be following him.

At the moment, Berthelot was under the Seine, just below the Ile de la Cité, and then, at the Metro station called Châtelet, under the Hôtel de Ville, he waited until the sliding doors of his car had opened and he stepped out onto the platform. Trying to appear nonchalant as he carried the brown envelope in his right hand, he passed through a tunnel and onto another platform to catch the train for Bastille. Five, ten minutes passed, and at last the train came roaring out of the tunnel. German soldiers filled the first-class coach to bursting. Berthelot walked down to the second-class coach—an enamel plaque on its outside said, "The train cannot leave until the doors are closed." Berthelot stepped onto the dirty floor inside, and the train lurched ahead, nearly throwing him off balance. He grabbed an overhead strap, then eased himself onto another slatted wooden bench. Five more minutes passed: it was now three-fifteen. The train reached Bastille, and Berthelot repeated the process, taking the Number 8 Line north to République, and another train under the heights of Montmartre. It was three-thirty. His new train passed under the Place Pigalle, Clichy, Place Blanche, the Moulin Rouge. The crowds on the platforms outside the dusty windows were thick; more and more Parisians, women in pompadours and wooden shoes, men in shabby raincoats, crowded aboard, slowing the progress of the train. Berthelot looked down at his watch: three-forty-five. He switched trains twice again, at Havre-Caumartin and Villiers, then he was under the residential Parc de Monceau, and, at last, L'Etoile. In a moment he was on the sidewalk upstairs, hearing the flap-flap of the huge swastika that hung from the keystone of the Arc de Triomphe.

Berthelot checked his watch again. It was just four o'clock, and the café where he would meet Renault was a good ten minutes away—if Renault was there at all.

(6)

The Gestapo were hot on Renault's trail. The day before they had arrested his sisters, Maisie and Isabelle, and raided the flat he had kept on the avenue de la Motte-Picquet. Fortunately he had just moved to a new apartment on the Square Henry-Paté, beside the Bois-de-Boulogne, but as he left that flat for the last time on the afternoon of May 14, and crossed the gravel walkway in the park outside, he had the feeling that someone was watching his every step.

Even as he sat down at a marble-topped table in a café on the avenue Carnot and sipped at a cup of bitter ersatz coffee, he felt nervous and uneasy. The Gestapo, he knew, planted undercover agents in cafés to watch for furtive meetings between members of the Resistance. A "French businessman" in Montparnasse had had his mind not on profits but on an intent conversation between two men at the next table; a "student" in a turtlenecked sweater lounging near the Place Victor Hugo had placed a telephone call about a single man seated next to him who had been glancing up and down the sidewalk as if he were waiting for somebody. Both of these incidents had led to arrests.

Renault glanced around the nearby tables. Some German soldiers, laughing and gabbling, were drinking beer and cognac in their peculiar fashion, a gulp of beer and a sip of cognac, a gulp of beer and a sip of cognac. A few French were there, too, drinking the only thing they could afford, the dreadful ersatz coffee, and for a moment Renault wondered if he looked as pale and undernourished as they. All the French women, he noticed, were wearing wooden shoes, and the men's trousers were unpressed and shiny.

But his stomach was still churning with worry, and he could feel the underarms of his dingy shirt soaking with sweat. One of those Frenchmen or one of those soldiers, he thought, was sure to notice him and wonder why he had been sitting at his table so long.

(7)

Marcel Berthelot was scurrying, as fast as he could go without attracting attention, along the avenue Carnot. His gold-rimmed glasses joggled up and down as he walked. Far down the street he could see a few German soldiers in gray uniforms giggling and nudging each other as they spun a rack of postcards in front of a newspaper stall. The pictures on the cards, Berthelot surmised, were lewd. He looked across the street from the postcard rack and noticed the maroon awning of a sidewalk café. That was where Renault should be waiting.

He hurried down the sidewalk of the avenue Carnot. Ordinarily the traffic, coming off the circle around the Arc de Triomphe, would be whishing along in what seemed one solid black ribbon of cars, but now the street was nearly empty, and the only vehicles that passed Berthelot, as he hurried along, were a few German Mercedes staff cars and the *vélocabs,* large tricycles with two-passenger seats in the back.

Berthelot was only a block away from the rendezvous point. He pulled back the cuff of his jacket to look at his watch: four-twelve. He walked even faster, and in his rush stumbled over the curb. And then he was lean-ing over the railing in front of a café, looking for Gilbert Renault.

He saw the German soldiers laughing coarsely and drinking their toasts of cognac and beer, and the crowds of Parisians, poorly attired, grimacing over their coffee, and looking around with vacant gray-white faces. But where was Renault? Berthelot glanced quickly from one table to the next, but saw no sign of him. Berthelot dared not stay long by the railing. He let his eyes sweep quickly over the tables again: still no Renault. Only when he had turned to go back up the sidewalk did he guess where Renault was. Berthelot turned back toward the café, looked toward the door that led inside, glanced over to the left, and peered into the shadow that covered the back corner. There he saw the square jaw and balding scalp of Gilbert Renault.

That evening Renault was on his way to Brittany, carrying the map of the wall in his cardboard suitcase.

(8)

Colonel Passy swiveled in his chair the next morning to watch the rain make streaks on the outside of his office window. He reached across the desk for his pipe, blew through it, stuffed in a wad of Scottish tobacco, lit it, then wheeled around again to face his dark-haired assistant, André Manuel.

Manuel was sitting in a chair facing the desk; he saw the cleft of worry between Passy's eyes.

The *Deuxième Bureau* had recently received a radiogram from Robert Delattre, Renault's chief radio operator in Brittany, a message that told the specific time the *Deux Anges*, bearing the Renault family, would set sail from the French coast and asked that the British send out a trawler to meet the boat.

"Do you think they have a chance?" Manuel asked.

"Should I speak frankly?" Passy responded.

"Certainly."

"Yes, of course, I think they have a chance," Passy said. "About one chance in five hundred."

Chapter 24

(1)

THE TYPEWRITERS OF CARLTON GARDENS WERE STILLED ON THE MORNING OF JUNE 10, 1942, AND THE MURMUR OF GREETINGS THAT NORMALLY ACCOMPANIED DE GAULLE'S ARRIVAL GAVE WAY TO SILENT AND RIGID salutes. As he proceeded stiffly toward his office that morning, battle-toughened veterans in the corridor shrank from his path. Never had his lips pressed tighter, never had his face seemed waxier or more inanimate, never had his eyes glowered more uncompromisingly straight ahead. He spoke to no one, barely acknowledged the salutes and then disappeared, distantly and fearsomely, behind the closed paneled door of his office.

A wave of awe and muted resentment spread through the building: why could not the General, his subordinates wondered, unbend, now, just for once? Now, of all times, they wanted reassurance, and that was precisely what the General seemed most determined not to give.

For the news had reached Britain from Libya: General Koenig was out of food, his men were exhausted, and General Rommel had unleashed his fiercest assault yet upon the defenders at Bir Hakeim. And the Free French were still being asked to hold out until the evening of June 10.

(2)

A thick fog had rolled over Bir Hakeim at dawn on June 8. Behind the mist the French could hear the clatter of tank treads and shouts in German as officers began lining up their infantry for the attack. The French crouched deeper into their trenches, loading their guns and placing their fingers in readiness on the triggers. The air was suddenly full of smoke and lead; artillery shells began to swish over the tops of the trenches. Machine-gun bullets zipped through the low scrub. Men in the trenches ripped off their shirts as they tried, with little success, to dig deeper into the hard bedrock that lay under the surface gravel of the desert. Then, an hour or two after dawn, the fog lifted, and the French saw the first wave of *Stukas* come swooping down across the horizon.

The German infantry charged next, heavily supported by tanks, sweeping in from the north, and forcing the *Bataillon de Marche*, that had gone out to meet the attack, back down a slight rise that overlooked the base. An Italian Colonel in an armored car was in the lead. Holding to the turret with one hand, he kept waving with the other and shouting, "*Avanti! Avanti!*"

By noon, however, the seventy-fives inside the base and the land mines outside had put most of the Axis vehicles out of order, and the attack ground to a halt.

Rommel was furious. Early in the afternoon he called upon the *Stukas* again. Plumes of dust and smoke mushroomed up from behind the French barricades. The German infantry charged again, knocking out a few of the French seventy-fives and driving a wedge between the two companies of the *Bataillon de Marche*. By nightfall one Axis combat group had fought its way to within two hundred yards of Bir Hakeim's barbed-wire perimeter.

(3)

Even before the sun rose the next morning the mist over the desert was thick with the dust churned up by the onrushing *Panzers*. General Rommel smelled blood. His tanks were everywhere now, rumbling out of the dust toward Bir Hakeim from every direction, looking monstrous and brutal as they emerged from the fog. Everytime the Free French looked up from their trenches now, they saw the same thing: the squat shape of the German Mark III's, turrets closed, crunching over the gravel closer and closer to the barbed-wire coils around the base.

Even when the remaining French artillery went into action, scoring a direct hat against a *Panzer*, lifting its turret high in the air, or hurling another tank on its side, or causing a great tongue of smoke and flame to leap skyward from deep inside a Mark III, even then more *Panzers* roared forth from the mist to continue the fight.

The French losses were heavy. Bombs and shells had ripped up most of the gravel terrain above the trenches, and one German bomb scored a direct hit upon a dressing station, killing nineteen of the wounded men lying inside. The gasoline tanks of several trucks exploded. Lieutenant-Colonel Broche and Captain de Bricourt died instantly when a German shell hit their command post.

The medical arrangements of the garrison were breaking down: plasma and anesthetics were dangerously low and the shortage of water prevented the doctors and nurses from washing the growing numbers of wounded bodies. One R.A.F. Bombay freight plane did somehow get through the German anti-aircraft fire to parachute in a load of medicine, but the chute failed to open and the wooden container plummeted off the ridge, shattering all the glass bottles that contained the vital supplies.

"Two or three times that day," wrote an observer, "the Germans over-ran the barbed-wire around Bir Hakeim; two times the French rose from the trenches to sweep them off," hurling hand grenades, firing machine guns, jabbing with bayonets, shooting with pistols, swinging with fists. Many Germans died in the assault but they outnumbered the French by more than ten to one, and the defenders could not continue forever without a pause. They needed food and they needed sleep and now they were getting neither.

And in the minefields far outside Bir Hakeim, General Rommel had ordered his artillery to step up its nighttime bombardment of Bir Hakeim. Nothing, he knew, could break morale more quickly than incessant racket and the lack of sleep.

(4)

A strange thing happened in Bir Hakeim, however, during the sleepless night of June 9–10. "General Koenig," de Gaulle had wired from London, "Know, and tell your troops, that the whole of France is looking at you, and you are her pride." And the men of Bir Hakeim responded to the message. There "was revived," wrote a journalist, "spontaneously in the desert all the spirit of the French soldier in the last war. In its small way there was a touch of Verdun about Bir Hakeim. . . . [The] French had fought with art and desperate comradeship and were gallant in their own way. All the bitter accusations against the French soldier after the fall of France were being denied and proved false under this little tri-color that kept hanging in dusty folds on the ridge of Bir Hakeim. Wherever you went in the desert, you found the rest of the men [in the Gazala Line] full of glowing pride for the French."

In the face of the German barrage that night, Koenig sent out his orders for the next morning: The men were to stay put at all costs; if necessary they were to let the tanks pass over them, then rise from the trenches to deal with the following enemy infantry. Koenig's command went out to the officers and the men, and unanimously they responded, "We'll do it! We'll hold on for one more day!"

(5)

The *Stukas* flew over at dawn the next morning.

"After one bombing," a Frenchman said, "I closed my eyes to sleep and so missed a lovely sight. An anti-aircraft gun got a direct hit on the bomb rack of a *Stuka*, and the slow silver plane burst in mid-air. They tell me it exploded with a huge orange flame shaped like a candle flame, and the two wings spiraled down to earth burning. The engine fell in the middle of a triangle formed by the tents of the officers at HQ. The pilot was thrown out of the cockpit, and his automatic parachute opened; he swung down to earth, blackened, burned to a cinder."

But then a German combat group, sweeping down in armored cars from the north, broke through the barbed wire around Bir Hakeim and the first line of defensive trenches. French Bren-gun carriers, under Lieutenant Dewey, rushed forward for the counterattack, and a violent fight took place. Rommel could see the struggle from a distance: the battling was ferocious, he wrote, "with the French desperately defending every single nest of resistance and suffering terrible casualties as a result." Through a supreme effort, Dewey's Legionnaires managed to contain the breakthrough.

Rommel threw "more and more metal into the attack," a French correspondent radioed out, "and though his losses grew proportionately greater, [more] of the tanks broke through our defenses and rolled right up to our guns. When our guns were overrun, it was men against tank. At one post, held by the Foreign Legion, a German tank scored a direct hit at twenty yards. The officer commanding the post—a calm young man from Saint-Cyr—burnt his regiment's standard so that it would not be captured, and then called on his men to attack. With incendiary grenades in their hands, they flung themselves on the tanks like infuriated hornets.

"There are some things," the correspondent continued, "I can never forget. The Legionnaire who, with blood streaming from his face, climbed onto a German tank and emptied his revolver through an aperture, killing all the occupants. The sergeant-major who destroyed seven tanks. The gun crew, who, when a shell stuck on the breach of their cannon at the height of the battle, gambled their lives by knocking the shell out with a hammer.

"In less than two hours Koenig's men destroyed thirty-seven tanks. Somehow, incredibly, the attack was repelled. The Germans and Italians retreated, seemingly appalled by the blind fury of the defenders. That moment will always live in my mind. The tanks withdrawing, screening the fleeing infantry. On the ground a ghastly chaos—a mingling of shell craters, dead and wounded Frenchmen, Germans and Italians. In that moment of victory, no cries of triumph, only the indescribable expression of defiance of the blackened, exhausted French.

"Since then, and up to thirty minutes ago, there was that uncanny silence. Now they are pounding us again, and hard. The shelling and bombing are rising to a crescendo. We are straining our eyes to see what they are preparing . . . beyond our lines."

The message, here, broke off.

Bir Hakeim was fast becoming untenable. Phalanxes of *Panzers* forming huge battering rams were thundering in from every side and in their wake came long lines of trucks bearing infantry and protected on both sides by columns of light tanks. Throughout the afternoon the enormous black juggernaut pushed in nearer and nearer with no break in tempo. *Stukas* were pouring in from the skies as well, a distant throbbing the French could hear even over the roar of gunfire, a distant throbbing that turned quickly into a harsh buzzing, getting louder and louder by the second in a terrifying crescendo until the planes came hurtling almost vertically downwards toward the vulnerable openings in the trenches. The remaining hospital tent in Bir Hakeim suffered a direct hit, most of the trucks and armored cars in the base exploded into towering mushroom clouds, and by late afternoon the French had run out of nearly everything, shells for their mortars, rounds for their field guns, water to quench thirsts and to cool machine guns, everything that was needed for further resistance. The men were calm but their blackened faces were showing the strain, and the enemy cannon were searching them out at will.

Then, at last, night fell, and Koenig's men knew that they had done their job. They had not won, but they had held on—for just as long as the British had asked them to hold. Despite their losses, out of the original thirty-six hundred, fifteen hundred men were killed or missing—they had refused to surrender.

But now they faced a still more dangerous task: they were going to try to escape. After sundown Koenig wired a coded message to Tobruk, saying that he would try to pass through the German lines that same night. Could the British send down a convoy of trucks and tanks to meet him at a point five miles west of Bir Hakeim? Yes, came back the answer, and Koenig set to work immediately preparing his men to flee under the cover of night.

There was, however, one major flaw in Koenig's plan: General Rommel knew he was coming.

Chapter 25

(1)

"**L**ISTEN, MY FRIEND," GILBERT RENAULT WAS SAYING AS HE TAPPED THE SHOULDER OF THE DRIVER OF THE HORSE-DRAWN CARRIAGE, "WOULD YOU OBJECT TO MAKING MORE MONEY?"

The driver, a peasant boy, kept his eyes on the road but cocked his head backwards to hear the proposal.

"*Eh bien,*" Renault said, "here's what I'd like you to do."

It was a warm, early summer evening, June 16, 1941, and after several nerve-wracking delays caused by failures in the *Deux Anges'* engine, the Renaults were ready at last to leave France. To cover their tracks they had taken rooms at the Hôtel Ostrea, in the secluded Breton village of Riec-sur-Belon, and now, on their last night together in France, Renault was treating Edith to a romantic carriage ride along the shore and dinner at the four-star Moulin Rosmadec, just down the coast at Pont-Aven. Renault had another reason, too, for going to the Moulin Rosmadec: there he would meet Alex Tanguy, who had docked the *Deux Anges* in Pont-Aven and who would brief the Renaults on the details of tomorrow morning's voyage. But the young driver of the carriage also fit into Renault's schemes.

"Could you pick us up," Renault was asking, "at five o'clock tomorrow morning? I'm taking my wife and children to Quimper for a picnic by the sea, and friends are going to pick us up in their car in Pont-Aven, but we don't have any way of getting from here to Pont-Aven. Could you help us out? I'll double your price because of the hour."

Renault leaned back in the carriage seat to await the boy's answer. He took Edith's hand. Her palm, he noticed, was damp. So, he suspected, was his own. For a long time the driver said nothing. The horse clip-clopped down a road from which one could see the breakers sweeping in from the sea, and at last pulled into view of a half-timbered, wisteria-covered inn beside a roaring weir. That was the Moulin Rosmadec. The driver reined the horse to a stop, then climbed out to help Edith Renault down from her seat. When she was safely upon the ground he turned his boyish face up to Renault and said, simply: "Yes, I'll be there. Five o'clock."

Renault himself climbed down from the carriage—and as he did he reached onto the seat beside him and picked up a tin biscuit box sealed shut with tape to keep moisture out. The box was about to leave on a sea-going voyage and its contents were invaluable: it contained the map of the Atlantic wall.

A waiter inside brought fat Bélon oysters to the long table at the back where the Renaults sat with Alex Tanguy, and then a plate piled high with Breton crabs, stuffed with herbs and mushrooms and garnished with lemon quarters. For the first time in months, Renault's cheeks began to take color. From the table he could see the water from the weir outside cascade over the ancient mill wheel and back into the stream again, and beyond that, he could see the square stone Breton houses that stretched in a row to the end of the quay. He took a sip of his cold dry Muscadet and turned, with great reluctance, to discuss the plans for tomorrow's escape.

Tanguy was talking, in his usual growl of a voice. The *Deux Anges* was docked out there, he said, at the end of the quay they could see through the window. If they left early enough tomorrow, few people would see them from the village.

"Be back here at six in the morning," he told the Renaults. "As you know, it's about an hour's ride in the carriage from Riec. You *have* to be here on time. We'll go along with the other fishing boats that way to Port-Manech at the mouth of the river—the Germans inspect the boats there. If we're with others we have a better chance of getting through unno-ticed."

"How do they do the inspection?" Edith asked, gripping her hus-band's hand under the table.

Tanguy's tone was blunt: "They check every other boat."

"And if they board ours," Edith persisted, "will they find us and the children?"

"Yes."

(2)

The hands of the alarm clock pointed to four the next morning: neither of the Renaults had slept, and although Gilbert had pretended to doze, he had felt Edith's body beside him, stiff and trembling with fear. And now it was time to leave the hotel. Only baby Michel, in his crib beside the bed, seemed to have slept that night.

While Edith went down to the kitchen to prepare the baby's bottle, Renault turned on the harsh light in the children's room next door. Catherine and Cécile were in the same bed, sleeping back to back; Jean-Claude was curled up in his own bed, with the sheet pulled over his head.

"Get dressed quickly, children," Renault said as the children were rubbing their eyes. He waited until they were fully awake before telling them of his plans.

"We're going on a trip," he explained. "We're going to get on a boat soon, and we're going to try to get out of here to England. Our chances of succeeding are small. But if we stay here the Gestapo will certainly catch us before long. I want you to obey me absolutely at every moment during the trip."

All three children were sitting straight up in bed, their eyes wide and attentive.

The proprietress of the Hôtel Ostrea, Renault went on, who believed they were starting at dawn for a picnic by the sea, had promised to leave the front door unlocked, and exactly at five o'clock the driver and his carriage would meet them at the front door.

"Now remember this, children," he said, "for the rest of the day our name is not Renault, but Recordier. Recordier. Can you remember that?"

Three young heads nodded in silence.

"Now say your prayers," he told them, "and get dressed at once."

By half-past four all the children were dressed and Renault was stealing down the staircase to make sure that the front door was open. He crossed the hotel lobby and turned the knob of the door. Then he cursed. The landlady had locked the door, after all.

He dashed from room to room, even racing into the kitchen, but every door in the place was locked and nowhere he looked could he find a key. It was now five-forty-five, fifteen minutes before the horse-drawn carriage was due to arrive and an hour and fifteen minutes before the Renaults were supposed to be aboard the *Deux Anges.* And Renault could not even get out of the hotel.

Perhaps he could find the landlady, he thought, and he pounded on the doors of all the rooms downstairs, trying to awaken her, wherever she was sleeping. But she failed to appear. Five o'clock came, and then five-fifteen, and still no landlady. And worse yet, Renault had heard nothing outside that resembled the kock-kock of horse's hoofs.

(3)

Then Renault heard a sound on the staircase: it was the landlady at last, in dressing gown and hair curlers, somehow managing to yawn and apologize both at the same time.

Renault cut her short, viciously, and told her to open the door immediately. She did—after glancing at him in angered surprise—and he stepped out onto the village square. He looked around, then came back in to speak to his family upstairs.

"It's too late," he told them in a tremulous voice, "the driver has forgotten, too."

It was now five-thirty, half an hour before scheduled sailing time.

Then, suddenly, Catherine and Jean-Claude ran to the window: "He's here," they shouted at their father. "The man with the horse is here."

Renault slipped the young driver a few hundred francs more than he had originally promised, and the horse went clip-clopping away in a fast trot. Soon the family was scurrying along the quay in Pont-Aven, Renault in the lead, wearing a shabby raincoat and carrying both the baby and the biscuit box with the map, the girls and Jean-Claude came next, and behind them ran their mother, trying to hustle the children along. They were late. It was six-fifteen, and already shutters were clattering back against the whitewashed stone walls of the houses along the quay.

The engine of the *Deux Anges* was sputtering away, unevenly, through the thick mist. Renault began to make excuses when they reached the boat, but Tanguy interrupted roughly.

"Just get aboard," he barked, "and do what I tell you to do. We don't have a second to spare."

The boat shoved off at once, chugging out between the high banks of the stream and the outcroppings of rock and yellow gorse. The throttle was open wide, racing to catch the other fishing boats that would be lining up at the Port-Manech inspection point. A chilly, salty Atlantic wind came up: Renault pulled Michel close to his raincoat to keep the baby warm.

A voice bellowed through the wind. It was Tanguy's: "Now get in your places. I'll show you where. Go on! Go on! Hurry up! We'll be at Port-Manech in ten minutes."

Tanguy made Edith and the older children lie down in the horizontal stern lockers—six feet long and three feet wide—and closed the sliding panels that sealed them off from the deck. Renault himself took Michel and the tin biscuit box with the map into the forward hold. He sat down between two gasoline drums, and then the door closed above him, leaving him in absolute blackness.

The smell of stale fish and gasoline vapor in the hold was nauseating. Holding Michel in his arms, Renault pitched forward, gagging. He cracked his elbow against something sharp and metallic, and swore.

The hatch swung open: Renault could see a square of daylight.

Tanguy's voice was commanding: "No noise at all now! We're approaching Control. They might come aboard!"

(4)

The blackness closed around Renault once more. He leaned back against something that felt rounded and hard like a gasoline drum; the floor of the hold was cold and slimy beneath the seat of his pants. Little Michel was lying stomach down and silent upon his father's chest, but his chubby fingers were busy exploring the buttons down the front of Renault's coat. The baby was wide awake, Renault sensed, and was bound at any moment to start calling out for his mother—and the Germans would certainly hear him if they came aboard for inspection.

There was only one thing to do—give the baby his bottle. Edith had filled it that morning before they left the hotel and, wrapping it in a thin woolen scarf, had given it to her husband to carry in the pocket of his raincoat. Renault extracted the bottle from his pocket, unfolded the scarf and could find no nipple. The fingers of his right hand fumbled in the depths of the pocket, clasped the folded tissue paper that contained the nipple. Just then the engine of the *Deux Anges* chugged loudly and shifted into low, slowing down for what was evidently the German Control post.

Renault had managed to get hold of the nipple, but the seesawing of the boat in the choppy waves and the complete blackness of the hold made it difficult for him to fit it onto the top of the bottle. The boat rolled and he spilled the still open bottle. A few drops of milk ran along the back of his hand and dripped on to the baby's cheek. With sharp, unmistakable clarity, Michel laughed. And the boat was bumping against a pier.

The nipple was finally in place, and Renault held the bottle securely in his right hand, turned Michel's head on its side with his left, and tried to slip the bottle into the baby's mouth. But Michel had already had his breakfast and his active hands pushed the bottle away; trying to squirm out of his father's arms, he started to gurgle.

Renault could hear voices outside the hold, guttural and official-sounding voices, then hobnailed boots, presumably German, clanged against the stone of a jetty. A German was talking to Alex Tanguy, in French: the voices sounded directly above the door of the hold.

It was then that Michel decided to let loose his first scream of the morning.

(5)

Someone on deck, thinking fast, dropped anchor to muffle the sound of Michel's voice. Renault leaned back against the gasoline drum, clamping his right hand over the baby's mouth, holding his own body motionless and still, listening. A guttural voice and Tanguy's were snapping back and forth, the German's obviously making some kind of demand. Then the voices died out and Renault heard a footstep overhead. It was a heavy tread, pounding across the deck, closer and closer to Renault until it stopped directly beside the trap door over his head.

Michel was squirming hard to get free, his legs kicking, his arms flailing, his torso twisting. He began to grunt. Renault pressed his hand harder over the baby's mouth, struggling to keep the child from making noise. The booted feet were shifting overhead—and Michel was fighting to yell out.

Renault had a thought. Two days before he had bought the children a bag of chocolate drops and he thought there might still be a few left. But where were they? Hadn't he left them in one of the pockets of his raincoat? His fingers explored the pocket where the bottle of milk had been. No chocolate drops. He reached into the pocket on his left side and felt around. His fingers touched crumpled paper—that was the bag. Quickly he popped a chocolate drop into Michel's mouth, hoping fervently that the baby would not choke or cough, holding his own breath again, and waiting.

A voice in German spoke out, loudly, just outside the trap door, no more than three feet from Renault's head. His mouth filled with saliva, he could not control it, it flowed down his chin. He thought he was going to vomit.

Then two things happened at once: Michel began to suck on the chocolate, and the heavy footsteps pounded away from the door of the hold. With a jerk, a movement of the boat threw Renault sideways into another gasoline drum. What, he wondered, was going on? The hold was now full of fumes and the engine was throbbing noisily. Renault refused to let himself hope. The *Deux Anges* heaved, it rose and fell and rocked — were the waves doing that? What seemed to be a second wave, then a third tilted the boat; it was seesawing faster and faster. It was gathering speed. It was up to two-thirds speed, now it seemed to be doing top speed. Was it true? Was it true?

Renault sat up straight and pounded on the door. It opened, he blinked in the sudden sunlight, and then he had his answer.

Alex Tanguy was looking down into the hold, and, for the only time Renault could ever remember, the man was grinning.

"They only wanted to look at our list," Tanguy hollered down. The Germans had searched the boat in front, Tanguy explained, and the one behind, but not the *Deux Anges.* "We're free," Tanguy yelled out. "We're free."

And then Michel cried out for his mother, and his father began to pray.

(6)

Two years later, after the liberation of Paris and long after the taped biscuit box that contained the map of the Atlantic wall had reached Great Britain, General Omar Bradley entered a restaurant in the rue de Lille in Paris, a restaurant frequented by men of the Resistance, and stopped at the table of one of the men who had worked with René Duchez in Caen back in 1942.

"I have something to say to you," Bradley began. "I must inform you of the gratitude of the American army in regard to your network. It was only after the reception in London of the plans of the coastal defenses of the Channel area that we chose our landing point and were able to make our arrangements. The information that this plan gave us was of such value that our landing operation succeeded with a minimum loss of men and *matériel.*"

Chapter 26

(1)

THE MAIN OFFICES OF CARLTON GARDENS WERE EMPTY ON THE MORNING OF JUNE 11, 1942: NO VOICES SPOKE INTO TELEPHONES, NO FINGERS TAPPED AT TYPEWRITERS, NO FOUNTAIN PENS SCRIBBLED ON DOCUMENTS, no eyes looked out at the trees and the flowers and the sunshine in St. James's Park. The usually bustling corridors were as empty and silent as if they had been bombed. And in a sense, a bomb *had* fallen. The receiver in the basement radio room had crackled that morning with the reports of the attempted escape from Bir Hakeim, and everybody in Carlton Gardens, secretaries, civilian officials, soldiers and sailors, everybody, that is, except General de Gaulle himself, had rushed to the basement to hear the news.

General de Gaulle had stayed in his office, secluded, remote, distant and fearsome. He had given the strictest orders that nobody disturb him other than the messenger with word of Bir Hakeim.

(2)

Early in the evening of June 10, General Koenig worked out his plan of escape. While the British Seventh Motor Brigade ran a convoy of tanks, trucks and ambulances down through the minefields, Koenig organized his columns and gave instructions to the two companies that had volunteered to stay behind as a deception party. He would launch the breakout at midnight: Koenig himself would lead the way in a half-track, four ambulances would follow, then one English Morris and ten empty munitions trucks loaded with stretchers of the wounded. The vehicles would drive in two tight columns, staying no more than a yard apart and followed by marching infantry, and as they passed through the narrow gap the sappers had cleared in the minefield, they would try to steer toward the blue flares of the British convoy, five miles off across the desert.

Koenig's messengers crawled along the trenches to deliver these instructions to the troops, and at nightfall, as the Free French converged upon the spot where Koenig was assembling the trucks, the sappers left the base in parties of two and three to clear the path through the mines.

(3)

But General Rommel was waiting. A French soldier his men had caught wandering in the minefield had given away valuable information: how the escape would be organized, where it would take place and when it was scheduled to start. And Rommel had prepared a surprise. He had just received six newly manufactured MG. 42's, machine guns that could rattle off twenty-five shots a second, and he had located them in fortified nests close to the point in the barbed wire where Koenig was planning to cross. Then he sent couriers running over the gravel terrain to pass on his orders in whispers, telling the machine gunners and artillery men and infantry captains and tank commanders exactly where they could expect the French to come.

(4)

Koenig had hoped to leave at midnight but the darkness and the shrapnel from the exploding shells made loading the vehicles slow work. Unless the men could squeeze a piece of equipment into their backpacks or tie it to the fenders of the trucks, they simply dropped it, abandoned, on the gravel floor of their camp. Not until two-thirty in the morning were Koenig's troops ready to go. Amidst great confusion, they piled into the backs of trucks, onto the sides of armored cars, onto the turrets of tanks or into the ranks of the infantry columns, with their remaining hand grenades ready and their bayonets fixed.

The infantry captains gave last-minute instructions; the drivers put their vehicles in neutral and made ready to turn their ignition keys. Koenig stood up in his armored car: in the flashes of the exploding shells he could see the black outlines of the trucks and men behind him.

He reached down, tapped his driver on the shoulder, giving the signal to start off, and amidst the rum-rumming of motors and the scrape of feet upon gravel, the Free French began moving toward the barbed-wire perimeter of Bir Hakeim.

(5)

Rommel's orders had gone out in whispers to his men flanking the escape path: every machine gun was loaded and trained on the breakout point, every infantry group was ready to charge, every tank was in position to roar off toward the Free French column. But, Rommel's orders had said, no one was to move yet. They were to wait, standing without noise and without revealing their presence until they saw the signal to fire, green stars preceded by a red flare. Only then were the German guns to speak.

(6)

The Free French column moved as quickly as it could toward the barbed-wire defenses. It passed the ruins of the old, rectangular Beau Geste fort, the rubble-filled squares of the two demolished hospital tents, the shells of the burned-out trucks and armored cars, the machine-gun nests, the slit trenches, the pillboxes, the observation posts and, at last, it reached the coils of barbed-wire that formed the great twisting defensive circle around the trenches of Bir Hakeim.

Infantrymen with shears raced forward to clip a hole in the barbed wire: and then the Free French column was out of the base, moving into the gap in the minefield that led, they hoped, to safety.

In that moment the black sky lit up, first with a red flare, and next with a veritable firmament of little green stars.

(7)

News of the battle's results reached the outer world in installments.

The first to learn anything were the crewmen and drivers of the British Seventh Motor Brigade, waiting in the night near Rommel's flank five miles northwest of Bir Hakeim. They had been waiting since midnight at the rendezvous point, seeing nothing of the Free French column, but at around two-forty-five the sky in front of them turned orange and white with the explosions of shells, and far off in the darkness they could hear the monotonous, awesome, incredibly rapid rat-tat-tat of Rommel's new machine guns. Then, an hour later, the Britishers began to learn what had happened.

The next reports reached Tobruk before dawn. Rommel had thrown his infantry and *Panzers* headlong into the ranks of the escaping Frenchmen. A wild melee had followed. The French had fought back with the only weapons they had left, revolvers, bayonets, hand grenades, spades, bare hands. But Rommel still pressed on with his forces scattering the French dangerously into the minefields, and disrupting communications between officers and men.

More information reached England by radio later that morning. Rommel had thrown more and more metal into the attack, *Panzer* armored cars, artillery, incessantly chattering machine-gun fire. Intelligence reports poured into Whitehall. The Germans had overrun Bir Hakeim, they said, Rommel had slaughtered every Frenchman he could find. Koenig, the messages said, had surrendered.

Then, at midday on June 11, the definitive report reached the radio room in Carlton Gardens, and a young messenger raced up the stairs to take the news to General de Gaulle.

(8)

As the youth again crossed the carpet in de Gaulle's spacious office, and reached the front edge of the wide mahogany desk, he stopped, nearly stumbled, stood straight and jerked his arm in a frightened salute. Like everyone else in the building, he was afraid of the General: he wondered if he could stammer out the words he had come to say.

The General looked up from his desk with an icy stare. His face was an impenetrable mask: his plastered-down black hair and his low narrow forehead seemed part of a wax statue; his small blackened eyes showed no trace of human feeling; his huge nose and tightly pressed lips seemed grotesque and unearthly. His mouth opened round, showing irregular teeth as he said, impatiently: "You may speak."

The messenger felt almost hypnotized by the power of the General's glare. He found he could not utter a word.

De Gaulle spoke again: "Yes?" he demanded. "What is it?"

The boy was still struggling to speak.

The General's voice commanded once again: "Tell me what you have come to say!"

Then the news, the real news, burst forth from the boy's lips. Of the two thousand Frenchmen who had left Bir Hakeim, he said, one hundred and thirty-nine were dead, one hundred and ninety-eight were wounded, eight hundred and twenty-nine were reported missing. The rest—including General Koenig—had escaped to Tobruk. There had never been the slightest question of surrender.

General de Gaulle said nothing. His stone mask of a face showed no emotion at all. He seemed almost not to have heard the messenger's words; he appeared riveted to his chair.

He rose from his desk at last, and went to the window, standing with his back to the room. He stood there for a long time. His back was straight and his long thin wrists, reaching the edge of his jacket, were as immobile as if they had been carved from stone. His gaze traveled out past the trees in St. James's Park. He stood stiffly, like a statue, scarcely breathing, and when he turned back from the window again, his eyes were still abstracted and his mouth as still as plaster. He had almost reached the chair behind his desk when the face of the statue shattered.

His small chin trembled with violence, his mouth tore open into a square, his nose became twisted and bent, and his long fingers flew up to cover his eyes.

General de Gaulle was crying.

Chapter 27

THEY WERE DESCENDING FROM EVERY DIRECTION, AT FIRST SINGLY OR IN PAIRS AS THEY WALKED THROUGH THE GATES OF PADDINGTON STATION OR PAST THE BRICK ROW HOUSES IN CHELSEA, THEN IN SMALL CLUSTERS as they passed under the green branches in Hyde Park or in front of the shops in Knightsbridge, and finally, in a huge sea of Foreign Legion uniforms, civilian suits and dresses and red naval pompons as they mounted the steps and filed through the massive doors of the Royal Albert Hall in London. It was the evening of June 18, 1942, exactly two years after General de Gaulle had first spoken to France from the underground studio of the B.B.C. Now, a large part of the French community in London had come to hear him again, and to celebrate the glories of the battle of Bir Hakeim. Although de Gaulle had not yet seized the reins of power in France, the audience sensed that Bir Hakeim marked the first great Gaullist success, the first real turning point, the end of the beginning. They knew with certainty now that the General's *mystique* would spread throughout France and that he was destined to become the symbol of the salvation of his country.

At precisely eight o'clock, a wave of tumultuous applause swept through the great auditorium. General de Gaulle was walking toward the podium.

He seemed as rigid as ever, and his chest squared like that of a wooden carving. His face, small when compared to his height, pointed uncompromisingly straight ahead. His eyes were distant and mouth was fixed and expressionless. He reached the podium and raised his long arms in the "V-for-Victory" gesture. The crowd of thousands roared in delight and exultation. He waited for silence, and then he began.

"Chamfort once said: 'Men of reason have endured. Men of passion have lived,'" de Gaulle spoke. His voice was high and quavering; his gestures, as always, choppy.

"For two years now," he continued, "France, surrendered and betrayed at Bordeaux, has nevertheless continued the war through the weapons, the territories, and the soul of Fighting France!"

At the mere use of his new name for Free France, the entire assemblage stood up to cheer.

Then he went on: "During these two years, we have lived greatly, for we are men of passion. But we have also endured, for we are men of reason.

"I say we are men of passion. Yet we have but one passion: France! Thousands of our people who, since the so-called armistice, have given their lives for her on the battlefields of Africa and the east, on every sea, in the skies over Britain, Eritrea and Libya . . . or on execution-grounds at dawn, have whispered the name of France with their last breath. The millions of our people who stand firm, whether making ready for revenge in their native land, striking at the enemy in battle, upholding in the free Empire, in their posts as administrators, magistrates, doctors, teachers, colonists, and missionaries, her sacred sovereignty and beneficent influence, or keeping watch abroad over her ties of friendship and her good name, have but one wish, to serve France, but one thought, to be loyal. And since nothing great can be accomplished without passion, the great task to which duty has pledged us demands a passion for France.

"I say we are men of reason. Indeed, we have chosen the hardest, yet easiest, path: the straight path. . . . Events have proved that this straightforwardness was, and remains, the best possible policy. Without doubt, a certain deviation from our duties, certain compromises with our responsibilities might at times have made us appear somewhat more accommodating. It might less often have been said of us: How tiresome they are! But at the same time we should have lost the very spark which is our *raison d'être*—honor, without compromise, in the service of our country. For with France reduced to her present straits neither surrender of principles nor deals are conceivable. What would have become of the country had Joan of Arc, Danton, or Clemenceau been willing to come to terms? From disaster to victory, the straight line is not only the shortest, but also the surest, way. . . .

"Yes, for two years now, the waves have not ceased to batter the France still in the fight. At home, oppression, propaganda and poverty have combined for her subjugation. Abroad, she has had to overcome countless material and moral difficulties. Yet invincible Fighting France emerges from the seas. When a ray of her reborn glory touched the bloodied brows of her soldiers at Bir Hakeim, the whole world recognized France.

"The ordeal, we know, is by no means over. We realize what strength and cunning the enemy still commands, and that some time must inevitably elapse before the defenders of liberty can deploy their full forces. But since France has made known her determination to triumph, there can be no doubting, flagging, or renunciation for us. United in battle, we shall loyally fulfill our duty towards France, never resting until national liberation is accomplished. Then, our task completed, our part played, following all who served her since the dawn of her history, precursors of all who will serve her in her eternal future, we shall say to France, simply, in the words of Péguy: *Mother, behold thy sons, who have fought so hard.*"

General de Gaulle had finished. For a moment the orchestra and balconies of the Albert Hall were silent. Faces frozen and bodies immobile. Then, here and there, by a seat in a balcony, and from a box on the side, and in an aisle on the floor, a few persons stood and a few choked voices began to sing. More and more people rose from their seats, more and more and more voices began to sing out, still more people stood and still more voices sounded until the entire congregation was up on its feet, at strict attention and singing as if from one throat the words of the anthem still forbidden in France:

> Allons, enfants de la Patrie,
> Le jour de gloire est arrivé,
> Contre nous, de la tyrannie,
> L'étendard sanglant est levé,
> L'étendard sanglant est levé.
> Entendez-vous, dans les campagnes,
> Mugir ces féroces soldats?
> Ils viennent jusque dans nos bras,
> Egorger nos fils, nos compagnes!
> Aux armes, citoyens,
> Formez vos bataillons!
> Marchons, marchons,
> Qu'un sang impur
> Abreuve nos sillons!

When they had reached the end of the *"Marseillaise,"* General de Gaulle left the podium, his legs stiff, his lips pressed tight, his glare as intransigent as ever, and then he disappeared behind the wings of the stage.

Epilogue

We must not overstate the Gaullist myth of a France beset by weakness and daunted by demons, then pulling itself together under the General's tutelage and climbing again the slope toward the final victory. Reality was more complicated than that. The Gaullists were by no means the only resisters: after Hitler's invasion of Russia in 1941, the embittered French Communist Party turned to violence and rebellion, and so did Christian Democrats, priests, army men, small businessmen throughout France, many of whom accepted de Gaulle as their symbol only, and not their leader, and who deeply resented his having chosen to carry on the fight from the comparative safety of London. Even in London there were always Frenchmen who refused to pledge allegiance to the General, for if his call to honor had attracted many, his coldness and arrogance had repelled others—one either loved or hated de Gaulle. Thousands more in France, furthermore, joined the "armies of the shadows" only in the last days of the war when it was manifestly clear that the Germans were on the run. And, it is obvious, de Gaulle needed others as much as they needed him. The exploits of men like René Duchez (who died a few years after the war—after receiving the Croix de Guerre), Gilbert Renault (who went on to become a best-selling and prolific memoirist) and, later, Jean Moulin, whom the Germans executed and who became the best-known Gaullist martyr, contributed nearly as much to the General's *mystique* as did de Gaulle's presence itself.

But still, the Gaullist myth was basically true. To a great extent, it was his metaphor, his legend, that shocked the French awake from their dream of a sheltered neutrality and showed them that their love affair with Pétain rested on delusion (in a burst of frenzied hatred after the Liberation in 1944, the new French government executed Laval and found Pétain guilty of treason— de Gaulle, as head of that government, pardoned the Marshal). And building on the style he had created during the first two years of the war, the General transformed himself and the Free French movement into the most potent force in postwar France: Leclerc, the hero of Chad, rose to the rank of General, led the first Allied units into Paris in 1944, and played a leading role in the fight against the Vietminh in Indo-China; Pierre Mendès-France, later a Premier of France, became part of Free France in February, 1942, and flew with General de Gaulle's Air Force; Geoffroy de Courcel, the aide-de-camp who flew with de Gaulle from Bordeaux to London, has served in several high diplomatic and governmental posts. And although he had no record of work in the Resistance, Georges Pompidou became a loyal member of the General's staff in Paris in 1944. He has since earned his reward.

But the question remains: How did de Gaulle do it? How did he advance from ignominy to fame? How did he rise from obscurity to become the Louis XIV or the Napoleon Bonaparte of modern France? How did he draw to himself the hopes and the wills of his countrymen "as the magnet draws iron"?

His appeal derived in part from his character. From his earliest days to the end, the loftiness and remoteness of his thinking, the arrogance of his scorn for the compromises and docilities of his fellows, the unworldliness of his obsession with destiny and the cold-bloodedness of his willingness to sacrifice anybody and anything, including his own career, to recapture the grandeur of France, had made him an outsider who invented and followed his own rules alone. These qualities had condemned him to spite and ridicule in the years before the fall of France because they cut across the entrenched prejudices and complacencies of the era. But these qualities were precisely what the French came to crave in the months and years after the débâcle of 1940. It was in the crisis of defeat that his call to honor began to strike deep chords; it was in the despair of occupation that his evocations of greatness began not to offend but to inspire; it was in the faraway yet discernible hope of liberation that his arrogance seemed the arrogance of creativity and his intransigence the pride of the nation. His uncannily accurate predictions of the course and results of the German invasion made him seem the prophet in the wilderness and he emerged from the trials and victories of 1940–1942 a hero pure, unbound and self-made. To many Frenchmen the General's sternness provided a warm and comforting discipline; they could avoid making complex decisions, they could narrow the focus of their lives, they could believe in the all-transcending importance of their work in the Resistance.

But character alone was not enough. The General de Gaulle of St. Stephen's House and Carlton Gardens had no constitutional claim to leadership, and he knew it. To save what he valued most deeply, the honor of France, he had rebelled against the state. He was, officially, a traitor. He had, therefore, to conjure up, out of his own weakness and poverty, a new basis of legitimacy. He had to *act out* the role of the rightful leader of France and with no resources other than the skill of his performance, make his audience suspend disbelief. De Gaulle's was a theatrical impulse, applied to a political stage, and like any other artist of note, he became a master of his craft.

His was a grand spectacle, fast moving, stage-managed with care, epic in proportion and designed in the seductiveness of its dreams and illusions to arouse the passions and morale of the audience. His quarrels with Churchill (and later with Presidents Roosevelt and Kennedy) often seemed deliberately contrived to magnify the obstacles he faced and to cast him in the part of the persecuted patriot, "too poor to bend," spiting others to save France. His decisions were bold and romantic, taken in the face of enormous odds and pitting a few ragged, ordinary Frenchmen such as Renault, Duchez and the troops at Bir Hakeim against an enemy both formidable, determined and evil. His stagecraft was suspenseful, a rousing tale of personal initiative, narrow escapes, dangers and pitfalls and ultimate success. His public appearances thrust him into the spotlight: he spoke with a mystical and lofty assurance, *as if* France were great again, *as if* he were truly her leader. His exits, withdrawals and silences heightened his stature through mystery and reproduced the distance of the relationship between awed subjects and their King. And so from behind the footlights of his stage in exile, he was able at last to implant in *most* Frenchmen, as he had once implied he would, "a sort of moral suggestion that [went] far beyond all reasoning and [crystallized] round his own person all their potentialities of faith, hope and devotion."

Such theatricality enabled the General to represent himself as the last of the giants of French history: the stilted rhetoric of his speeches resembled the rhythms of Richelieu, the stiffness of his gestures evoked the dignity of Henri IV, the mystery and ritual of his public appearances suggested the pomp of Napoleon, and the *panache* with which he defied the world brought to mind the antics of Cyrano de Bergerac. The General was thus able to draw up upon himself the mantle of myth, to associate himself with the most sacred symbols of French culture.

It had its costs, however, at least for de Gaulle. The gods of tragedy punished pride by fulfilling man's wishes too well, and by the very magnitude of his success the General condemned himself to a lifetime of loneliness. He became indeed the symbol he had wished to become and so, in the end, he had no one outside his family whom he could call friend. For if he commanded respect, he also instilled fear. His ferocious concentration of both intellect and character upon a single, abstract target, the greatness of France, threatened the casual, sprawling shapes of ordinary men's lives.

But his country did, and does, hold him in awe. Hundreds of thousands of tourists have visited Colombey in the years since his death, and there they behave like tourists at any other national shrine: they pose for photographs in front of his house, they buy up souvenirs such as the ballpoint pen molded into a uniformed torso and topped with a huge nose and two-starred kepi, and they gawk at the huge stone Cross of Lorraine that dominates the village today. But then they enter the graveyard behind the ancient stone church and pause at the headstone that reads simply: "CHARLES DE GAULLE 1890–1970." And, as the General himself once wrote of Napoleon, "in spite of the time that had gone by, of opposing sentiments and new subjects for mourning, crowds from every part of the world render homage to his memory and near his grave abandon themselves to a shiver of greatness!"

Reference Notes

The bibliography that follows lists the works (only a fraction of those that have dealt with the fall of France and the career of General de Gaulle) that I have used to a greater or lesser extent in the course of writing this book. I feel I should, however, indicate which sources were of especially great help in which chapters, and add certain notes of explanation, qualification and elaboration. The works are cited below by name of author and refer, unless otherwise indicated, to the books listed in the Bibliography. The numbers alongside the names of certain authors indicate that more than one work by them is mentioned in the Bibliography. In such cases, the numbers following the author's names refer to the sequential listing of their works in the Bibliography.

Although I have been in touch, personally or by correspondence, with numerous persons who were involved with the Free French movement, I have relied most heavily in my researches upon works published during the Second World War or shortly thereafter. The Gaullist myth grew and grew over time until it became the semiofficial ideology of the Fifth Republic, and like all such myths, it stands like a brick wall between memory and fact. The capacity of English and French alike excessively to laud or denounce the General was stunning. I have, therefore, used conversations and correspondence primarily to supplement, double-check, and clarify points already made in contemporary source material.

Chapter 1: Baudouin, Gamelin, Guderian (1), Reynaud (1 and 2), Sevareid. This chapter raises the question of *why* the High Command was so reluctant to act. I touch on the answer in Chapter 2, but a thorough response would fill (and has filled) whole libraries. The most widely accepted theories are: (1) that the High Command felt cold-shouldered by the French public and so believed it lacked the support needed for an aggressive military policy; (2) that the members of the High Command were old men and so incapable of devising and accepting new policies; (3) that the High Command, consisting as it did of officers who had experienced the trench warfare of the First World War, was horrified at the thought that the violence might be repeated, and so stood by hypnotized until it was too late; (4) that certain high-ranking French officers, secretly allied with Pierre Laval and other civilians, deliberately sabotaged the country's defense efforts in the hope of readying France for a *coup d'état*. For a quick summary of the voluminous literature on this subject, see Samuel M. Osgood, *The Fall of France, 1940* (New York, 1965).

Chapter 2: De Gaulle (1, 2, 3, 4, 5), François-Poncet (1 and 2), Laffargue, Nicolson (1), Tournoux. Despite the great number of biographies of de Gaulle (most of which are, more properly speaking, hagiographies), we know very little about his early life. We do have official school and military records, and scattered commentary by persons who knew him in his youth, but nothing systematic and certainly nothing to suggest, as do some biographers, that even as a small boy he was obsessed with the idea of his own destiny—that seemed to come sometime in late adolescence. Most of the facts about his childhood seem lost now in the mists of the past.

Chapter 3: Aron (1), Bankwitz, de Gaulle (5), Reynaud (1), Weygand (2).

Chapter 4: De Gaulle (5) Murphy, Reynaud (1), Rommel, Spears (1). Weygand (1 and 2). General Weygand (1) has denied the precise wording of his conversation with de Gaulle but not its central thrust: in attempting to exonerate himself for his part in the defeat of France, Weygand maintains that he told de Gaulle emphatically that strategic retreat was impossible. Whether Weygand's analysis was correct is a subject of controversy to this day among French military historians. See Bankwitz on this point.

Chapter 5: Baudouin, Chautemps, Horne, Liebling (2 and article 1), Pawle, Reynaud (1), Spears (1). It was Weygand's remark, "In three weeks, England's neck will be wrung like a chicken" that led Churchill, while speaking some time later before the Canadian Houses of Parliament, to spit out: "Some chicken! Some neck!"

Chapter 6: Baudouin, Chautemps, Churchill (5), de Gaulle (5), Liebling (2), Reynaud (1 and 2), Spears (1).

Chapter 7: This chapter is based on two sources, de Gaulle (5) for the General's mood and Spears (1) for the events of the night of June 16–17, 1940. De Gaulle's War Memoirs pass over the question of whether he was in danger of arrest, but Spears, in personal correspondence, has reaffirmed the authenticity of his version of the escape from Bordeaux.

Chapter 8: Aglion (1 and 2), Auphan and Mordal, Bourdan (1 and 2), Churchill (5), de Gaulle (5), Flanner (article), Gary, Henrey, Mengin, Oberlé (2), Panter-Downes, Reynolds (article), Sevareid, Shirer (1), Spears (1).

Some members of the Chamber of Deputies did set forth in June for North Africa aboard the steamer *Massilia*—Georges Mandel and Pierre Mendès-France among them. The deputies, however, were arrested upon landing in Algiers, the Jews among them incarcerated and the rest released to Marseille where they were prevented from speaking out against the Vichy regime.

The events at Mers-el-Kébir were more complex than I have portrayed them since, before the British had actually reached the harbor, Churchill's flagship had radioed ultimata to the French shore command—demands for surrender that the French had rejected. (For details, see White and Auphan and Mordal.) I have presented my simplified version of the attack in order to convey the sense of shock that beset the French military everywhere.

Those readers who know French might be interested in the original version of the General's broadcast of June 18, 1940; no English translation quite gets across the stilted, old-fashioned quality of de Gaulle's phrases or the way they evoked the feel of seventeenth-century French letters:

"Les chefs qui, depuis de nombreuses années, sont à la tête des armées françaises ont formé un gouvernement.

Ce gouvernement alléguant la défaite de nos armées, s'est mis en rapport avec l'ennemi pour cesser le combat.

Certes, nous avons été, nous sommes, submergés par la force mécanique, terrestre et aérienne, de l'ennemi.

Infiniment plus que leur nombre, ce sont les chars, les avions, la tactique des Allemands qui nous font reculer. Ce sont les chars, les avions, la tactique des Allemands qui ont surpris nos chefs au point de les amener là où ils en sont aujourd'hui.

Mais le dernier mot est-il dit? L'espérance doit-elle disparaître? La défaite est-elle définitive? Non!

Croyez-moi, moi qui vous parle en connaissance de cause et vous dit que rien n'est perdu pour la France. Les mêmes moyens qui nous ont vaincus peuvent faire venir un jour la victoire.

Car la France n'est pas seule! Elle n'est pas seule! Elle n'est pas seule! Elle a un vaste Empire derrière elle. Elle peut faire bloc avec l'Empire britannique qui tient la mer et continue la lutte. Elle peut, comme l'Angleterre, utiliser sans limites l'immense industrie des Etats-Unis.

Cette guerre n'est pas limitée au territoire malheureux de notre pays. Cette guerre est une guerre mondiale. Toutes les fautes, tous les retards, toutes les souffrances, n'empêchent pas qu'il y a, dans l'universe, tous les moyens pour écraser un jour nos ennemis. Foudroyés aujourd'hui par la force mécanique, nous pourrons vaincre dans l'avenir par une force mécanique supérieure. Le destin du monde est là

Moi, général de Gaulle, actuellement à Londres, j'invite les officiers et les soldats français qui se trouve en territoire britannique on qui viendraient à s'y trouver, avec leurs armes ou sans leurs armes, j'invite les ingénieurs et les ouvriers spécialistes des industries d' armement qui se trouve en territoire britannique ou qui viendraient à s'y trouver, à se mettre en rapport avec moi.

Quoi qu'il arrive, la flamme de la résistance français ne doit pas s'éteindre et ne s'éteindra pas.

Chapter 9: "Passy," "Rémy" (3, 6, and 7).

Chapter 10: Abetz, Baudouin, Curie, de Gaulle (5), De Larminat, Laval (1 and 2), Mengin, Murphy, Muselier, Oberlé (2), Sevareid, *The Times.* Two works of fiction portray well the mood and feel of Vichy France during the first two years of the War, Jean Dutourd's *The Best Butter* and the movie, *The Sorrow and the Pity (Le Chagrin et la pitié)*, directed by Marcel Ophuls and recently released in the United States. See also Robert O. Paxton, *Vichy France*, for an excellent, unemotional and balanced treatment of the motives of Vichy's major political figures.

Chapter 11: Castilho, "Passy," "Remy" (3, 6, and 7)

Chapter 12: Aglion (1 and 2), Boisseau, Churchill (5), Curie, de Gaulle (5), Mordal (1 and article), Spears (2), Soustelle, *The Times*, White. It was during the preparation for and execution of the Dakar operation that de Gaulle acquired the reputation among many British military types of being a courageous dunderhead who had first proposed an impossible overland attack upon Dakar, then insisted on attacking the port despite insuperable odds. This reputation seems to persist even today in the British military. General Weygand would certainly have concurred.

Chapter 13: De Gaulle (2, 4 and 5), Grinnell-Milne, Thompson.

Chapter 14: D'Astier (1), Castilho, Ehrlich, Flanner (article), Liebling (1), "Rémy" (2, 3, 4, 5 and 6).

Chapter 15: Barker, Bourdan (1 and 2), Burman (1), Dansette, Hassoldt Davis, de Gaulle (5), De Larminat, Denis, Kennedy Shaw, Lambermont, Mengin, Moran, Nicolson (2), Schmidt, Soustelle, *The Times.*

Chapter 16: D'Astier (1), Castilho, Churchill (5), Ehrlich, Flanner (1), Liebling (1), "Rémy" (2, 3, 4, 5, 6, and 9).

Chapter 17: Borden, Catroux, Collet, de Gaulle (5), Ismay, Kirk, Lyttleton, Muselier, Playfair, Rommel, Schmidt, Spears (2), Wilson.

Chapter 18: D'Astier (1), Castilho, Ehrlich, Liebling (1), "Rémy" (2, 3, 4, 5, 6 and 9).

Chapter 19: Borden, Catroux, Lyttleton, Collet, Curie, de Gaulle (5), Ismay, Kirk, Morehead, Playfair, Wilson.

Chapter 20: Aglion (1 and 3), Borden, Burman (1 and 2), Carell, Carver, Castilho, Catroux, Cowles (1), Dansette, Hassoldt Davis, De Gaulle (2 and 5), De Larminat, Denis, Gary, Grand'Combe, Holmes, Lambermont, Lyttleton, Mengin, Muselier, Playfair, Schmidt, Soustelle, Stratton, Young.

Chapter 21: Collier, "Passy," "Rémy" (3, 4, 6 and 7). The portions of this chapter devoted to Duchez's escapade are based almost exclusively on a single source, Richard Collier's *Ten Thousand Eyes*. "Rémy's" books allude to the theft of the map and to the crucial role Duchez and Girard played in getting it to London, but the details of the operation are preserved today only in Collier's work.

Chapter 22: Aglion (1 and 3), Borden, Carell, Carver, Catroux, Dansette, Hassoldt Davis, de Gaulle (5), De Larminat, Denis, Grand'Combe (1), Holmes, Mengin, Playfair, Schmidt, Soustelle, Stratton, Weil-Curiel (1 and 2), Young.

Chapter 23: Collier, "Passy," "Rémy" (2, 3, 4, 6, 7, 8, 9, 10 and 11).

Chapter 24: Aglion (1 and 3), Borden, Carell, Carver, Catroux, Dansette, De Larminat, Denis, Grand'Combe (1), Holmes, Mengin, Playfair, Schmidt, Soustelle, Stratton, Weil-Curiel (1 and 2), Young.

Chapter 25: Castilho, "Rémy" (6, 7, 8).

Chapter 26: Here I used the same sources as in Chapter 24.

Chapter 27: De Gaulle (5), Mengin, *The Times.*

Epilogue: My interpretation here rests heavily upon the fascinating insights in Gary (2), Hoffmann (all of his works mentioned below have been extremely helpful), Thomson, Tucker, White, Willner (1 and 2).

Bibliography

BOOKS

Abetz, Otto, *Das Offene Problem* (Cologne, 1951).

Accart, J. M., *Chasseurs du ciel* (Paris, 1945).

Aglion, Raoul, *L'Epopée de la France combattante* (New York, 1943; also published in English under the title, *The Fighting French* (New York, 1943).

———, *The War in the Desert* (New York, 1941).

Allard, Paul, *L'Enigme de la meuse: la verité sur l'affaire Corap* (Paris, 1941).

Amouroux, Henri, *Pétain avant Vichy* (Paris, 1967).

Armstrong, Hamilton Fish, *Chronology of Failure* (New York, 1941).

Aron, Robert, *An Explanation of de Gaulle* (New York, 1966).

———, *De Gaulle before Paris* (London, 1962).

———, *De Gaulle Triumphant* (London, 1964).

———, *Les grandes dossiers de l'histoire contemporaine* (Paris, 1964).

———, *Histoire de Vichy* (Paris, 1954).

Ashcroft, Edward, *De Gaulle* (London, 1962).

Auphan, Paul, and Jacques Mordal, *The French Navy in World War II* (Annapolis, 1959).

Avon, the Rt. Hon. the Earl of, *The Eden Memoirs; the Reckoning* (London, 1965).

Balbaud, René, *Cette drôle de guerre* (Oxford, 1941).

Baldwin, Hanson W., *World War I* (New York, 1962).

Bankwitz, Philip C. F., *General Weygand and French Civil-Military Relations* (Cambridge, Mass., 1967).

Bardoux, Jacques, *Journal* (Paris, 1957).

Barker, A. J., *Eritrea 1941* (London, 1966).

Barlone, D., *A French Officer's Diary* (Cambridge, Mass.,1948).

Barnett, Correlli, *The Desert Generals* (New York, 1960).

Barrès, Philippe, *Charles de Gaulle* (Montreal, 1941).

Baudouin, Paul, *Private Diaries: March 1940–January, 1941* (London, 1948).

Bauer, Major Eddy, *La guerre des blindés* (Paris, 1947).

Bayac, J. Delperrie de, *La milice, 1918–1945* (Paris, 1969).

Bayle, Jean-Louis Loubet del, *Les non-conformistes des années 30* (Paris, 1969).

Beaufre, Général, *Le drame de 1940* (Paris, 1965).

Beer, Max, *La guerre n'a pas eu lieu* (New York, 1941).

Benoist-Méchin, Jacques, *Soixante jours qui ébranlèrent l'Occident* (Paris, 1956).

Bidault, Georges, *Resistance* (London, 1965).

Bloch, Marc, *L'Etrange défaite* (Paris, 1946).

Bloch, Pierre, *Charles de Gaulle, le premier ouvier de France* (Paris, 1945).

Blum, Léon, *De Munich à la guerre, 1937–1940* (Paris, 1965).

——, *Mémoires* (Paris, 1955).

Boillot, Félix, *The Three Years of Fighting France* (London, 1943).

Bois, Elie J., *The Truth on the Tragedy of France* (London, 1941).

Boisseau, Colonel René, *Les trois glorieuses de l'empire, 26–28 soût, 1940* (Paris, 1945).

Bonheur, Gaston, *Charles de Gaulle* (Paris, 1958).

——, *Le glaive nu, Charles de Gaulle et son destin* (Paris, 1958).

Bonnet, Georges, *De Munich à la guerre* (Paris, 1967).

Boothe, Clare, *Europe in the Spring* (New York, 1940).

Borchert, Hubert W., *Panzerkampf im Westen* (Berlin, 1940).

Borden, Mary, *Journey down a Blind Alley* (London, 1946).

Bourdan, Pierre, *Carnets des jours d'attente* (Paris, 1945).

——, *Les commentaires de Pierre Bourdan* (Paris, 1947).

——, *The English Way* (London, 1946).

Bouthillier, Yves, *Le drame de Vichy* (Paris, 1950).

Bret, Paul-Louis, *Au feu des événements* (Paris, 1959).

Broad, Lewis, *Winston Churchill; The Years of Achievement* (New York, 1963).

Brogan, D. W., *The Development of Modern France* (London, 1940).

——, *The French Nation from Napoleon to Pétain: 1814–1940* (New York, 1957).

Brown, Cecil, *Suez to Singapore* (New York, 1942).

Brugère, Raymond, *Veni, vidi, Vichy et la suite* (Paris, 1953).

Bryant, Arthur, *The Turn of the Tide* (Garden City, 1957).

Buckmaster, Maurice, *They Fought Alone* (New York, 1958).

Bullard, Robert Lee, *Personalities and Reminiscences of the War* (Garden City, 1925).

Bullock, Alan, *Hitler: A Study in Tyranny* (New York, 1953).

Burman, Ben Lucien, *The Generals Wear Cork Hats* (New York, 1963).

——, *Miracle on the Congo* (New York, 1941).

Cantril, Hadley, *The Psychology of Social Movements* (New York, 1963).

Carell, Paul, *The Foxes of the Desert* (London, 1960).

Carver, Michael, *Tobruk* (London, 1964).

Castilho, Catherine de, *Mon père était Rémy* (Paris, 1970).

Catroux, Georges, *Dans la bataille de la Méditeranée* (Paris, 1949).

Cattaui, Georges, *Charles de Gaulle: l'homme et le destin* (Paris, 1960).

Chambrun, René Aldebart, Comte de, *I Saw France Fall* (New York, 1940).

Charles-Roux, F., *Cinq mois tragiques aux affaires étrangères* (Paris, 1949).

Chautemps, Camille, *Cahiers secrets de l'armistice* (Paris, 1963).

Chenet, Daniel, *Qui a sauvé l'Afrique?* (Paris, 1949).

Christian, William A., Jr., *Divided Island: Faction and Unity on Saint-Pierre* (Cambridge, Mass., 1969).

Christophe, E. C., *Wir Stossen mit Panzern Zum Meer* (Berlin, 1940).

Churchill, Peter, *Dual of Wits* (London, 1953).

———, *Of Their Own Choice* (London, 1950).

Churchill, Winston S., *Blood, Sweat and Tears* (New York, 1941).

———, *The Gathering Storm* (Boston, 1948).

———, *The Grand Alliance* (Boston, 1950).

———, *The Hinge of Fate* (Boston, 1950).

———. *Their Finest Hour* (Boston, 1949).

Clark, Stanley, *The Man Who Is France* (New York, 1960).

Clostermann, Pierre, *The Big Show* (New York, 1951).

Cole, Hubert, *Laval* (New York, 1963).

Collet, Ann, *The Road to Deliverance* (Beirut, 1942).

Collier, Richard, *Ten Thousand Eyes* (New York, 1958).

Connell, John, *Auchinleck* (London, 1959).

Cookridge, E. H., *Set Europe Ablaze* (New York, 1966).

Cooper, Duff, *Old Men Forget* (London, 1953).

Cot, Pierre, *Le procès de la république* (New York, 1944).

Cotta, Michèle, *La collaboration* (Paris, 1964).

Cowles, Virginia, *The Phantom Major* (New York, 1958).

———, *Winston Churchill: The Era and the Man* (New York, 1953).

Crozier, Michel, *The Bureaucratic Phenomenon* (Chicago, 1964).

Curie, Eve, *Journey among Warriors* (Garden City, 1943).

Dansette, Adrien, *Leclerc* (Paris, 1952).

D'Astier de la Vigérie, Emmanuel, *De la chute à la libération de Paris, 25 août 1944* (Paris, 1965).

———, *Les grandes* (Paris, 1961).

———, *Sept fois, sept jours* (Paris, 1961).

D'Astier de la Vigérie, François, *Le ciel n'était pas vide* (Paris, 1952).

Davis, Forrest, and Ernest K. Lindley, *How War Came* (New York, 1962).

Davis, Hassoldt, *Feu d'Afrique* (Paris, 1945).

De Beauvoir, Simone, *The Prime of Life* (London, 1963).

De Chambrun, René, *I Saw France Fall* (New York, 1940).

De Cugnac, Général, *Les quarante jours; 1 mai–19 juin, 1940* (Paris, 1948).

De Daruvar, Yves, *De Londres à la Tunisie: Carnet de route de la France libre* (Paris, 1945).

De Gaulle, Charles, *La discorde chez l'ennemi* (Paris, 1944).

——, *Le fil de l'épée* (Paris, 1932); English translation, *The Edge of the Sword* (New York, 1960).

——, *France and Her Army* (London, 1938).

——, *Vers l'armée de métier* (Paris, 1934); English translation, *The Army of the Future* (Philadelphia, 1941).

——, *War Memoirs* (London, 1955).

De la Gorce, Paul, *De Gaulle entre deux mondes* (Paris, 1964).

Delange, René, *La vie de Saint-Exupéry* (Paris, 1948).

De Larminat, René-Marie-Edgar, *Chroniques irrévérencieuses* (Paris, 1962).

Denis, Pierre, *Souvenirs de la France libre* (Paris, 1947).

De Saint-Exupéry, Antoine, *Flight to Arras* (New York, 1942).

De Villefosse, Héron, *Souvenirs d'un marin de la France libre* (Paris, 1951).

Dorgelès, Roland, *La drôle de guerre* (Paris, 1957).

Draper, Theodore, *The Six Weeks' War* (New York, 1944).

Du Gard, Maurice Martin, *La carte impériale* (Paris, 1949).

——, *La chronique de Vichy* (Paris, 1948).

——, *Le drame de l'Afrique française* (Paris, 1941).

Durand, Paul, *La S.N.C.F. pendant la guerre* (Paris, 1968).

Dutourd, Jean, *The Best Butter* (New York, 1955).

Eade, Charles (Ed.), *Churchill by His Contemporaries* (New York, 1954).

Ehrenburg, I., *Eve of War, 1933–1941* (London, 1963).

Ehrlich, Blake, *Resistance; France, 1940–1945* (Boston, 1965).

Eisenhower, Dwight D., *Crusade in Europe* (Garden City, 1948).

Ellis, Major L. F., *The War in France and Flanders* (London, 1953).

Farmer, Paul, *Vichy; Political Dilemma* (New York, 1955).

Feis, Herbert, *Churchill, Roosevelt, Stalin: The War They Waged and the Peace They Sought* (Princeton, 1957).

Flandin, Pierre-Etienne, *Politique française, 1919–1940* (Paris, 1947).

François-Poncet, André, *De Versailles à Potsdam* (Paris, 1948).

——, *The Fateful Years* (London, 1949).

Freeman, C. Denis, and Douglas Cooper, *The Road to Bordeaux* (London, 1940).

Fry, Varian, *Surrender on Demand* (New York, 1945).

Fuller, Jean Overton, *Madeleine* (London, 1952).

Funk, Arthur Layton, *Charles de Gaulle: The Crucial Years, 1943–1944* (Norman, 1959).

Galante, Pierre, *The General!* (New York, 1968).

Galimand, Lucien, *Origine et déviations du gaullism* (Paris, 1950).

Gamelin, Général, *Servir — les armées françaises de 1940* (Paris, 1946).

Garas, Félix, *Charles de Gaulle: seul contre les pouvoirs* (Paris, 1957).

Gary, Romain, *Promise at Dawn* (New York, 1961).

Gauché, Maurice Henri, *Le deuxième bureau au travail* (Paris, 1953).

Gaulmier, Jean, *Charles de Gaulle, écrivain* (Paris, 1946).

Gavin, Catherine, *Liberated France* (New York, 1955).

Gide, André, *Journal, 1939–1949* (Paris, 1954).

———, *Journal, 1942–1945* (Paris, 1950).

Girard, Louis-Dominique, *La guerre franco-française* (Paris, 1950).

Giraud, Général, *Mes évasions* (Paris, 1946).

Gourdon, Pierre, *Le Général de Gaulle, serviteur de la France* (Paris, 1945).

Grand'Combe, Félix de, *Bir Hakeim; 26 mai–10 juin, 1942* (Paris, 1945).

———, *The Three Years of Fighting France* (London, 1963).

Grinnell-Milne, Duncan, *The Triumph of Integrity* (New York, 1962).

Groussard, Colonel, *Chemins secrets* (Paris, 1948).

Guderian, Heinz, *Achtung-Panzer* (Stuttgart, 1937).

———, *Mit Den Panzern in Ost und West* (Stuttgart, 1942).

———, *Panzer Leader* (London, 1952).

Habe, Hans, *A Thousand Shall Fail* (London, 1942).

Halifax, the Earl of, *Fullness of Days* (London, 1957).

Halleguen, Joseph, *Aux quatre vents du gaullisme* (Paris, 1953).

Hartley, Anthony, *Gaullism: The Rise and Fall of a Political Movement* (New York, 1971).

Heckstall-Smith, Anthony, *Tobruk: The Story of a Siege* (New York, 1960).

Henrey, Mrs. Robert, *London under Fire 1940–45* (London, 1969).

Herriot, Edouard, *Episodes, 1940–1944* (Paris, 1950).

Holmes, Richard, *Bir Hakim* (New York, 1971).

Hooker, Nancy Harbison, *The Moffat Papers* (Cambridge, 1956).

Horne, Alistair, *To Lose a Battle: France 1940* (Boston, 1969).

Huddleston, Sisley, *France: The Tragic Years, 1939–1947* (New York, 1955).

Hughes, H. Stuart, *The Obstructed Path* (New York, 1968).

Hull, Cordell, *The Memoirs of Cordell Hull* (New York, 1948).

Ingold, Général, *Le chemin* (Paris, 1958).

Ismay, Lord, *The Memoirs of General the Lord Ismay* (London, 1960).

Jäckel, Eberhard, *La France dans l'Europe de Hitler* (Paris, 1968).

Kammerer, Albert, *La passion de la flotte française* (Paris, 1951).

———, *La vérité sur l'armistice* (Paris, 1945).

Kennedy Shaw, W. B., *Patrouilles au désert* (Paris, 1949).

Kérillis, Henri de, *De Gaulle, dictateur* (Montreal, 1945).

Kessel, Joseph, *L'Armée des ombres* (Paris, 1945).

Kirk, George, *The War in the Middle East* (London, 1952).

Koeltz, Général Louis, *Comment s'est joué notre destin: Hitler et l'offensive du 10 mai, 1940* (Paris, 1947).

Koestler, Arthur, *Scum of the Earth* (London, 1941).

Labarthe, André, *Retour au feu* (New York, 1943).

Labat, René, *Le Gabon devant le gaullisme* (Bordeaux, 1941).

Lacouture, Jean, *De Gaulle* (Paris, 1965).

Laffargue, André, *Fantassin de Gascogne* (Paris, 1962).

Lambermont, Paul, *Lorraine Squadron* (London, 1956).

Langer, William L., *Our Vichy Gamble* (New York, 1947).

Lania, Leo, *The Darkest Hour* (Boston, 1941).

Lapie, Pierre Olivier, *Les déserts de l'action* (Paris, 1946).

Laval, Pierre, *The Diary of Pierre Laval* (New York, 1948).

———, *Laval parle* (Paris, 1948).

Lazareff, Pierre, *Deadline* (New York, 1942).

Leahy, Admiral William, *I Was There* (New York, 1950).

Lebrun, Albert, *Témoignage* (Paris, 1945).

Lewin, Ronald, *Rommel as Military Commander* (New York, 1968).

Liddell Hart, B. H., *The Other Side of the Hill* (London, 1948).

———, *Reputations Ten Years After* (Freeport, 1968).

Liebling, A. J., and Eugene Jay Sheffer, *La république du silence* (New York, 1946).

———, *The Road Back to Paris* (Garden City, 1944).

Longrigg, Stephen, *Syria and Lebanon under the French Mandate* (New York, 1958).

Lyttleton, Oliver, *Memoirs of Lord Chandos* (New York, 1963).

Machin, Lucien, *Charles de Gaulle* (Paris, 1944).

MacIntyre, Donald, *The Battle for the Mediterranean* (London, 1964).

Mackenzie, Compton, *Eastern Epic* (London, 1951).

Macmillan, Harold, *The Blast of War, 1939–1945* (New York, 1967).

———, *Winds of Change* (New York, 1966).

Malaquais, Jean, *Jean Malaquais' War Diary* (Garden City, 1944).

Malraux, André, *Anti-memoirs* (New York, 1968).

———, *Les chênes qu'on abat* (Paris, 1971).

Marlow, James, *De Gaulle and the Coming Invasion of Germany* (New York, 1940).

Marshall, Bruce, *The White Rabbit* (Boston, 1952).

Maugham, Somerset, *France at War* (London, 1940).

Mauriac, François, *De Gaulle* (Paris, 1964).

Maurois, André, *Tragedy in France* (New York, 1940).

Mellenthin, Major-General F. W. von, *Panzer Battles, 1939–1945* (London, 1955).

Mende, Karl Heinz, *Briefs aus dem Westen* (Berlin, 1940).

Mendès-France, Pierre, *The Pursuit of Freedom* (London, 1956).

Mengin, Robert, *No Laurels for de Gaulle* (New York, 1966).

Michel, Henri, *Histoire de la Résistance* (Paris, 1950).

Michelet, Edmond. *Le gaullisme passionnante aventure* (Paris, 1962).

Middleton, Drew, *Our Share of Night* (New York, 1946).

Millet, Raymond, *Charles de Gaulle, trois époques, trois guerres, trois hommes* (Lyon, 1946).

Minart, Jacques, *Charles de Gaulle tel que je l'ai connu* (Paris, 1945).

Montmorency, Alec de, *The Enigma of Admiral Darlan* (New York, 1943).

Moorehead, Alan, *The March to Tunis* (New York, 1967).

Moran, Lord Charles M. W., *Churchill* (Boston, 1966).

Mordal, Jacques, *La bataille de Dakar* (Paris, 1956).

Morgan, William J., *The O.S.S. and I* (New York, 1957).

Morize, André, *France, été 1940* (New York, 1941).

Moulton, J. L., *The Norwegian Campaign of 1940* (London, 1966).

Moynet, Paul, *L'Epopée du Fezzan* (Algiers, 1944).

Murphy, Robert, *Diplomat among Warriors* (New York, 1964).

Muselier, Emile, *De Gaulle contre le gaullisme* (Paris, 1946).

Nicolson, Harold, *Peacemaking, 1919* (London, 1933).

———, *The War Years, 1939–1945* (New York, 1967).

Noguères, Louis, *La haute cour de la libération* (Paris, 1965).

———, *Le véritable procès du Maréchal Pétain* (Paris, 1955).

Novick, Peter, *The Resistance versus Vichy* (New York, 1958).

Oberlé, Jean, *Images anglaises* (London, 1942).

———, *Jean Oberlé vous parle* (Paris, 1945).

Panter-Downs, Mollie, *London War Notes, 1939–1945* (New York, 1971).

Passy, Colonel, *Souvenirs* (Monte Carlo, 1947).

Pawle, Gerald, *The War and Colonel Warden* (New York, 1963).

Paxton, Robert O., *Parades and Politics at Vichy* (Princeton, 1966).

———, *Vichy France: Old Guard and New Order, 1940–1944* (New York, 1972).

Pendar, Kenneth, *Adventure in Diplomacy* (New York, 1945).

"Pertinax," *Les fossoyeurs* (New York, 1943).

Pierre-Gosset, Renée, *Conspiracy in Algiers, 1942–1943* (New York, 1945).

Pineau, Christian, *La simple vérité* (Paris, 1960).

Playfair, Major General I. S. O., *The Mediterranean and Middle East*, Volume III (London, 1960).

Plumyène, Jean, *Pétain*, (Paris, 1964).

Prételat, Général, *Le destin tragique de la ligne Maginot* (Paris, 1950).

Rémond, René, *The Right Wing in France: From 1815 to de Gaulle* (Philadelphia, 1966).

"Rémy," *Bruneval, Opératin Coup de Croc* (Paris, 1968).

———, *Comment meurt un réseau* (Monte Carlo, 1947).

———, *Compagnons de l'honneur* (Paris, 1964).

———, *Courage and Fear* (London, 1950).

———, *De Gaulle, cet inconnu* (Monte Carlo, 1947).

———, *Memoirs of a Secret Agent of Free France* (New York, 1948).

———, *On m'appelait Rémy* (Paris, 1951).

———, *Passeurs Clandestins* (Paris, 1954).

———, *Portrait of a Spy* (London, 1955).

———, *Ten Steps to Hope* (London, 1959).

———, *Une affaire de trahison* (Monte Carlo, 1948).

Reynaud, Paul, *Au coeur de la mêlée* (Paris, 1951).

———, *Mémoires: envers et contre tous, 7 mars, 1936–16 juin, 1940* (Paris 1964).

Reynolds, Quentin, *The Wounded Don't Cry* (New York, 1940).

Riveloup, A., *The Truth about de Gaulle* (New York, 1944).

Rommel, Field Marshal Erwin, *The Rommel Papers.* B. H. Liddell Hart, Ed. (London, 1951).

Roskill, Captain S. W., *The War at Sea, 1939–45* (London, 1954).

Rouillon, Léon, *Les compagnons du priemier jour* (Paris, 1952).

Rouleau-Dugage, Jacques, *Deux ans d'histoire secrète en Afrique du nord* (Geneva, 1945).

Roy, Jules, *The Trial of Marshal Pétain* (New York, 1966).

Sandhal, Pierre, *De Gaulle sans Képi* (Paris, 1948).

Sarraz-Bournet, Colonel, *Témoignage d'un silencieux G.Q.G. 2ᵉ bureau* (Paris, 1948).

Sautot, Henri, *Grandeur et décadence du gaullism dans le Pacifique* (London, 1949).

Schmidt, H. W., *With Rommel in the Desert* (London, 1951).

Schoenbrun, David, *The Three Lives of Charles de Gaulle* (New York, 1966).

Shuman, Frederick L., *Europe on the Eve* (New York, 1939).

Schumann, Maurice, *Honneur et patrie* (Paris, 1946).

Sevareid, Eric, *Not So Wild a Dream* (New York, 1946).

Sheean, James Vincent, *Between the Thunder and the Sun* (New York, 1943).

Sherwood, John M., *Georges Mandel and the Third Republic* (Stanford, 1970).

Sherwood, Robert E., *Roosevelt and Hopkins* (New York, 1948).

Shiber, Etta, *Paris—Underground* (New York, 1943).

Shirer, William L., *Berlin Diary* (New York, 1941).

———, *The Collapse of the Third Republic* (New York, 1969).

———, *The Rise and Fall of the Third Reich* (New York, 1959).

Sicé, Médecin-Général A., *L'A.E.F. et le Cameroon au service de la France, 26–28 août, 1940* (Paris, 1946).

Siegfried, André, *De la 3ᵉ à la 4ᵉ République* (Paris, 1956).

Siriex, Hertrich, *L'Empire au combat* (Paris, 1945).

Soulairol, Jean, *Charles de Gaulle, le libérateur* (Paris, 1944).

Soustelle, Jacques, *Envers et contre tout* (Paris, 1950).

Spears, Sir Edward, *Assignment to Catastrophe* (London, 1954).

——, *Two Men Who Saved France* (London, 1966).

Sulzberger, C. L., *The Last of the Giants* (New York, 1970).

Thompson, Lawrence, *The Greatest Treason: The Untold Story of Munich* (New York, 1968).

Thomson, David, *Two Frenchmen, Pierre Laval and Charles de Gaulle* (London, 1951).

Tissier, P., *The Riom Trial* (London, 1942).

Tournoux, Jean-Raymond, *Pétain et de Gaulle* (Paris, 1964).

Truchet, André, *L'Armistice de 1940 et l'Afrique du Nord* (Paris, 1955).

Van Moppès, Maurice, *Chansons de la B.B.C.* (Paris, 1944).

Vaucel, Médecin-Général, *La France d'outremer dans la guerre* (Paris, 1949).

Viorst, Milton, *Hostile Allies: For and against Charles de Gaulle* (New York, 1965).

Warner, Geoffrey, *Pierre Laval and the Eclipse of France* (London, 1968).

Weber, Eugen, *The Nationalist Revival in France, 1905–1914* (Berkeley, 1959).

Weil-Curiel, André, *Le jour se leve à Londres* (Paris, 1945).

——, *Le temps de la honte* (Paris, 1945).

Welles, Sumner, *Seven Decisions that Shaped History* (New York, 1950).

Werth, Alexander, *De Gaulle* (New York, 1965).

——, *The Last Days of Paris* (London, 1940).

——, *The Twilight of France* (New York, 1966).

Weygand, Maxime, *En lisant les mémoires de guerre du Général de Gaulle* (Paris, 1955).

——, *Mémoires: rappelé au service* (Paris, 1950).

Wheeler-Bennett, John W., *Munich: Prologue to Tragedy* (New York, 1948).

White, Dorothy Shipley, *Seeds of Discord* (Syracuse, 1964).

Williams, John, *The Ides of May* (London, 1968).

Willner, Ann Ruth, *Charismatic Political Leadership: A Theory* (Princeton: Center of International Studies, Monograph no. 28, 1968).

Wilson, Sir Henry Maitland, *Eight Years Overseas* (London, 1948).

Wolfenstein, E. Victor, *The Revolutionary Personality* (Princeton, 1967).

Woodward, Llewellyn, *British Foreign Policy in the Second World War* (London, 1970).

Woollcombe, Robert, *The Campaigns of Wavell, 1939–1943.*

Wright, Gordon, *The Reshaping of French Democracy* (New York, 1948).

Young, Desmond, *Rommel: The Desert Fox* (New York, 1950).

ARTICLES

Atkins, Paul M., "Dakar and the Strategy of West Africa," *Foreign Affairs* (January, 1942).

———, "French West Africa in Wartime," *National Geographic* (March, 1942).

Bess, Demaree, "Our Undeclared War," *Saturday Evening Post* (January 3, 1942).

Cairns, John C., "Along the Road Back to France, 1940," *American Historical Review* (April, 1959).

Chamberlain, William Henry, "France in June: The Collapse," *Atlantic Monthly* (September, 1940).

Crémieux-Brilhac, J. L., "Les émissions françaises à la B.B.C. pendant la guerre," *Revue d'histoire de la deuxième guerre mondiale* (November, 1950).

Davray, H. D., "France in Reverse," *Contemporary Review* (October, 1940).

D'Hoop, J. M., "La politique française du réarmament," *Revue d'histoire de la deuxième guerre mondiale* (April, 1954).

Edinger, Lewis, "Political Science and Political Biography," *The Journal of Politics* (May and August, 1964).

Flanner, Janet, "Soldats de France, debout!" *The New Yorker* (February 1, 1941).

Friedrich, Carl J., "Political Leadership and Charismatic Power," *The Journal of Politics* (February, 1961).

Gary, Romain, "The Man Who Stayed Lonely to Save France," *Life* (December 8, 1958).

Gaskill, Gordon, "Europe's Man without a Country," *American Magazine* (January, 1942).

Harmon, D., "Free France Booms in Africa," *Christian Science Monitor* (January 7, 1942).

Hoffmann, Stanley, "Aspects du régime de Vichy," *Revue française de science politique* (January–March, 1956).

———, "Collaborationism in Vichy France," *Journal of Modern History* (September, 1968).

———, "De Gaulle's Memoirs: The Hero as History," *World Politics* (October, 1960).

———, "Heroic Leadership: The Case of Modern France," in Lewis J. Edinger, *Political Leadership in Industrial Societies* (New York, 1967).

———, "On *The Sorrow and the Pity*," *Commentary* (September, 1972).

———, "Paradoxes of the French Political Community," *In Search of France*, (Cambridge, Mass., 1963).

Hoffmann, Stanley and Inge, "The Will to Grandeur: De Gaulle as a Political Artist," *Daedalus* (Summer, 1968).

Kaskeline, Egon, "Félix Eboué and the Fighting French," *Survey Graphic* (November, 1942).

Liebling, A. J., "Generalissimo," *The New Yorker* (May 11 and May 18, 1940).

———, "A Reporter at Large," *The New Yorker* (June 21, 1958).

Madaule, Jacques, "La France en guerre," *Esprit* (February, 1940).

Mordal, Jacques, "La bataille navale de Dakar," *Revue des deux mondes* (September 15, 1955).

Muraccilo, J., "La conquête de la base africaine," *La France et son empire dans la guerre* (Paris, 1947).

Nicolson, Harold, "Ici Londres," *Atlantic Monthly* (March, 1945).

———, "Marginal Comment," *Spectator* (October 27, 1944).

Oberlé, Jean, "A Londres le 18 juin, 1940," *Lectures pour tous*, No. 78 (1960).

Panter-Downes, Mollie, "Letter from London," *The New Yorker* (June 11, 1940).

Pierre, "We Escaped from France by Canoe," *Life* (October 27, 1941).

Ratnam, K. J., "Charisma and Political Leadership," *Political Studies* (1964).

Reynolds, Quentin, "The Man Who Didn't Quit," *Collier's* (Augsust 10, 1940).

Rollot, Général, "La bataille de Sedan," *Revue d'histoire de la deuxième guerre mondiale* (October, 1958).

Ronan, "L'Arrivée du Colonel Leclerc à Fort Lamy," *Cahiers de Charles de Foucauld*, 3ᵉ série, (1949).

Searing, Donald, "Models and Images of Man in Society in Leadership Theory," *The Journal of Politics* (February, 1969).

Stratton, Arthur Mills, "Ambulance at Bir Hacheim," *Atlantic Monthly* (November, 1942).

Tournoux, Général, "Les origines de la ligne Maginot," *Revue d'histoire de la deuxième guerre mondiale* (January, 1959).

Townroe, B. S., "The Free French Colonial Empire," *Asiatic Review* (July, 1941).

Tucker, Robert C., "The Theory of Charismatic Leadership," *Daedalus* (Summer, 1968).

Villate, R., "Changement de commandment de mai, 1940," *Revue d'histoire de la deuxième guerre mondiale* (January, 1952).

Wanty, E., "La défense des Ardennes en 1940," *Revue d'histoire de la deuxième guerre mondiale* (April, 1961).

Weber, Max, "The Three Types of Legitimate Rule," *Berkeley Publications in Society and Institutions* (Summer, 1958).

Wild, Roger, "De Vaugirard au quartier latin," *Revue des deux mondes* (March, 15, 1962).

Willner, Ann Ruth and Dorothy, "The Rise and Role of Charismatic Leaders," *The Annals of the American Academy of Political and Social Science* (March, 1965).

Wormser, O., "The War Effort of the Fighting French Empire," *Asiatic Review* (April, 1943).

OTHER SOURCES

Bulletin of the Department of State.

The Christian Science Monitor.

Délégation française aupres de la Commission Allemande d'Armistice, *Recueil de documents public par le gouvernement français* (Paris, 1947–1959).

Documents on American Foreign Relations.

Le Figaro

The Free French Year Book.

The French Yellow Book: Diplomatic Documents, 1938–1939 (New York, 1940).

History of the Second World War.

Illustrated London News.

Journal officiel de l'Afrique equatorial française.

Journal officiel de la France libre.

Life.

London Gazette.

The Manchester Guardian.

Newsweek.

The New Yorker.

The New York Times.

Paris-Match.

Royal Institute of International Affairs, *Survey of International Affairs,* IV (London, 1952–1954).

Time.

The Times.

United States Foreign Relations.

Index